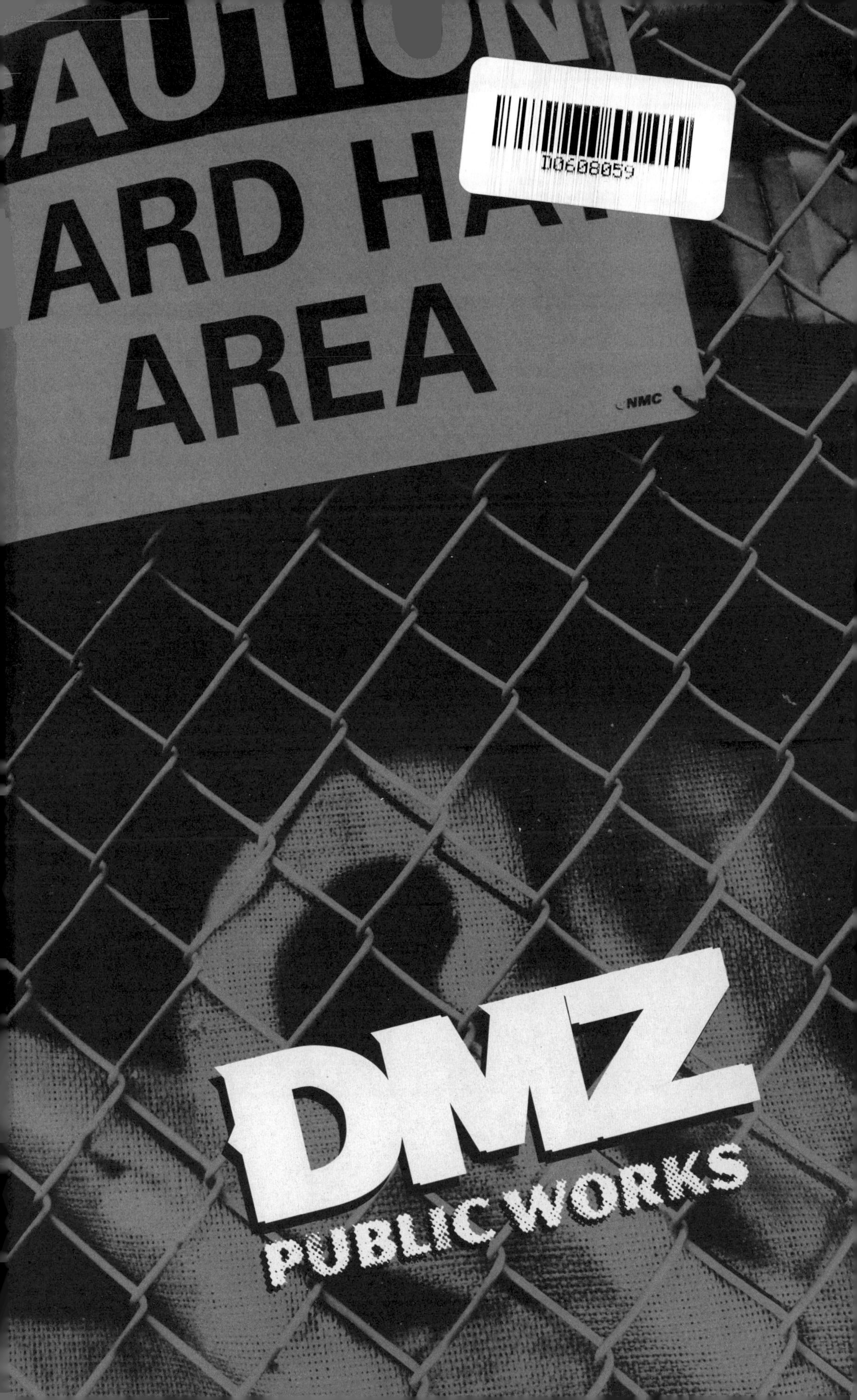
AUTION
ARD HA
AREA
NMC
DMZ
PUBLIC WORKS

**Karen Berger** Senior VP-Executive Editor
**Will Dennis** Editor-original series
**Casey Seijas** Assistant Editor-original series
**Bob Harras** Editor-collected edition
**Robbin Brosterman** Senior Art Director
**Paul Levitz** President & Publisher
**Georg Brewer** VP-Design & DC Direct Creative
**Richard Bruning** Senior VP-Creative Director
**Patrick Caldon** Executive VP-Finance & Operations
**Chris Caramalis** VP-Finance
**John Cunningham** VP-Marketing
**Terri Cunningham** VP-Managing Editor
**Alison Gill** VP-Manufacturing
**Hank Kanalz** VP-General Manager, WildStorm
**Jim Lee** Editorial Director-WildStorm
**Paula Lowitt** Senior VP-Business & Legal Affairs
**MaryEllen McLaughlin** VP-Advertising & Custom Publishing
**John Nee** VP-Business Development
**Gregory Noveck** Senior VP-Creative Affairs
**Sue Pohja** VP-Book Trade Sales
**Cheryl Rubin** Senior VP-Brand Management
**Jeff Trojan** VP-Business Development, DC Direct
**Bob Wayne** VP-Sales

Cover illustration and logo design by Brian Wood
Publication design and additional photography by Amelia Grohman

**DMZ: PUBLIC WORKS**

Published by DC Comics. Cover, introduction and compilation
copyright © 2007 DC Comics. All Rights Reserved.
Originally published in single magazine form as DMZ 13-17.
Copyright © 2007 Brian Wood and Riccardo Burchielli.
All Rights Reserved. VERTIGO and all characters, their
distinctive likenesses and related elements featured
in this publication are trademarks of DC Comics.
The stories, characters and incidents featured
in this publication are entirely fictional.
DC Comics does not read or accept unsolicited
submissions of ideas, stories or artwork.

DC Comics
1700 Broadway, New York, NY 10019
A Warner Bros. Entertainment Company
Printed in Canada. First Printing.
ISBN: 1-4012-1476-2
ISBN 13: 978-1-4012-1476-0

**BRIAN WOOD**
WRITER

**RICCARDO BURCHIELLI**
ARTIST

**JEROMY COX**
COLORIST

**JARED K. FLETCHER**
LETTERER

**BRIAN WOOD**
ORIGINAL SERIES COVERS

INTRODUCTION BY
**CORY DOCTOROW**

DMZ CREATED BY
**BRIAN WOOD** AND
**RICCARDO BURCHIELLI**

# DMZ
## PUBLICWORKS

# INTRODUCTION

BY CORY DOCTOROW

**There are two sides in every war: combatants and non-combatants.**

Oh, I know it's not a popular belief, but it's true. There's not much ideological distance between, say, a bunch of bearded religious fanatics who want to suicide-bomb skyscrapers and a bunch of suited fanatics who want to wiretap, RFID-tag, and imprison every human being on earth and deny the right to travel to anyone whose name sounds anything like the name of anyone who ever said anything nice about terrorism.

At least not when compared to the ideological distance between both of these packs of sociopathic monsters and the rest of us people who just want get onto an airplane without having our colons examined, who want to go to work, church or a mosque without having some nutjob daisy-cutter us for being in the wrong place at the wrong time.

The real "other" isn't brown people with turbans: it's people of all colors with guns, airplanes and wiretaps, no matter what side they fight on.

And tell you what, it's *mutual*. They hate and fear us like anything, those small people with small ideas, the authoritarians who know better than we do. They blame every single problem in their lives on *us*, the nebulous other who comes to their town, takes their jobs, speaks some foreign tongue (whether that's Persian or Brooklynese doesn't matter). A rape? That migrant worker looks suspicious. A theft? How about that out-of-towner with his big-city ways? Poverty, disease—even traffic jams—all the fault of some *other* who needs to be ethnically cleansed to restore us all to our pre-lapsarian glory.

Which is not to say that they're above sticking up for us if it gives them the excuse to tighten the noose. Islamic fanatics who thought of Saddam Hussein as the devil incarnate are delighted to use his toppling as the excuse to inspire another generation of jihadists. Just like the shitkickers who wouldn't have pissed on Manhattan if it was on fire are nevertheless proud to stick a yellow ribbon magnet on their Hummers and proclaim Never Forget, even as they forget that the 9/11 attacks were directed at Sodom on the Hudson, a city filled with gayers, women in bifurcated garments and brown people who smell like curry.

DMZ is a special kind of angry comic, the kind of angry war comic that tells the story of the other side in the war. Non-combatants aren't just cannon fodder or collateral damage. We've got every bit as much agency, as much control over our destinies, as the guys with the guns and the satellite photos. But you wouldn't know it from how we're depicted in the press—instead, we're the bodies blown apart on street corners, the shoeless sheep having our hemorrhoid cream confiscated at the airport.

DMZ is an inspiration to we who refuse to be dismembered and unshod. It's a wake-up call to stop letting greedy profiteers sell fresh wars to cement their authority and profitability.

If I had my way, this comic would be required reading in every civics class in America.

Cory Doctorow is an award-winning author, blogger, journalist and co-editor of the blog *Boing Boing*. His novels include *Down and Out in the Magic Kingdom*, *Eastern Standard Tribe* and *Someone Comes to Town, Someone Leaves Town*.

# CHAPTER ONE

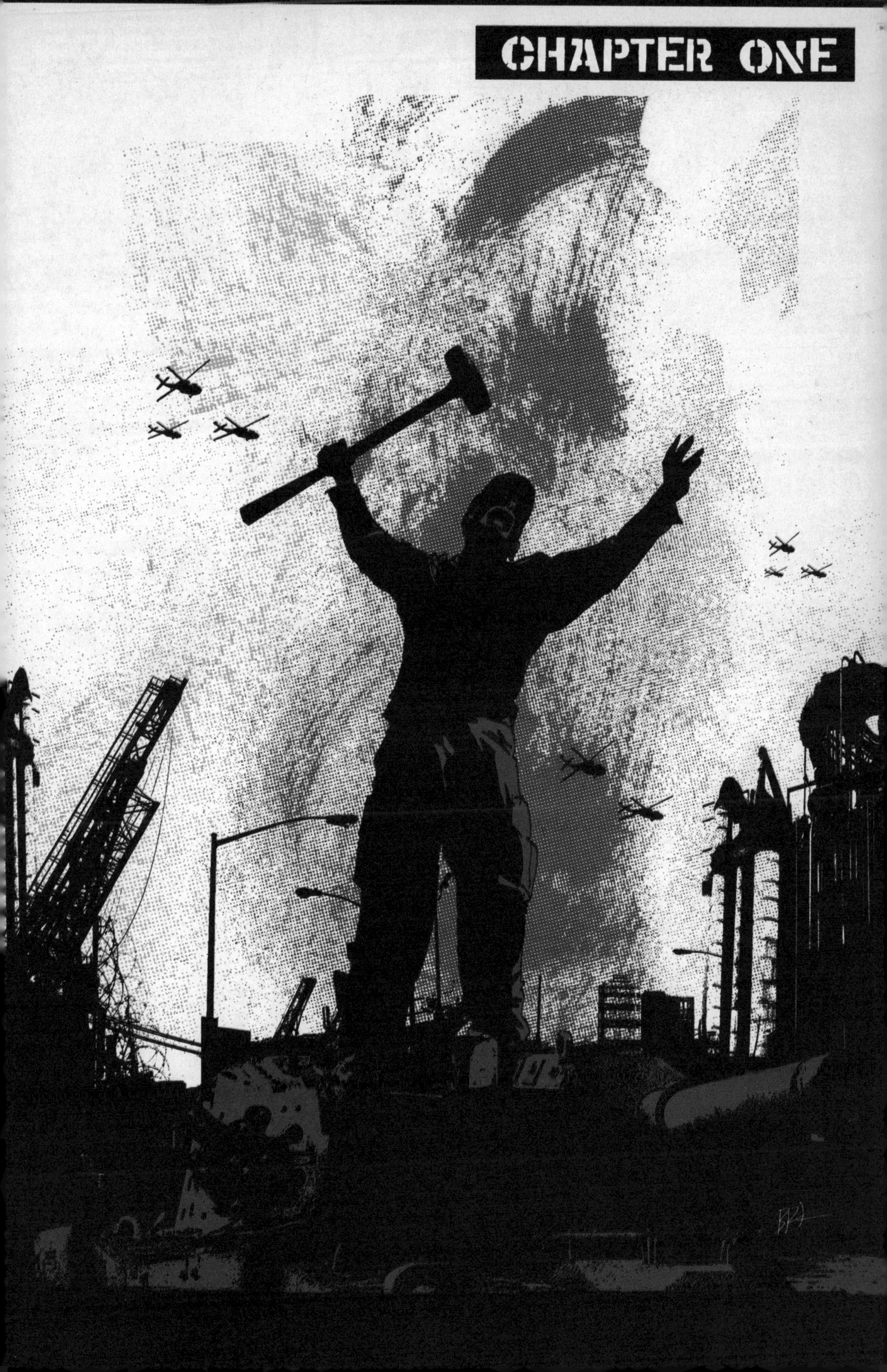

...Top of the news hour this morning: *U.N. Peacekeepers* reported trading small arms fire overnight with *Trustwell security forces.*

*No casualties were reported, but this most recent incident further complicates the already uneasy situation both groups find themselves in...*

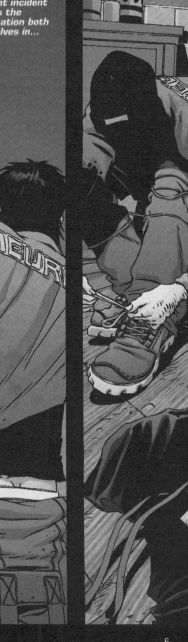

*...providing security for the reconstruction, but answering to different authorities with very different mandates.*

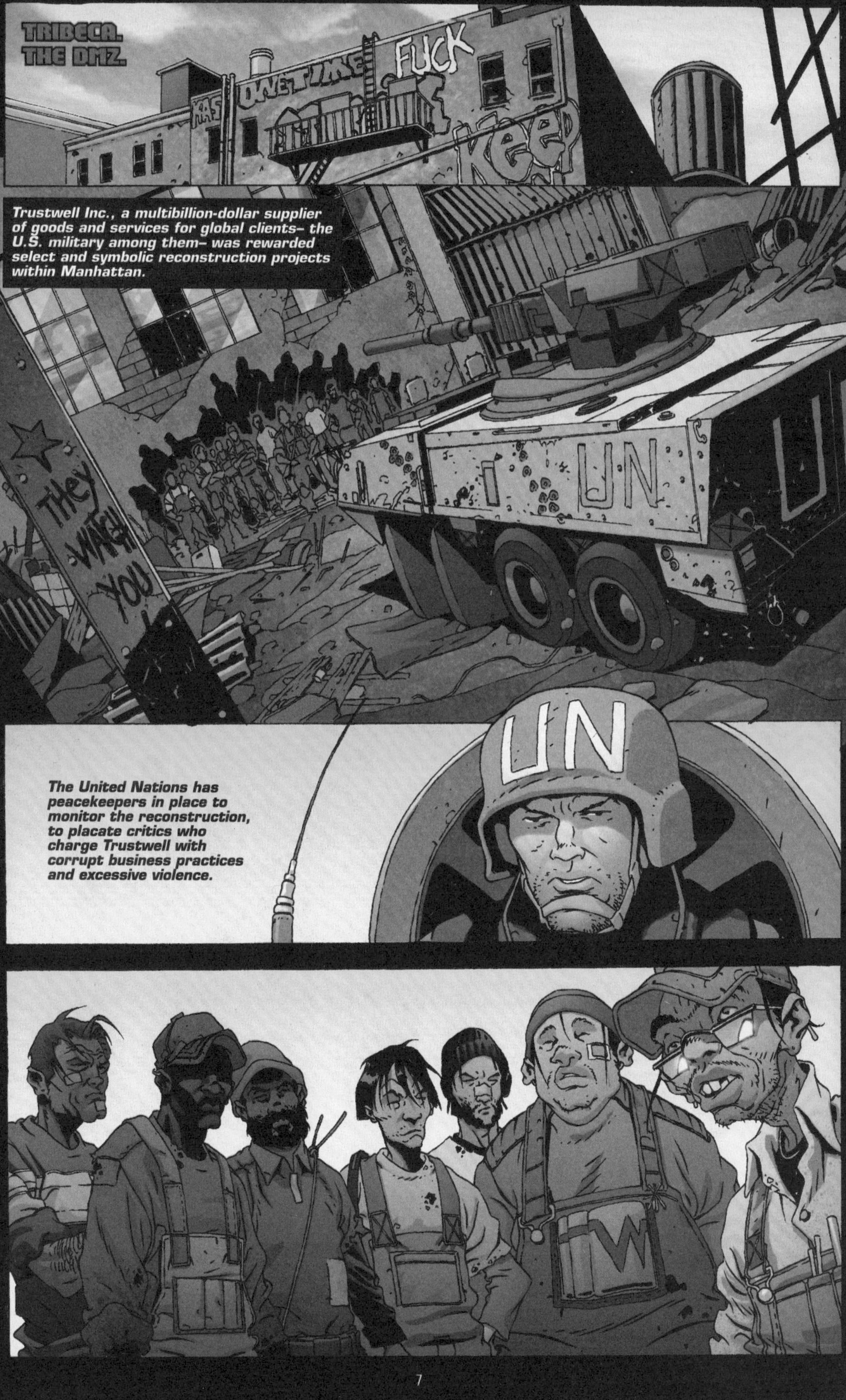
TRIBECA.
THE DMZ.
ONETIME
FUCK
KEEP
Trustwell Inc., a multibillion-dollar supplier of goods and services for global clients– the U.S. military among them– was rewarded select and symbolic reconstruction projects within Manhattan.
THEY WATCH YOU
UN
UN
UN
The United Nations has peacekeepers in place to monitor the reconstruction, to placate critics who charge Trustwell with corrupt business practices and excessive violence.
TW

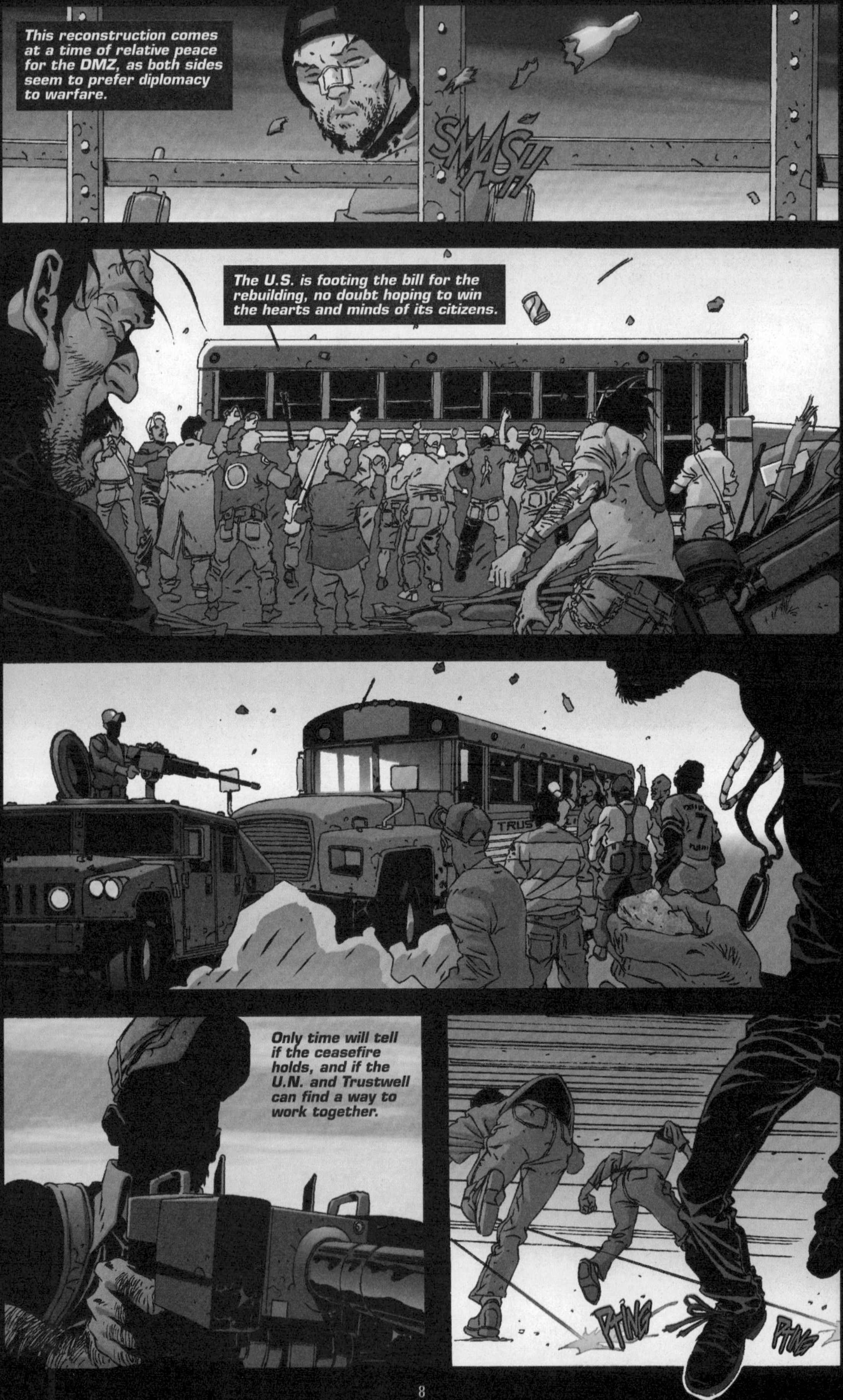
This reconstruction comes at a time of relative peace for the DMZ, as both sides seem to prefer diplomacy to warfare.
SMASH
The U.S. is footing the bill for the rebuilding, no doubt hoping to win the hearts and minds of its citizens.
Only time will tell if the ceasefire holds, and if the U.N. and Trustwell can find a way to work together.
PTING
PTING

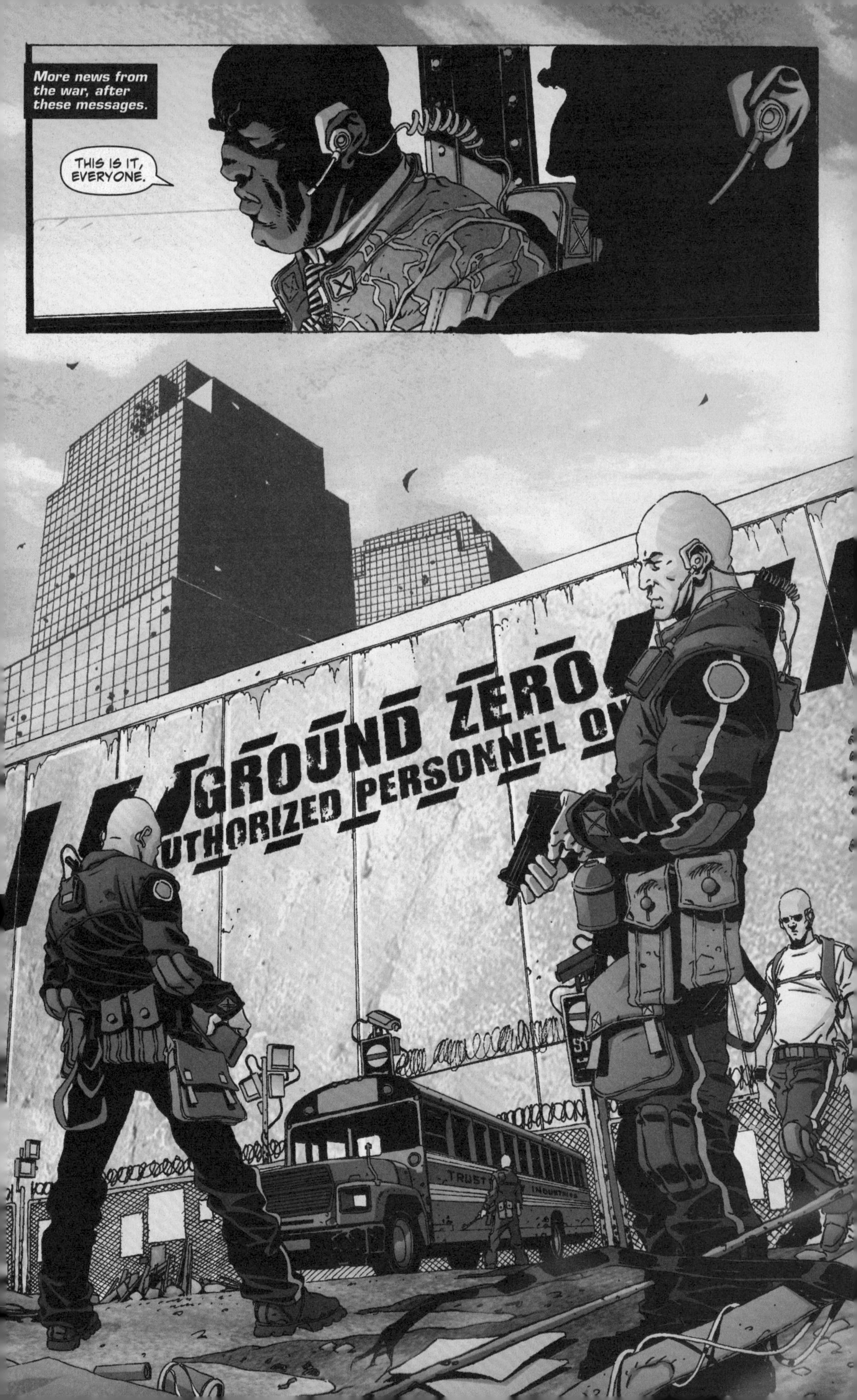
More news from the war, after these messages.
THIS IS IT, EVERYONE.
GROUND ZERO
UTHORIZED PERSONNEL

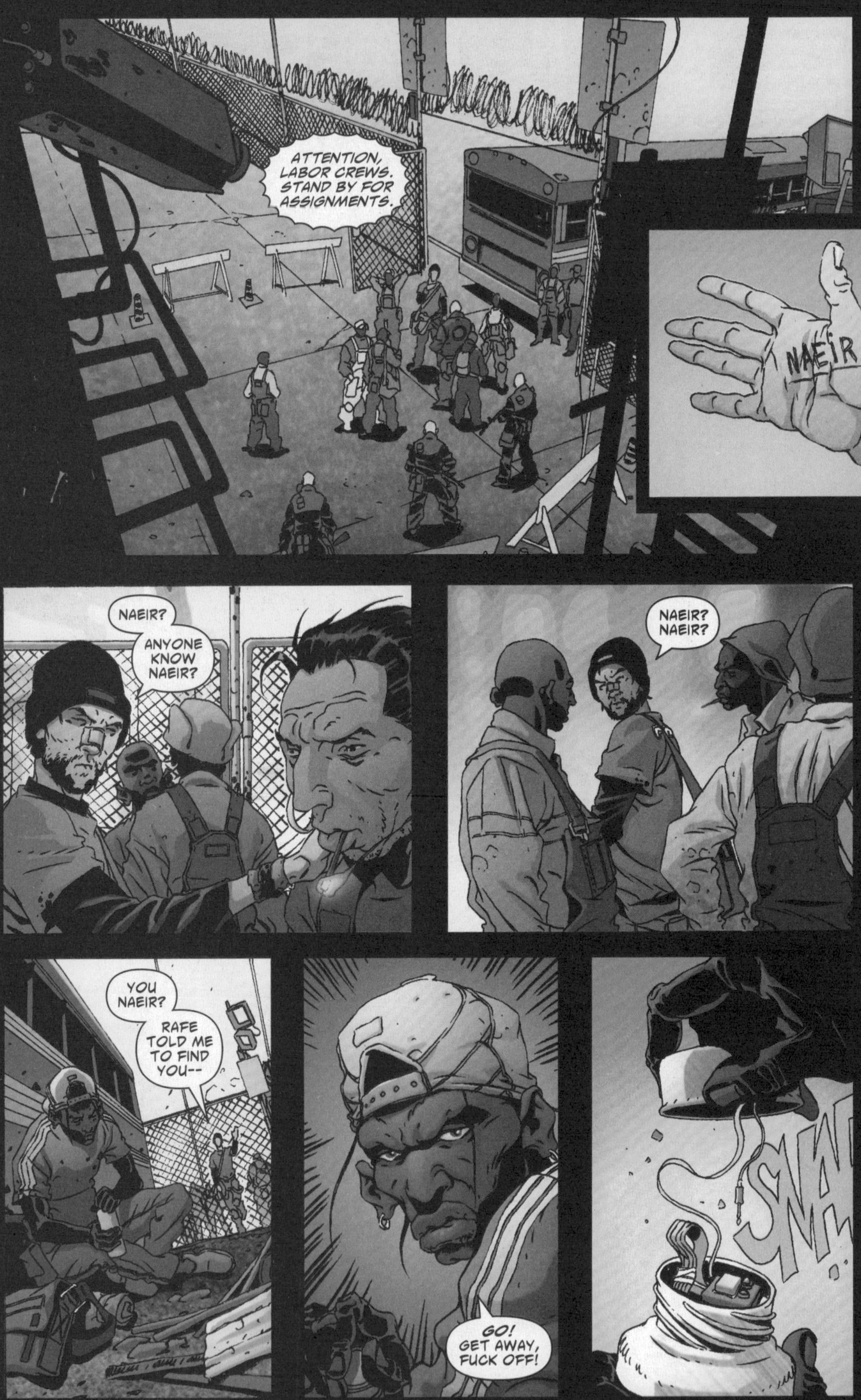

ATTENTION, LABOR CREWS. STAND BY FOR ASSIGNMENTS.
NAEIR
NAEIR?
ANYONE KNOW NAEIR?
NAEIR? NAEIR?
YOU NAEIR?
RAFE TOLD ME TO FIND YOU--
GO! GET AWAY, FUCK OFF!

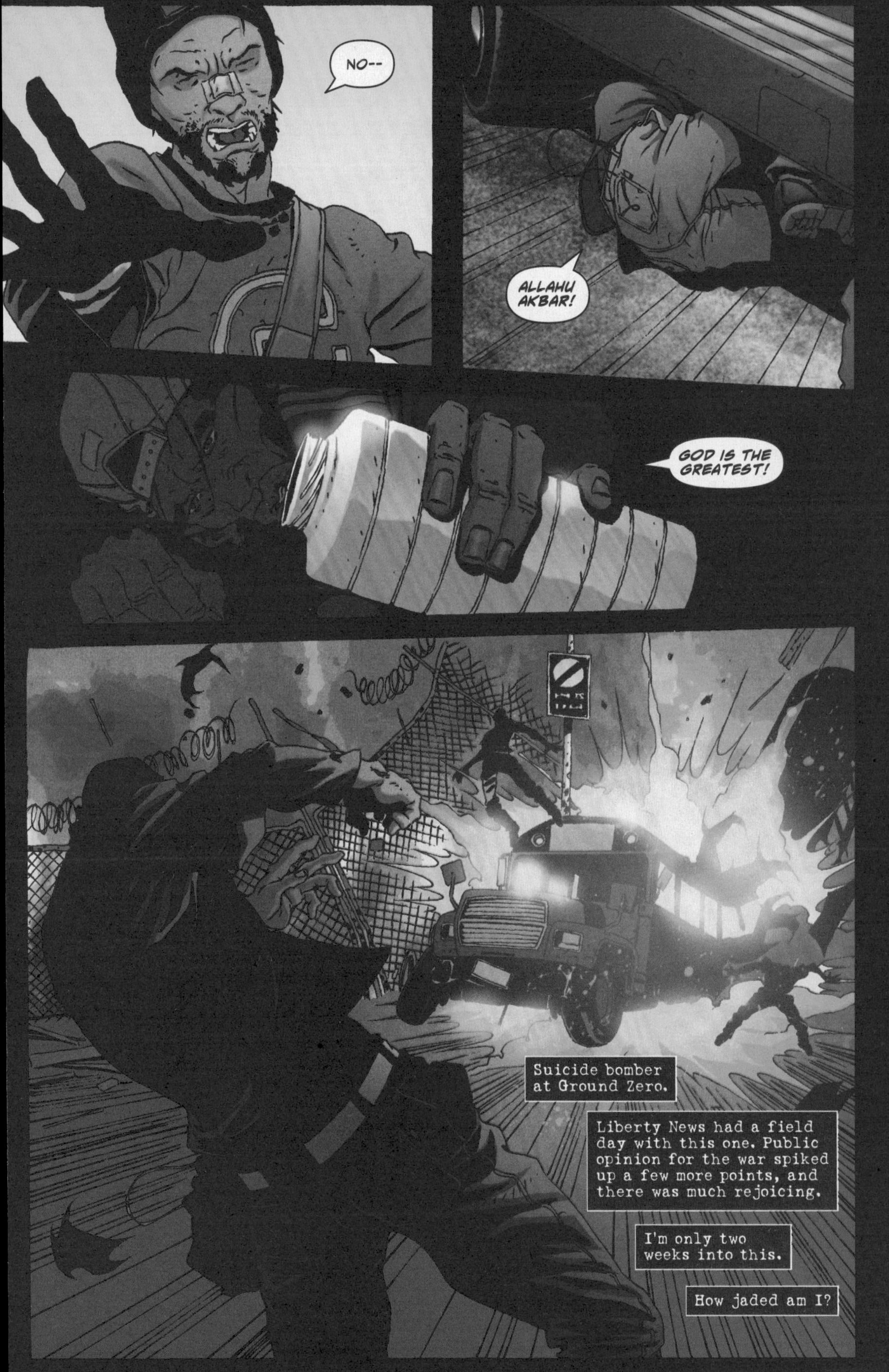
NO--
ALLAHU AKBAR!
GOD IS THE GREATEST!
Suicide bomber at Ground Zero.
Liberty News had a field day with this one. Public opinion for the war spiked up a few more points, and there was much rejoicing.
I'm only two weeks into this.
How jaded am I?

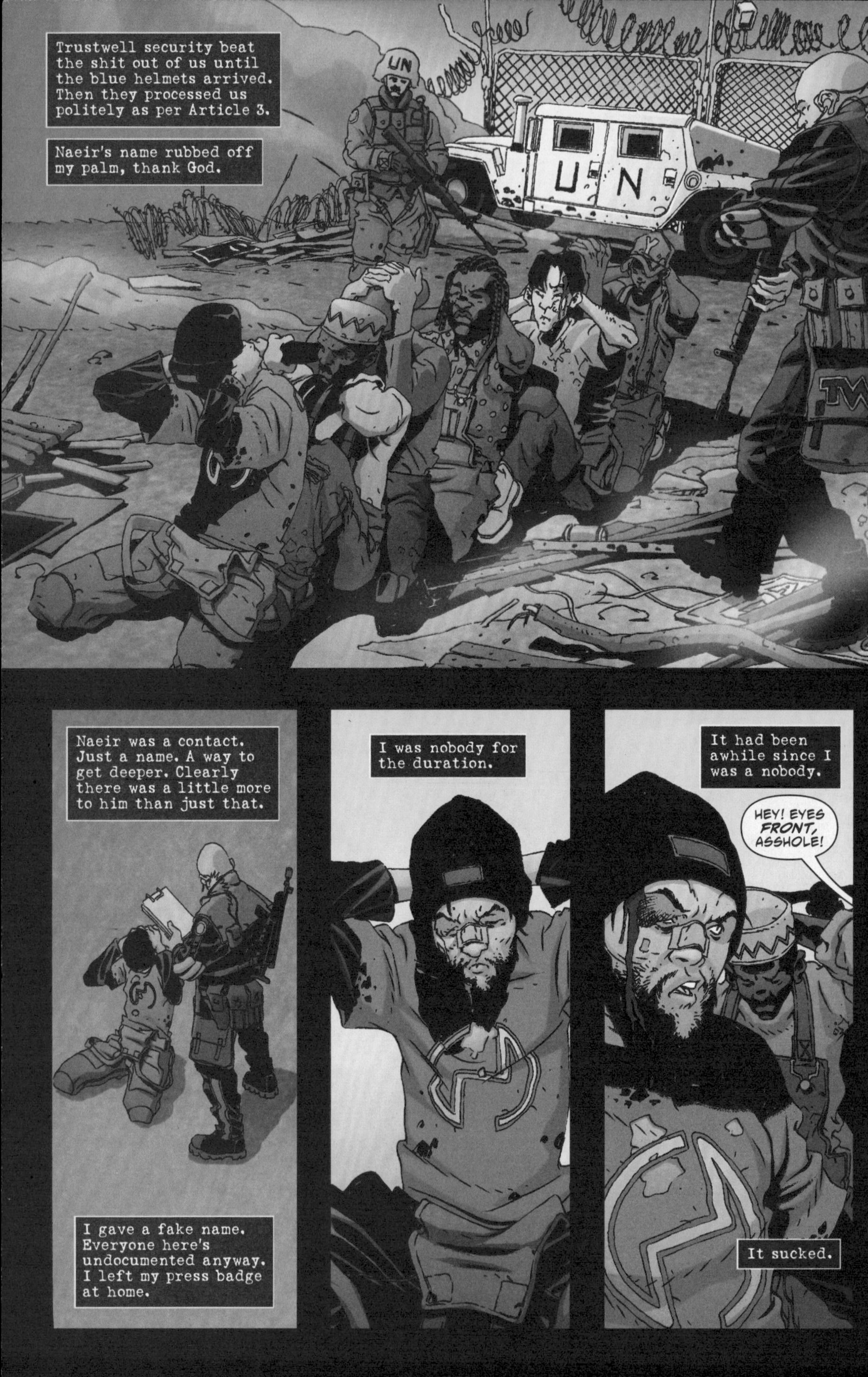
Trustwell security beat the shit out of us until the blue helmets arrived. Then they processed us politely as per Article 3.
Naeir's name rubbed off my palm, thank God.
UN
U N
Naeir was a contact. Just a name. A way to get deeper. Clearly there was a little more to him than just that.
I gave a fake name. Everyone here's undocumented anyway. I left my press badge at home.
I was nobody for the duration.
It had been awhile since I was a nobody.
HEY! EYES FRONT, ASSHOLE!
It sucked.

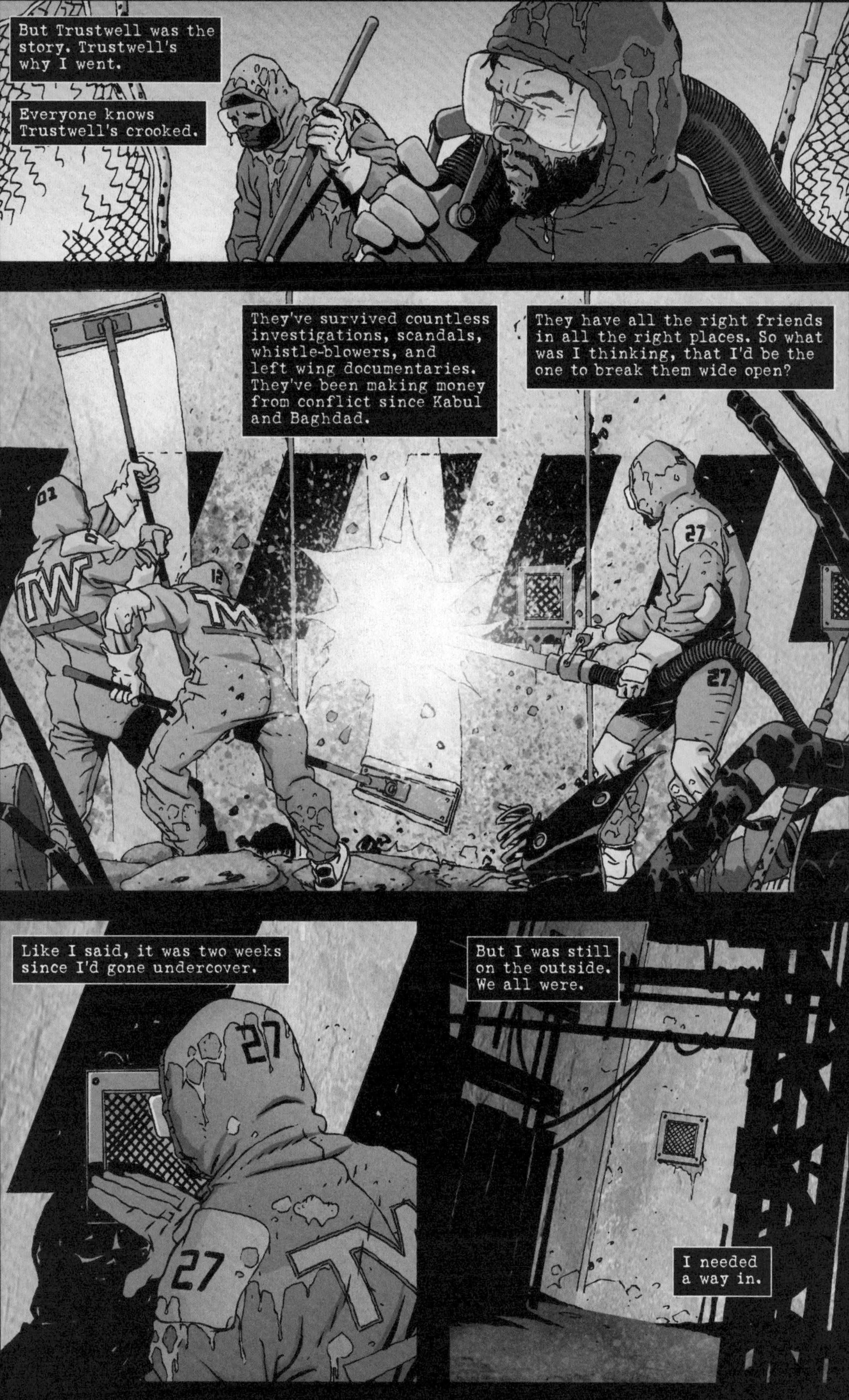

But Trustwell was the story. Trustwell's why I went.
Everyone knows Trustwell's crooked.
They've survived countless investigations, scandals, whistle-blowers, and left wing documentaries. They've been making money from conflict since Kabul and Baghdad.
They have all the right friends in all the right places. So what was I thinking, that I'd be the one to break them wide open?
TW
TW
Like I said, it was two weeks since I'd gone undercover.
27
27
But I was still on the outside. We all were.
I needed a way in.

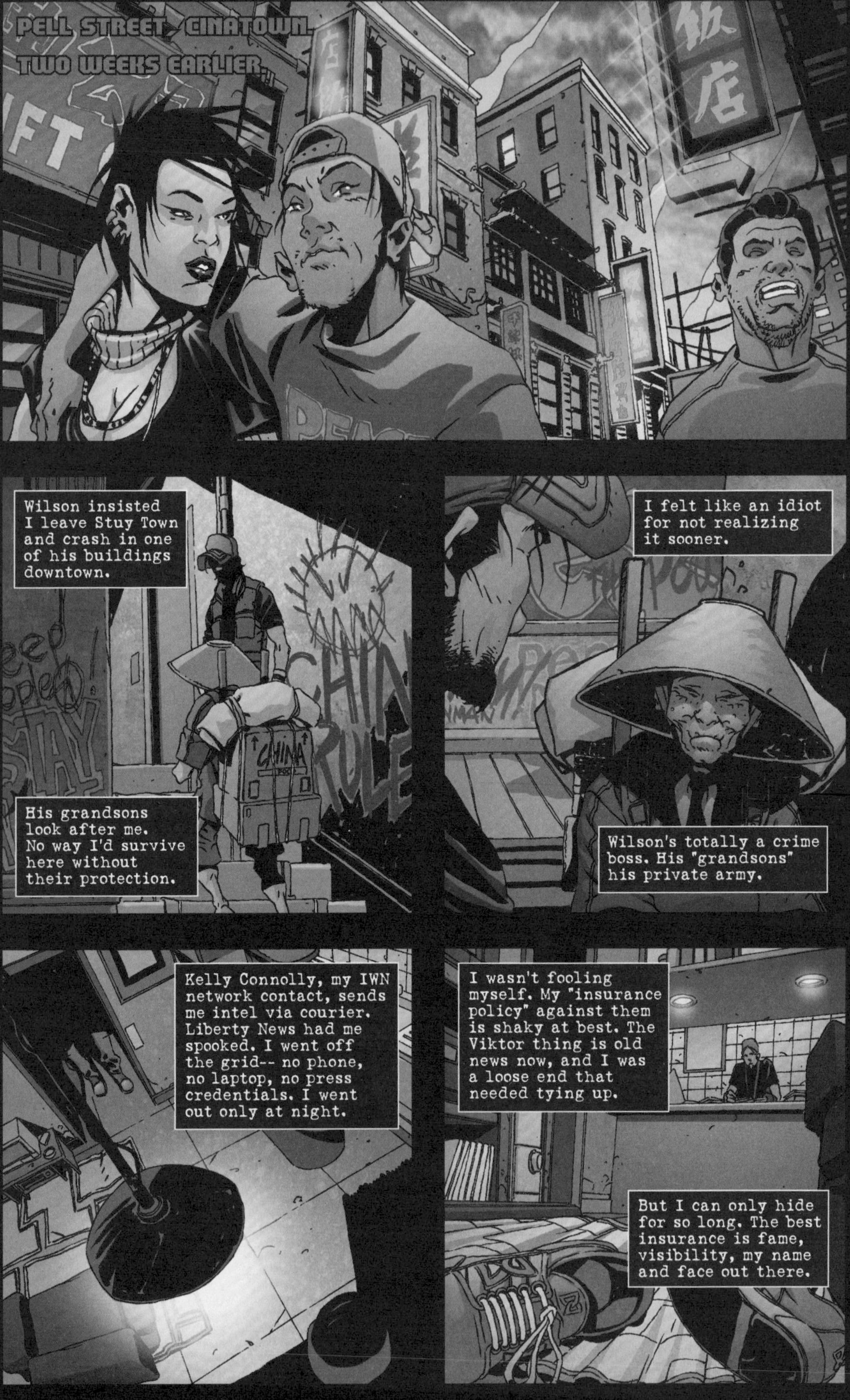
PELL STREET, CINATOWN.
TWO WEEKS EARLIER.
Wilson insisted I leave Stuy Town and crash in one of his buildings downtown.
His grandsons look after me. No way I'd survive here without their protection.
I felt like an idiot for not realizing it sooner.
Wilson's totally a crime boss. His "grandsons" his private army.
Kelly Connolly, my IWN network contact, sends me intel via courier. Liberty News had me spooked. I went off the grid-- no phone, no laptop, no press credentials. I went out only at night.
I wasn't fooling myself. My "insurance policy" against them is shaky at best. The Viktor thing is old news now, and I was a loose end that needed tying up.
But I can only hide for so long. The best insurance is fame, visibility, my name and face out there.

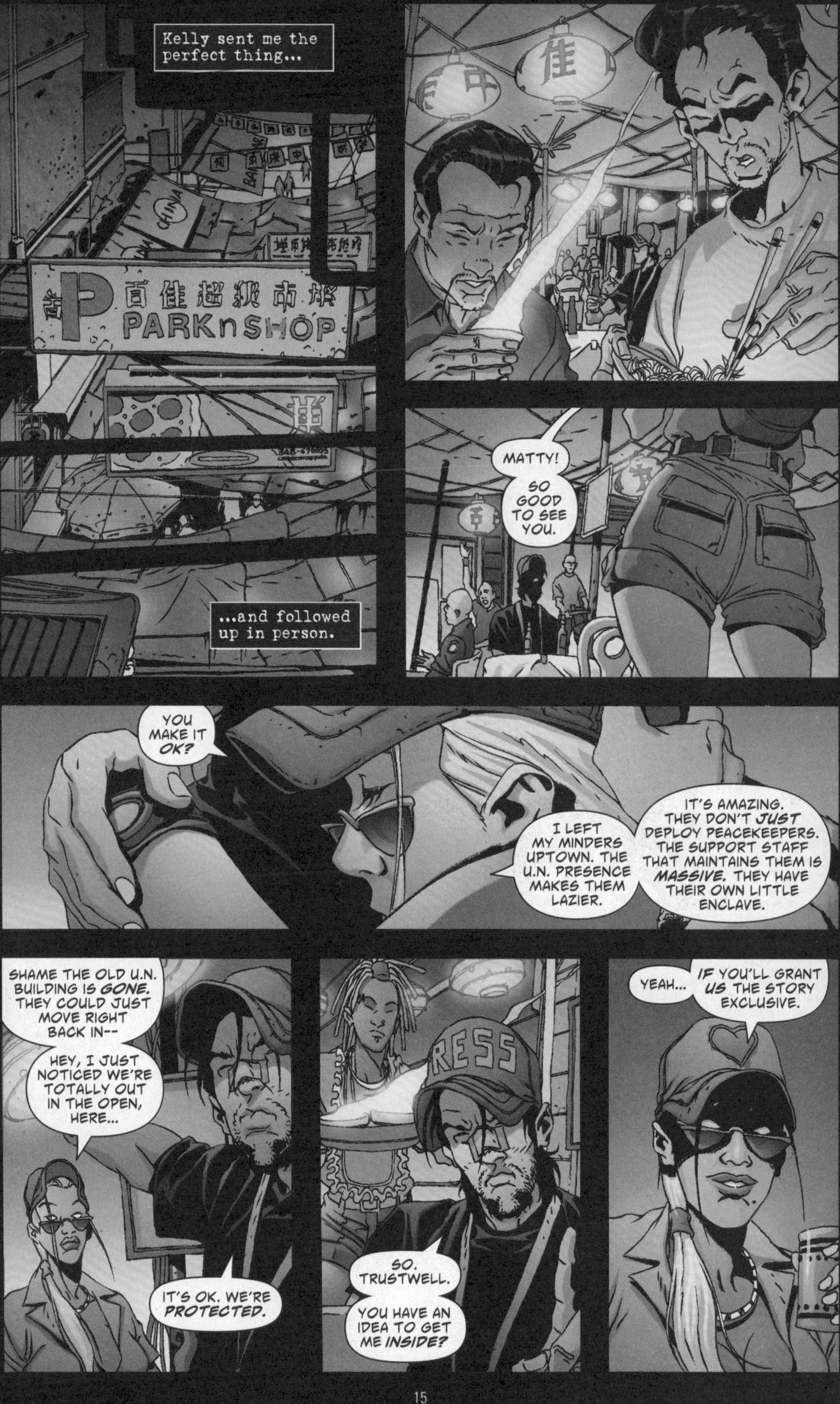
Kelly sent me the perfect thing...
百佳超級市場
PARKnSHOP
...and followed up in person.
MATTY!
SO GOOD TO SEE YOU.
YOU MAKE IT OK?
I LEFT MY MINDERS UPTOWN. THE U.N. PRESENCE MAKES THEM LAZIER.
IT'S AMAZING. THEY DON'T JUST DEPLOY PEACEKEEPERS. THE SUPPORT STAFF THAT MAINTAINS THEM IS MASSIVE. THEY HAVE THEIR OWN LITTLE ENCLAVE.
SHAME THE OLD U.N. BUILDING IS GONE. THEY COULD JUST MOVE RIGHT BACK IN--
HEY, I JUST NOTICED WE'RE TOTALLY OUT IN THE OPEN, HERE...
IT'S OK. WE'RE PROTECTED.
RESS
SO. TRUSTWELL.
YOU HAVE AN IDEA TO GET ME INSIDE?
YEAH...
IF YOU'LL GRANT US THE STORY EXCLUSIVE.

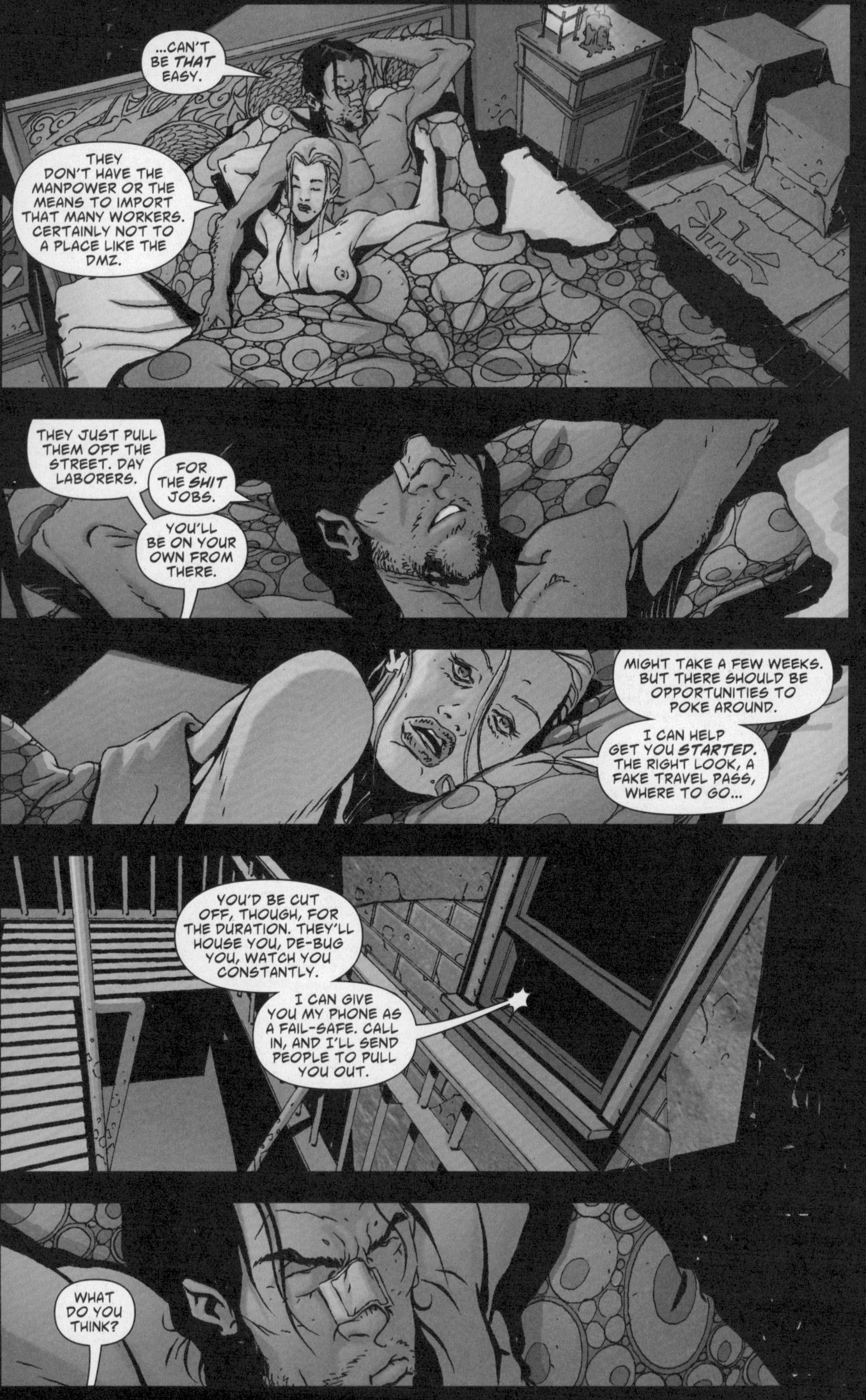
...CAN'T BE THAT EASY.
THEY DON'T HAVE THE MANPOWER OR THE MEANS TO IMPORT THAT MANY WORKERS. CERTAINLY NOT TO A PLACE LIKE THE DMZ.
THEY JUST PULL THEM OFF THE STREET. DAY LABORERS.
FOR THE SHIT JOBS.
YOU'LL BE ON YOUR OWN FROM THERE.
MIGHT TAKE A FEW WEEKS. BUT THERE SHOULD BE OPPORTUNITIES TO POKE AROUND.
I CAN HELP GET YOU STARTED. THE RIGHT LOOK, A FAKE TRAVEL PASS, WHERE TO GO...
YOU'D BE CUT OFF, THOUGH, FOR THE DURATION. THEY'LL HOUSE YOU, DE-BUG YOU, WATCH YOU CONSTANTLY.
I CAN GIVE YOU MY PHONE AS A FAIL-SAFE. CALL IN, AND I'LL SEND PEOPLE TO PULL YOU OUT.
WHAT DO YOU THINK?

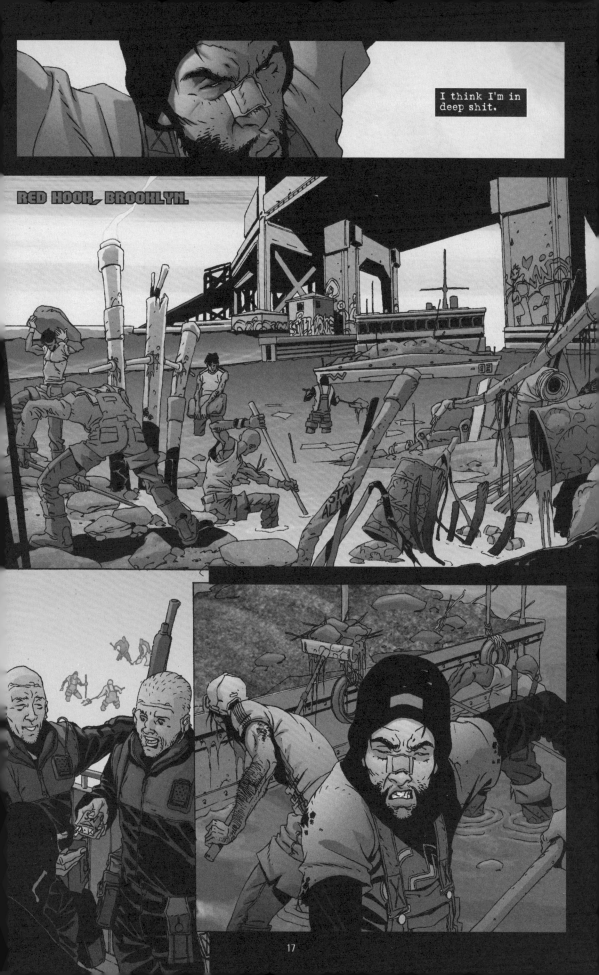

I think I'm in deep shit.

RED HOOK, BROOKLYN.

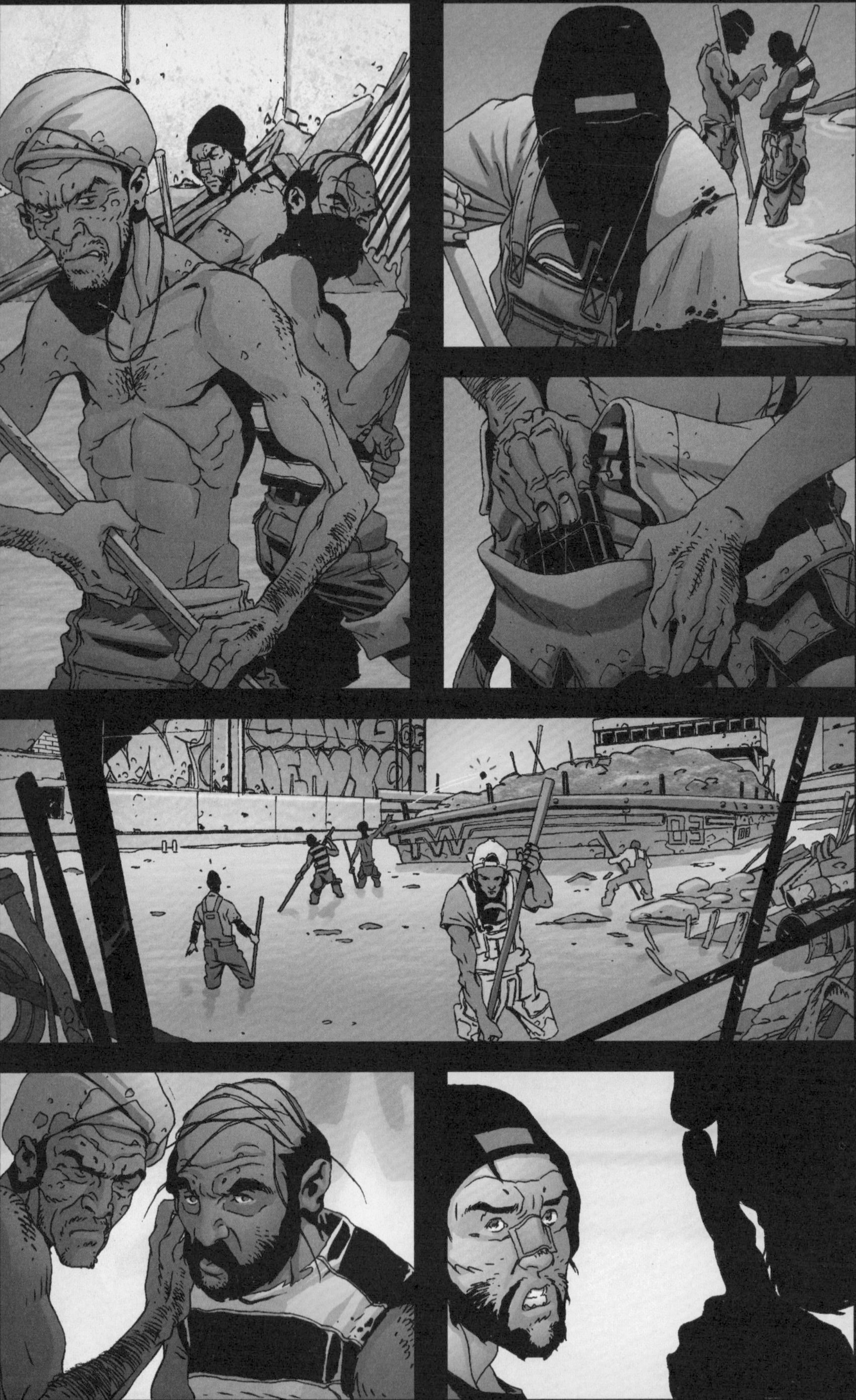

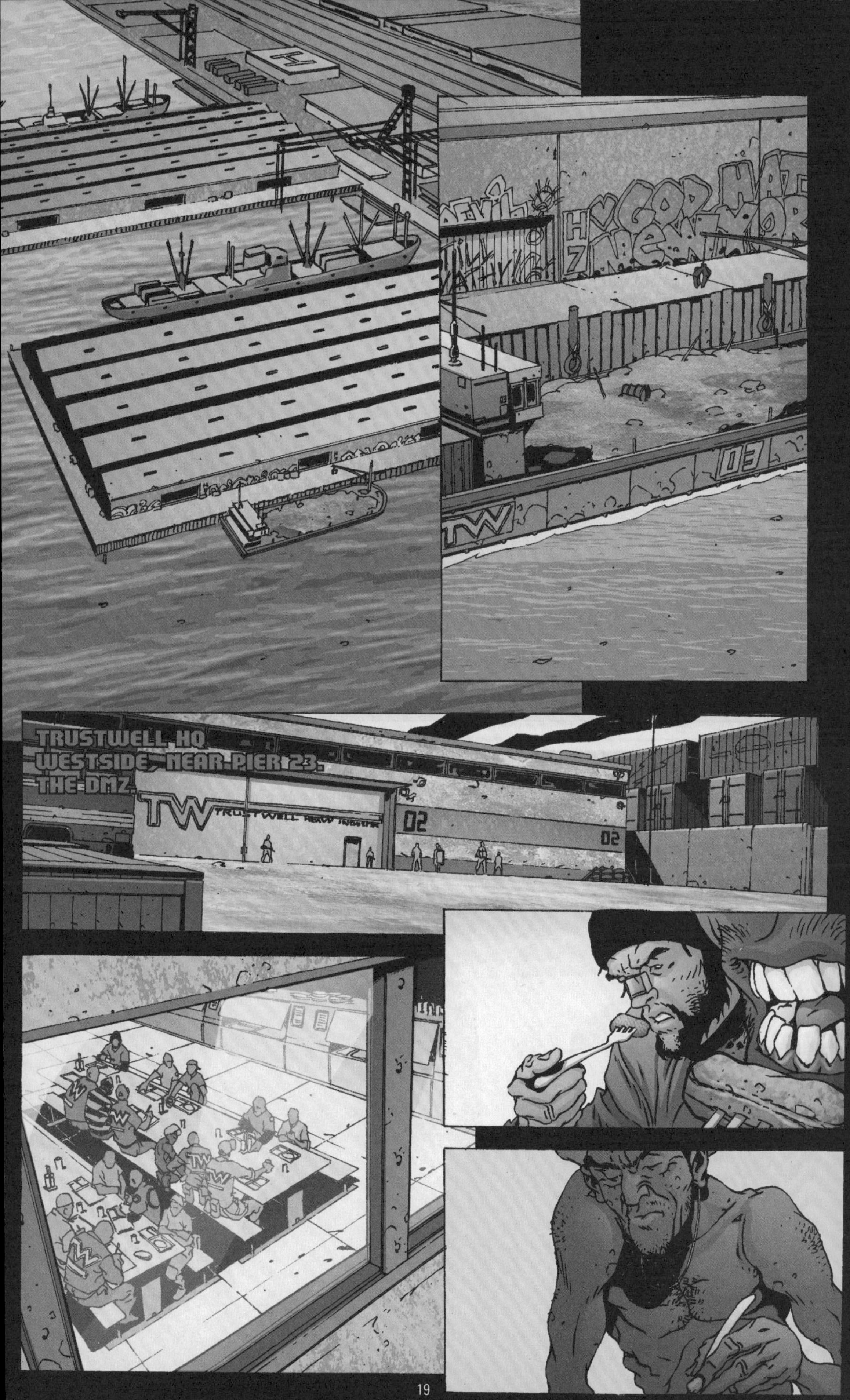

TRUSTWELL HQ
WESTSIDE, NEAR PIER 23.
THE DMZ.

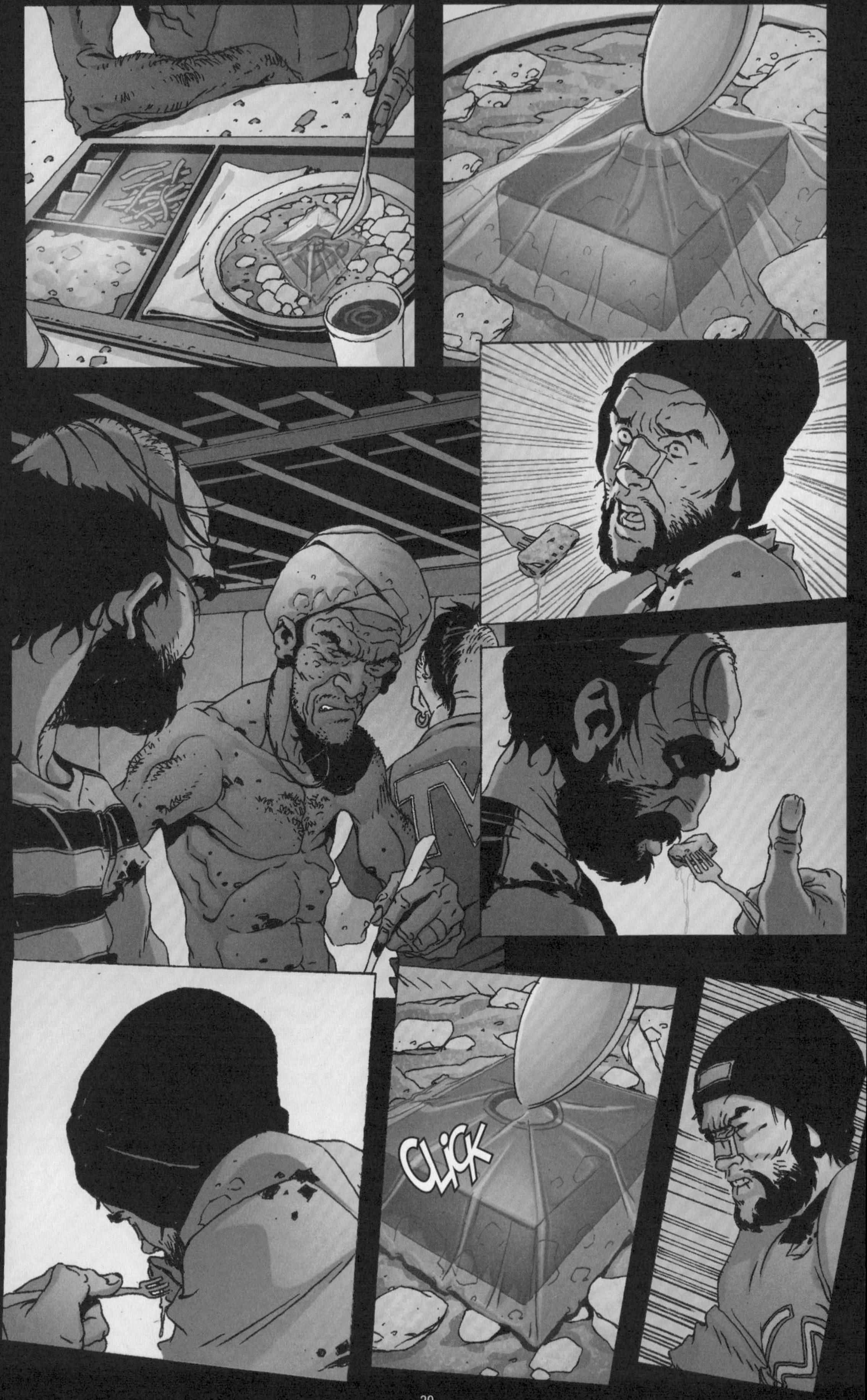
CLICK

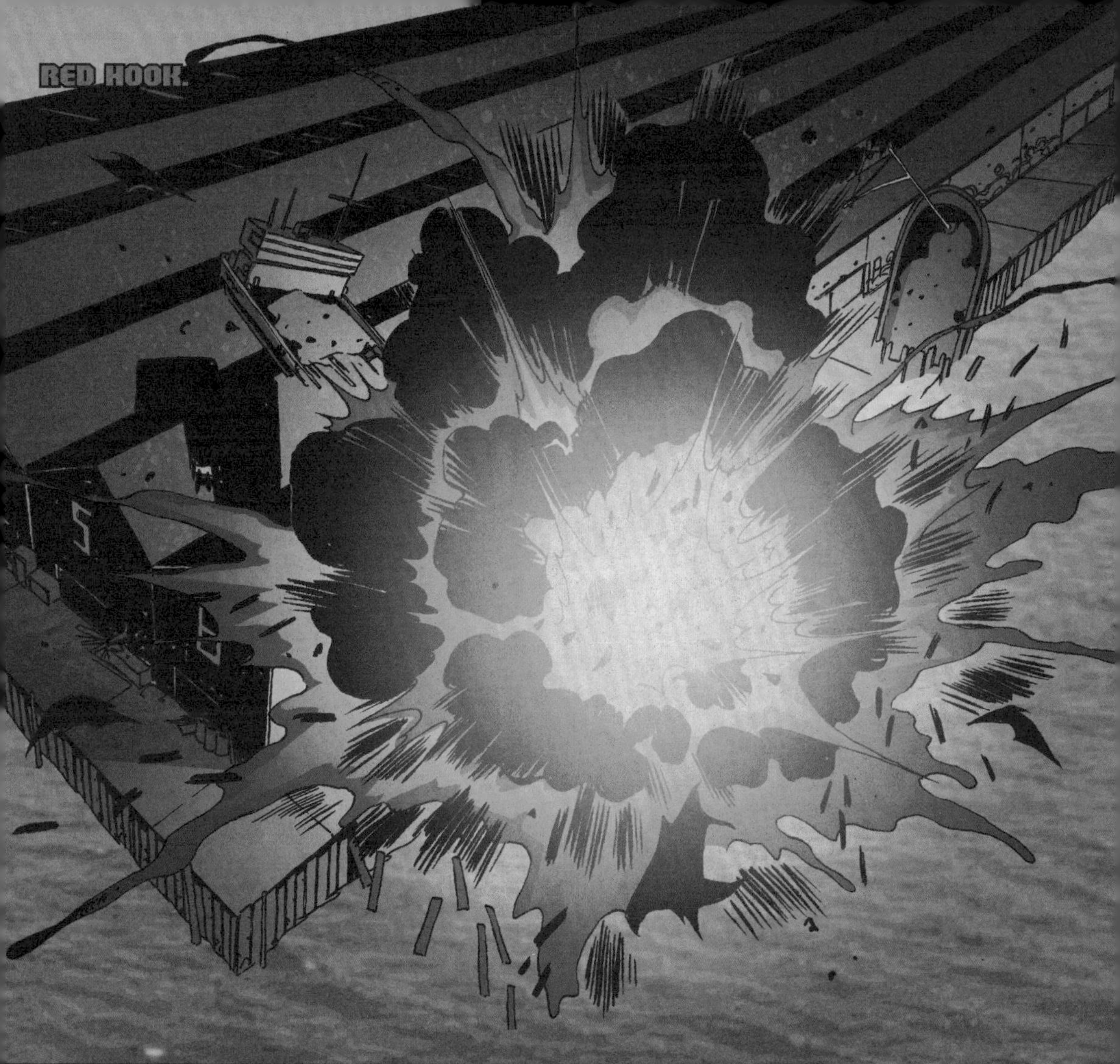
RED HOOK.

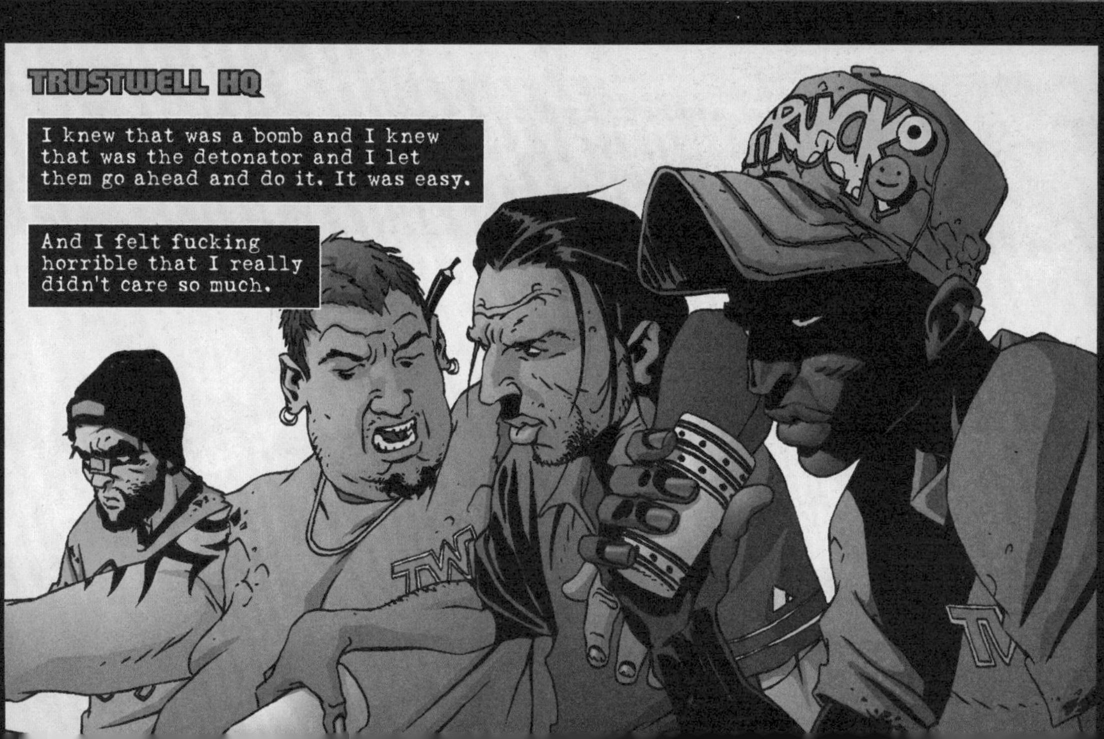
TRUSTWELL HQ
I knew that was a bomb and I knew that was the detonator and I let them go ahead and do it. It was easy.
And I felt fucking horrible that I really didn't care so much.

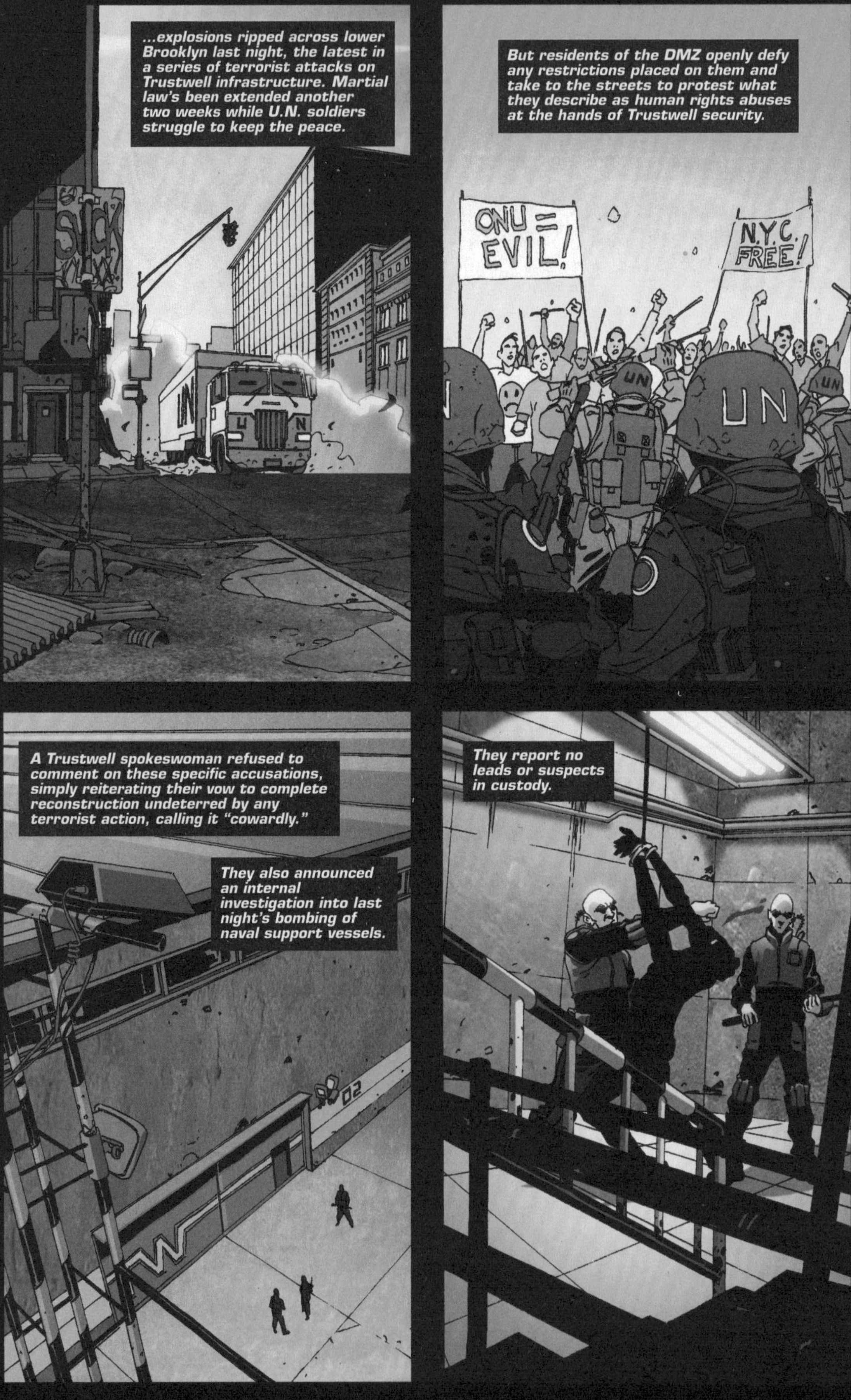
...explosions ripped across lower Brooklyn last night, the latest in a series of terrorist attacks on Trustwell infrastructure. Martial law's been extended another two weeks while U.N. soldiers struggle to keep the peace.
SICK
UN
But residents of the DMZ openly defy any restrictions placed on them and take to the streets to protest what they describe as human rights abuses at the hands of Trustwell security.
ONU = EVIL!
N.Y.C. FREE!
UN
A Trustwell spokeswoman refused to comment on these specific accusations, simply reiterating their vow to complete reconstruction undeterred by any terrorist action, calling it "cowardly."
They also announced an internal investigation into last night's bombing of naval support vessels.
02
They report no leads or suspects in custody.

With work temporarily halted at Ground Zero, resources are now being focused on the Empire State building...

...yet another sensitive site for New Yorkers, and the mere presence of Trustwell there is an emotional trigger.

With violence on the rise, Trustwell's commitment is also under attack.

A TRUSTWELL
For a new

STWELL PROJECT
new beginning

But the multibillion-dollar company is showing no signs of weakness, no signs of backing down.

This is Liberty News, back in sixty seconds.

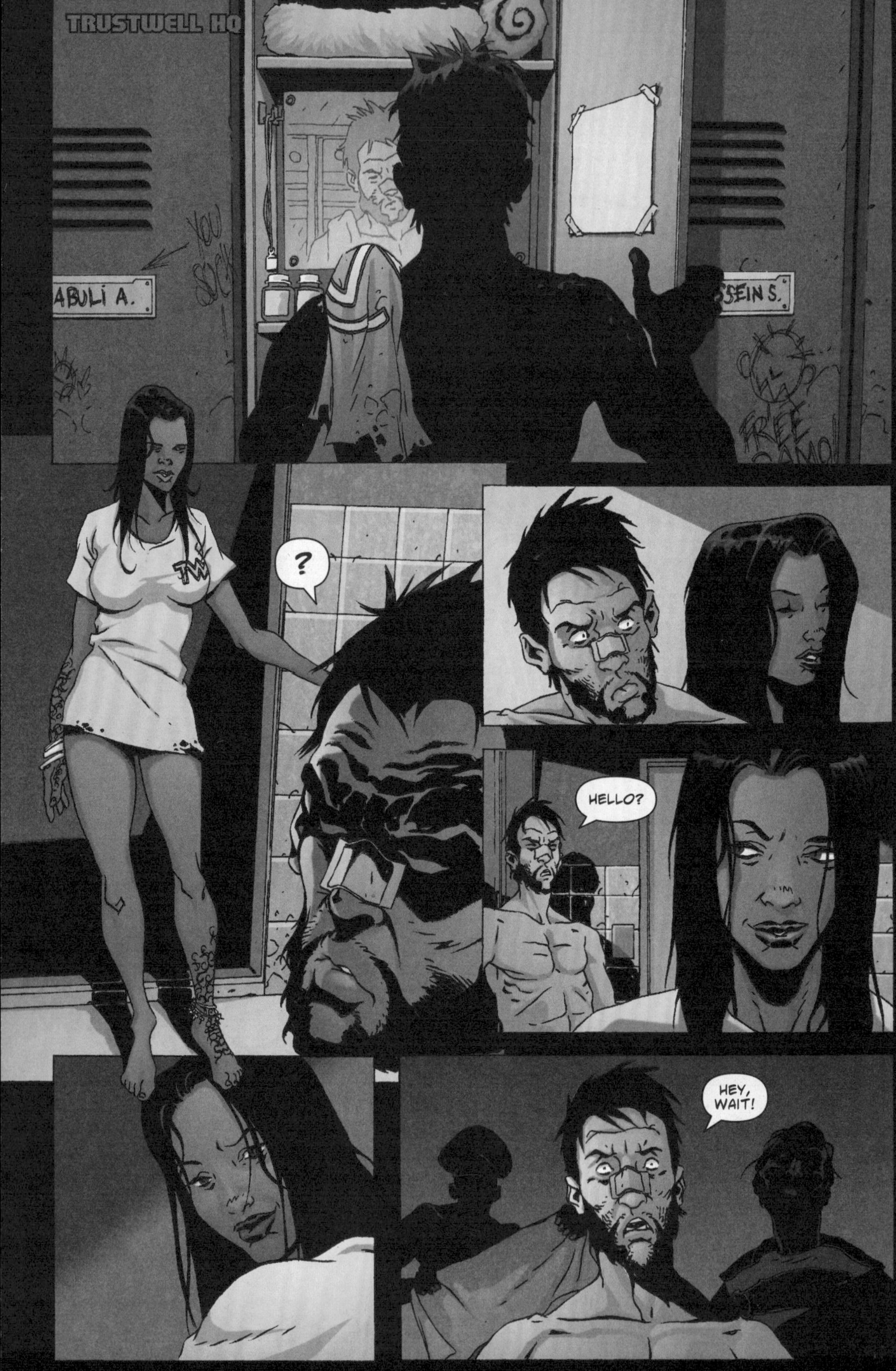
TRUSTWELL HQ
YOU SUCK
ABULI A.
SSEIN S.
FREE SAMOI
?
HELLO?
HEY, WAIT!

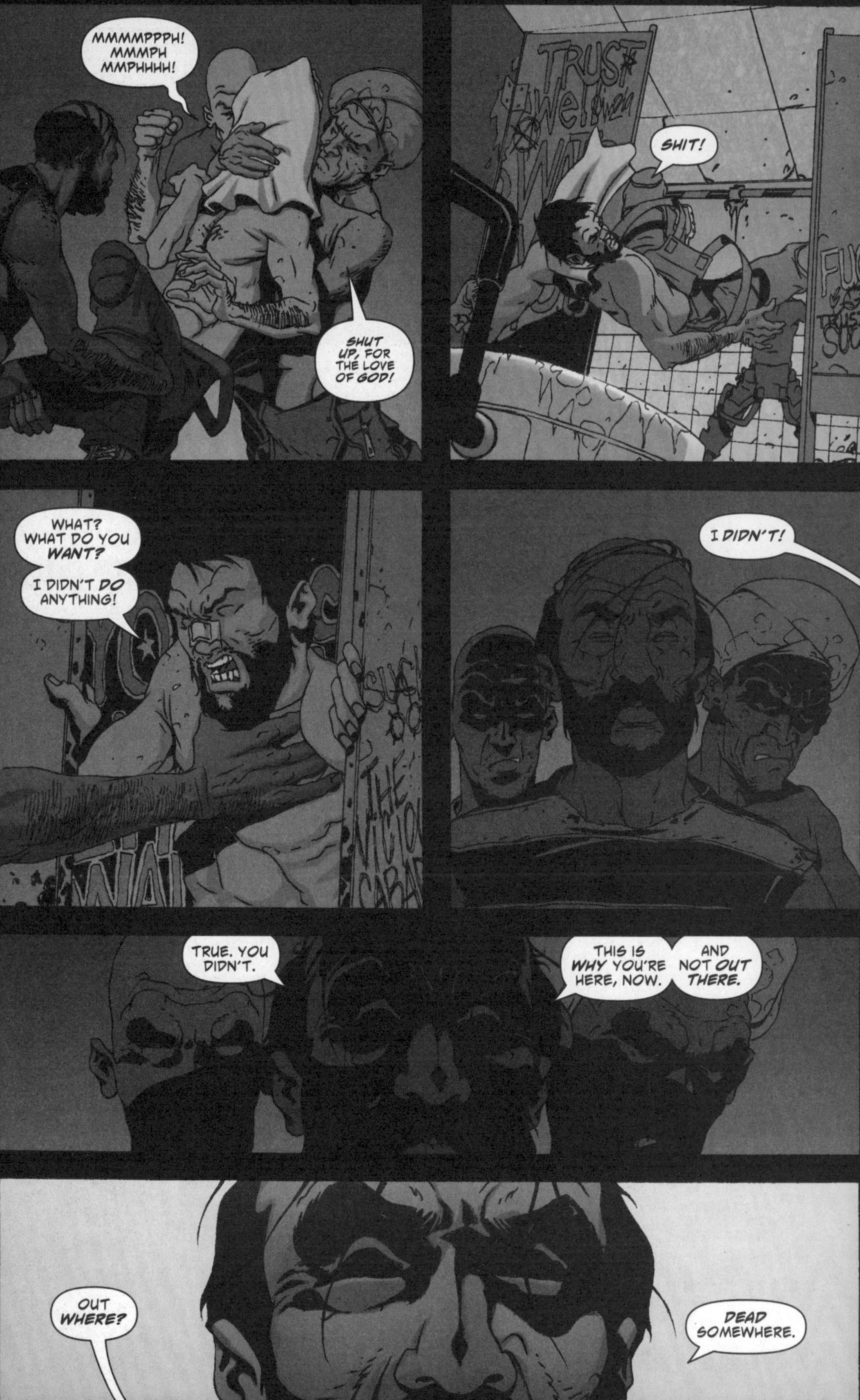
MMMMPPPH! MMMPH MMPHHHH!
SHUT UP, FOR THE LOVE OF GOD!
SHIT!
WHAT? WHAT DO YOU WANT?
I DIDN'T DO ANYTHING!
I DIDN'T!
TRUE. YOU DIDN'T.
THIS IS WHY YOU'RE HERE, NOW.
AND NOT OUT THERE.
OUT WHERE?
DEAD SOMEWHERE.

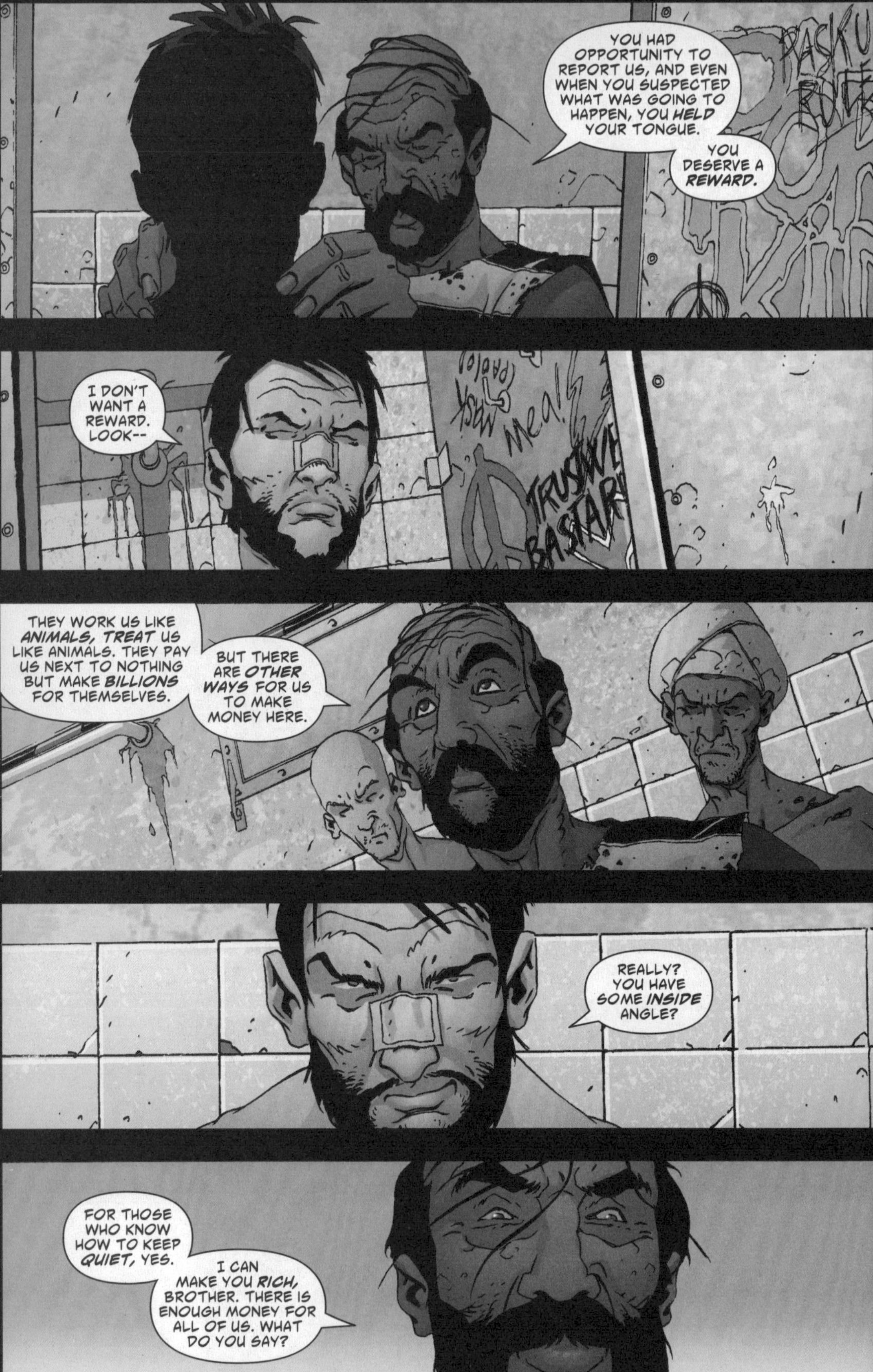

YOU HAD OPPORTUNITY TO REPORT US, AND EVEN WHEN YOU SUSPECTED WHAT WAS GOING TO HAPPEN, YOU HELD YOUR TONGUE.
YOU DESERVE A REWARD.
I DON'T WANT A REWARD. LOOK--
THEY WORK US LIKE ANIMALS, TREAT US LIKE ANIMALS. THEY PAY US NEXT TO NOTHING BUT MAKE BILLIONS FOR THEMSELVES.
BUT THERE ARE OTHER WAYS FOR US TO MAKE MONEY HERE.
REALLY? YOU HAVE SOME INSIDE ANGLE?
FOR THOSE WHO KNOW HOW TO KEEP QUIET, YES.
I CAN MAKE YOU RICH, BROTHER. THERE IS ENOUGH MONEY FOR ALL OF US. WHAT DO YOU SAY?

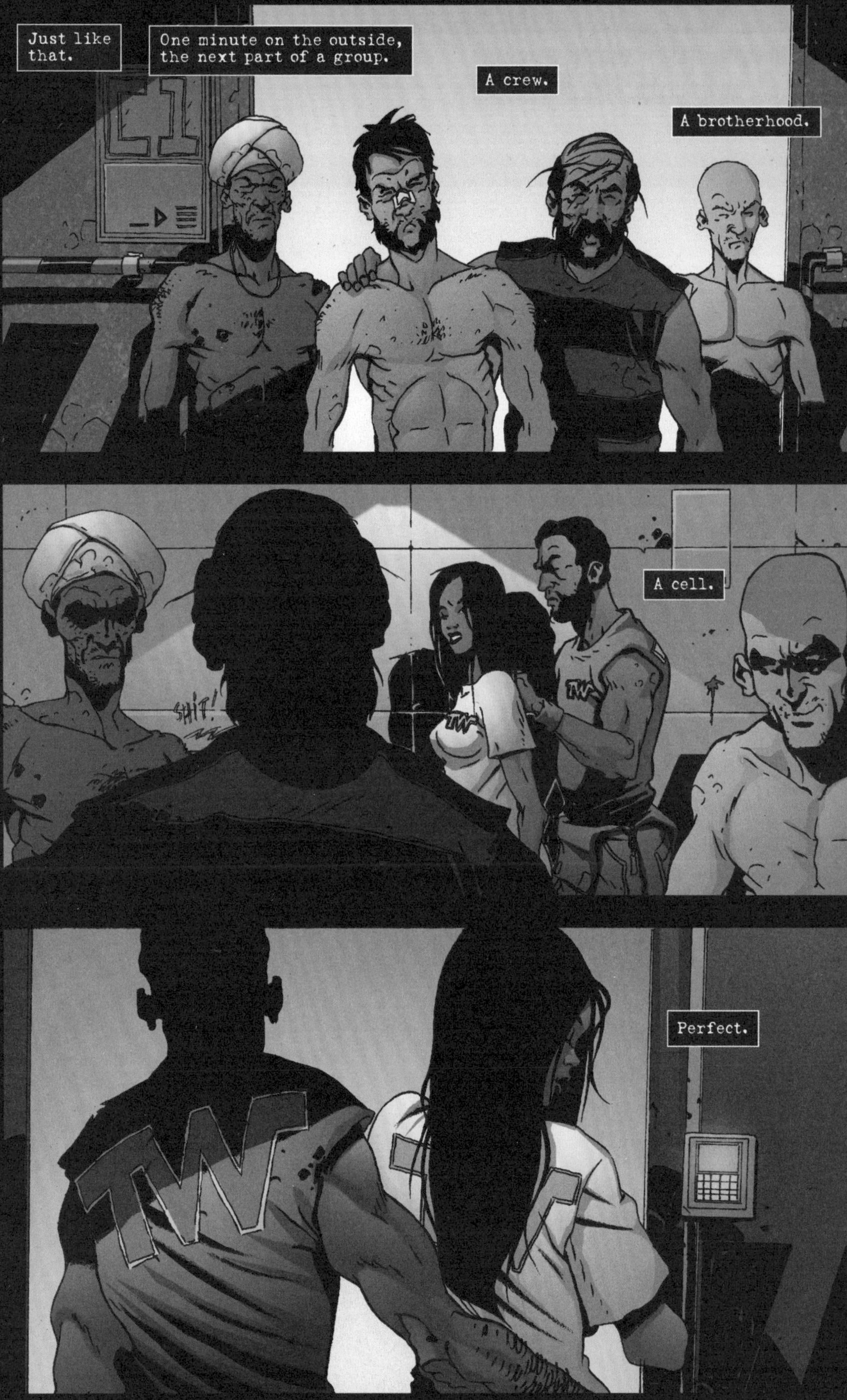
Just like that.
One minute on the outside, the next part of a group.
A crew.
A brotherhood.
SHIT!
A cell.
Perfect.

# CHAPTER TWO

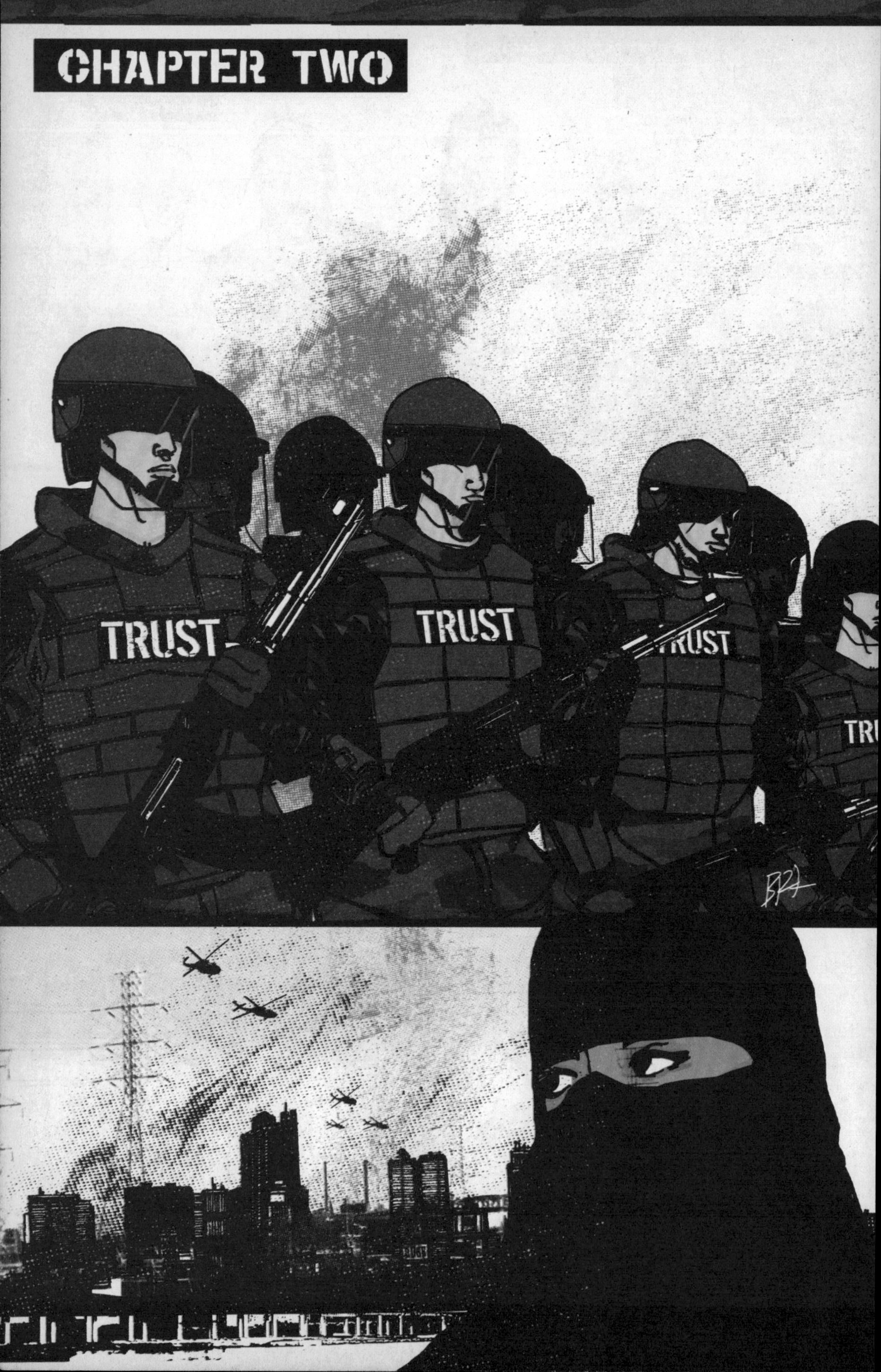

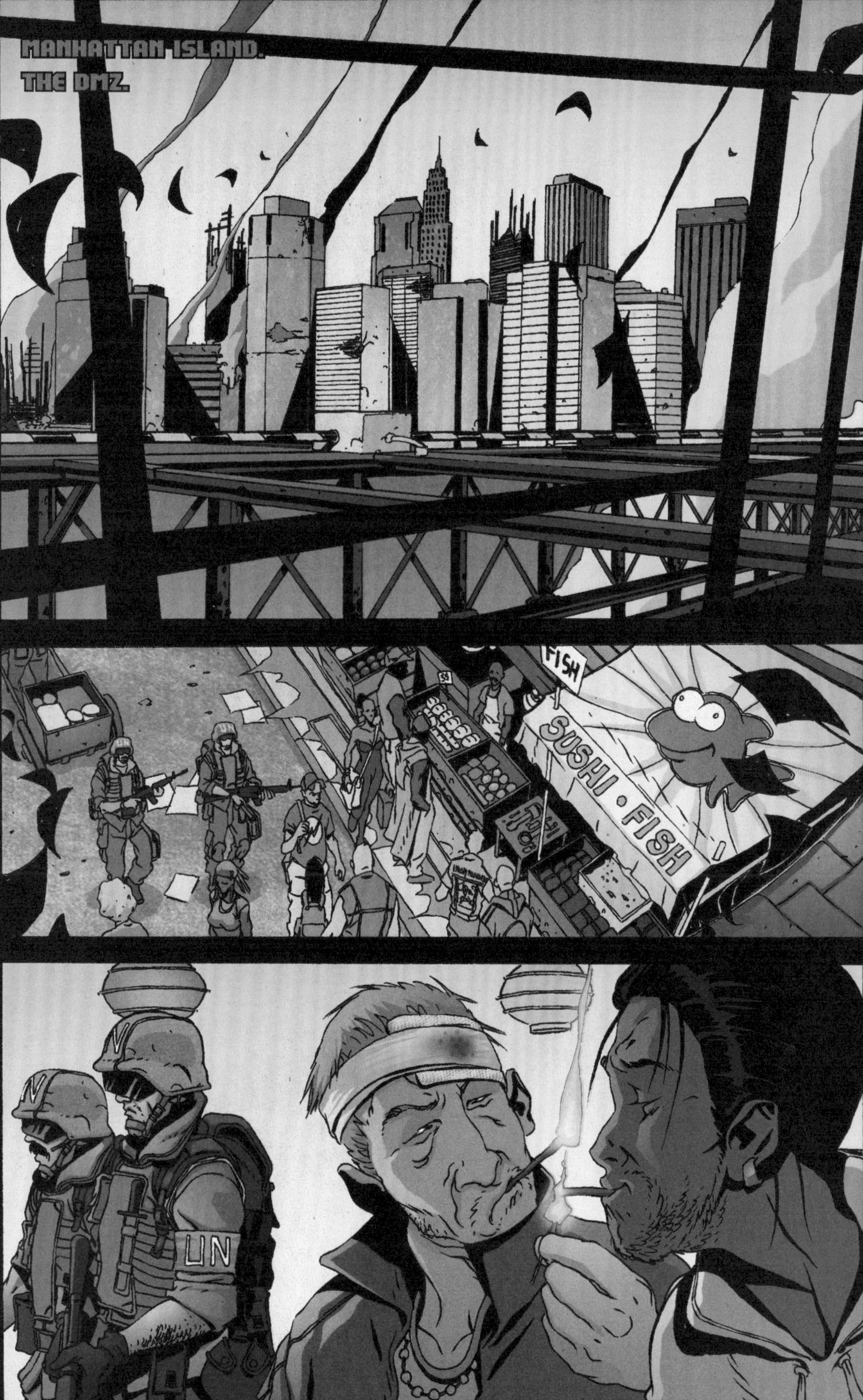
MANHATTAN ISLAND.
THE DMZ.
FISH
SUSHI • FISH
UN
UN

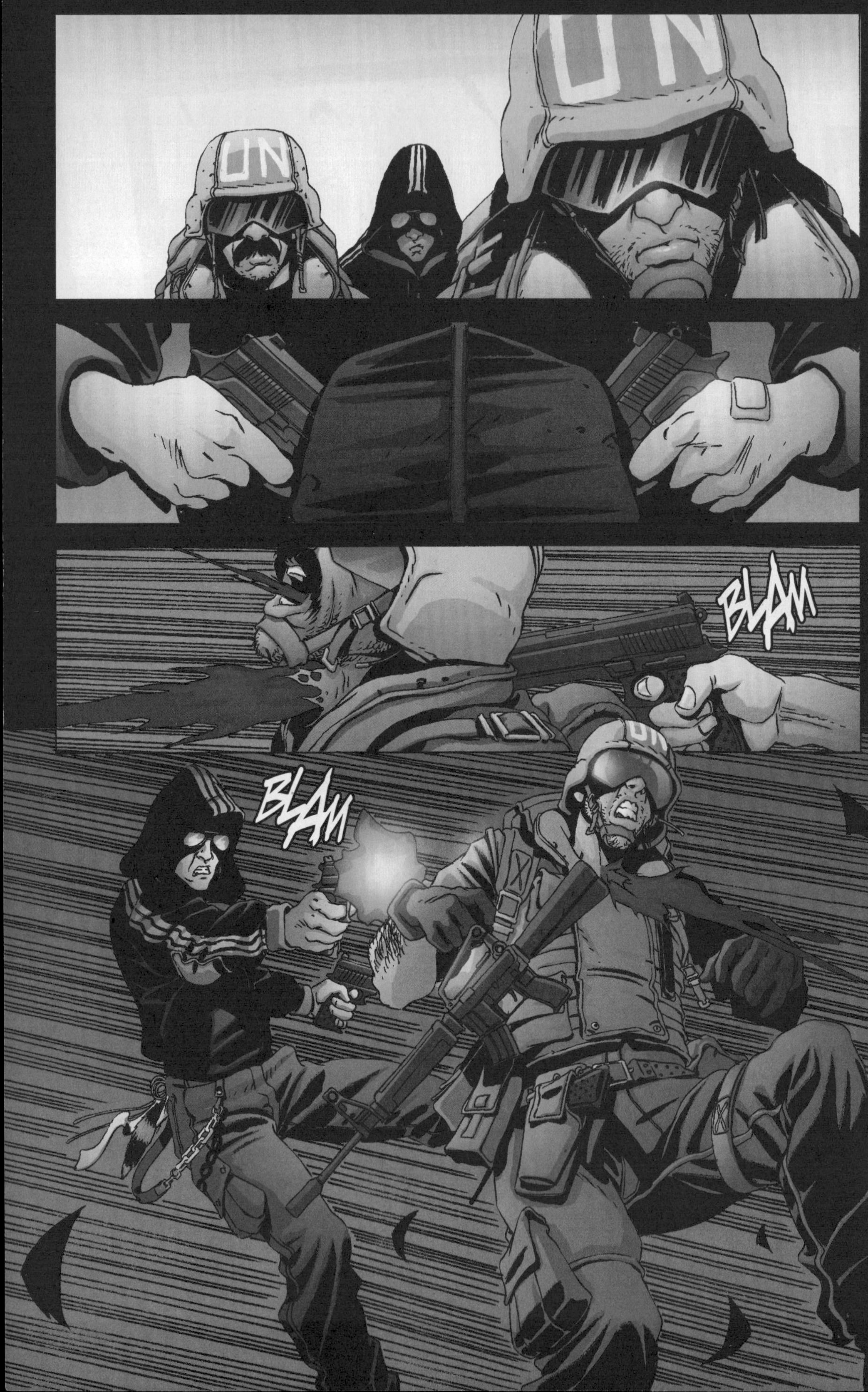
BLAM
BLAM

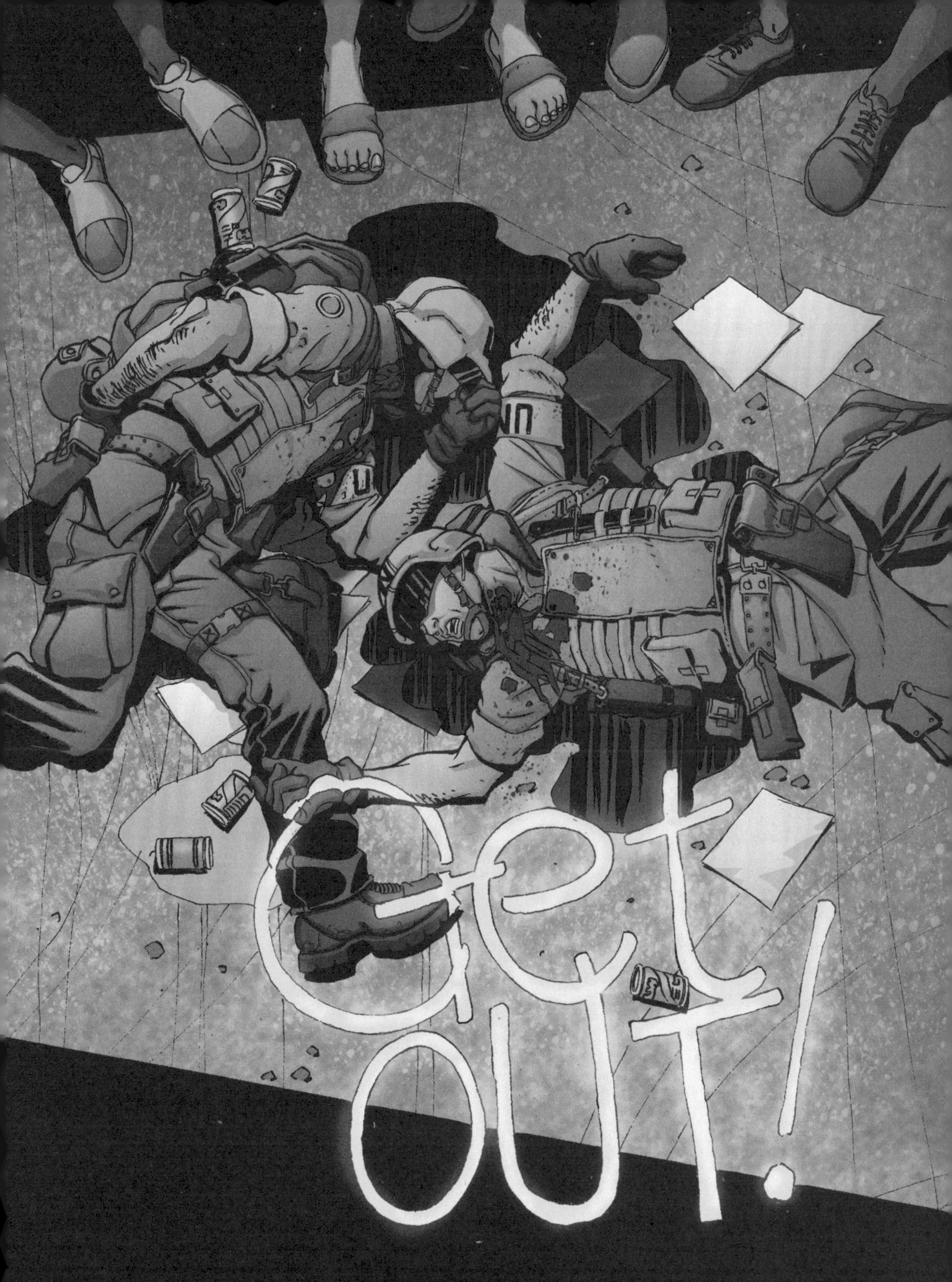
Get out!

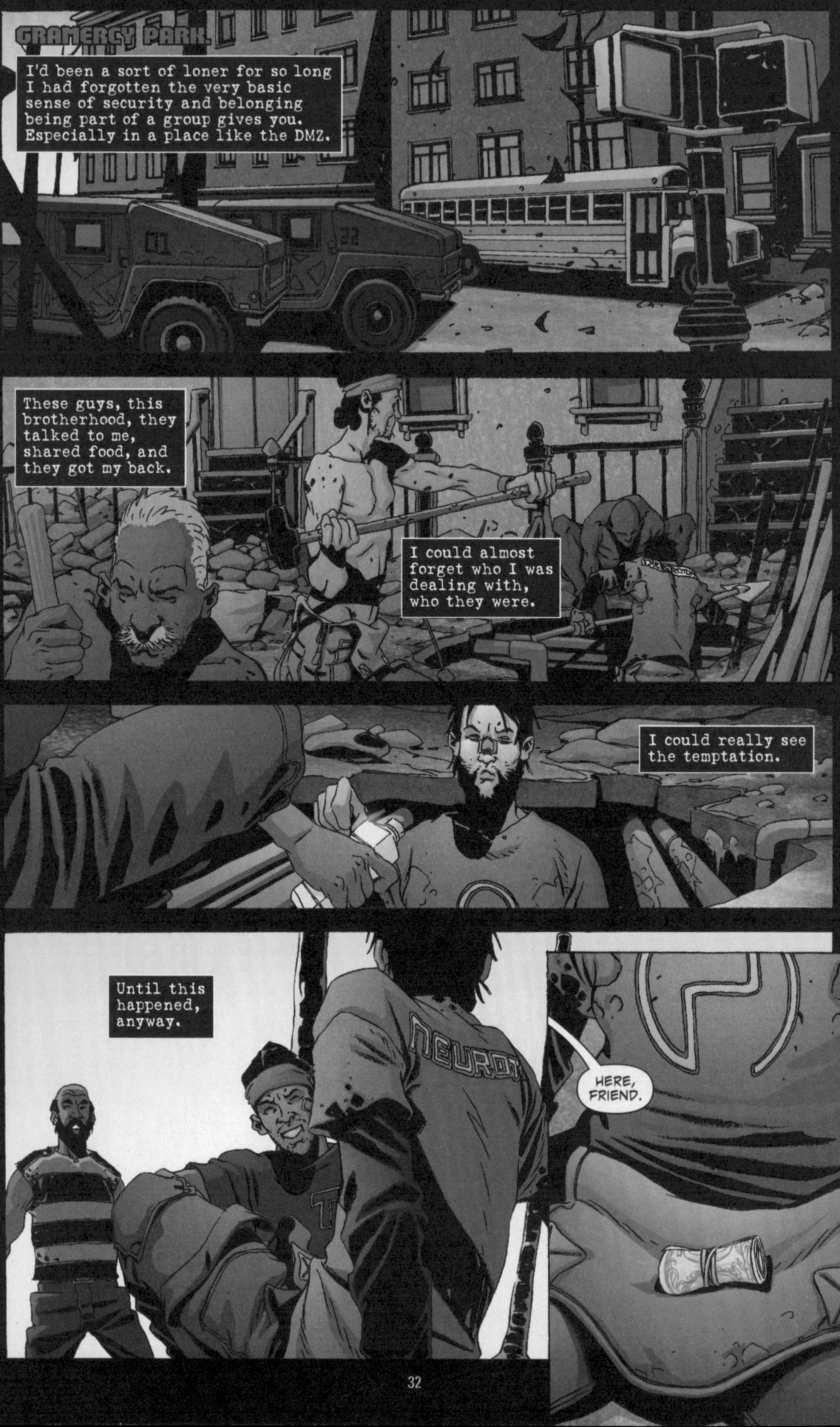
GRAMERCY PARK
I'd been a sort of loner for so long I had forgotten the very basic sense of security and belonging being part of a group gives you. Especially in a place like the DMZ.
These guys, this brotherhood, they talked to me, shared food, and they got my back.
I could almost forget who I was dealing with, who they were.
I could really see the temptation.
Until this happened, anyway.
HERE, FRIEND.

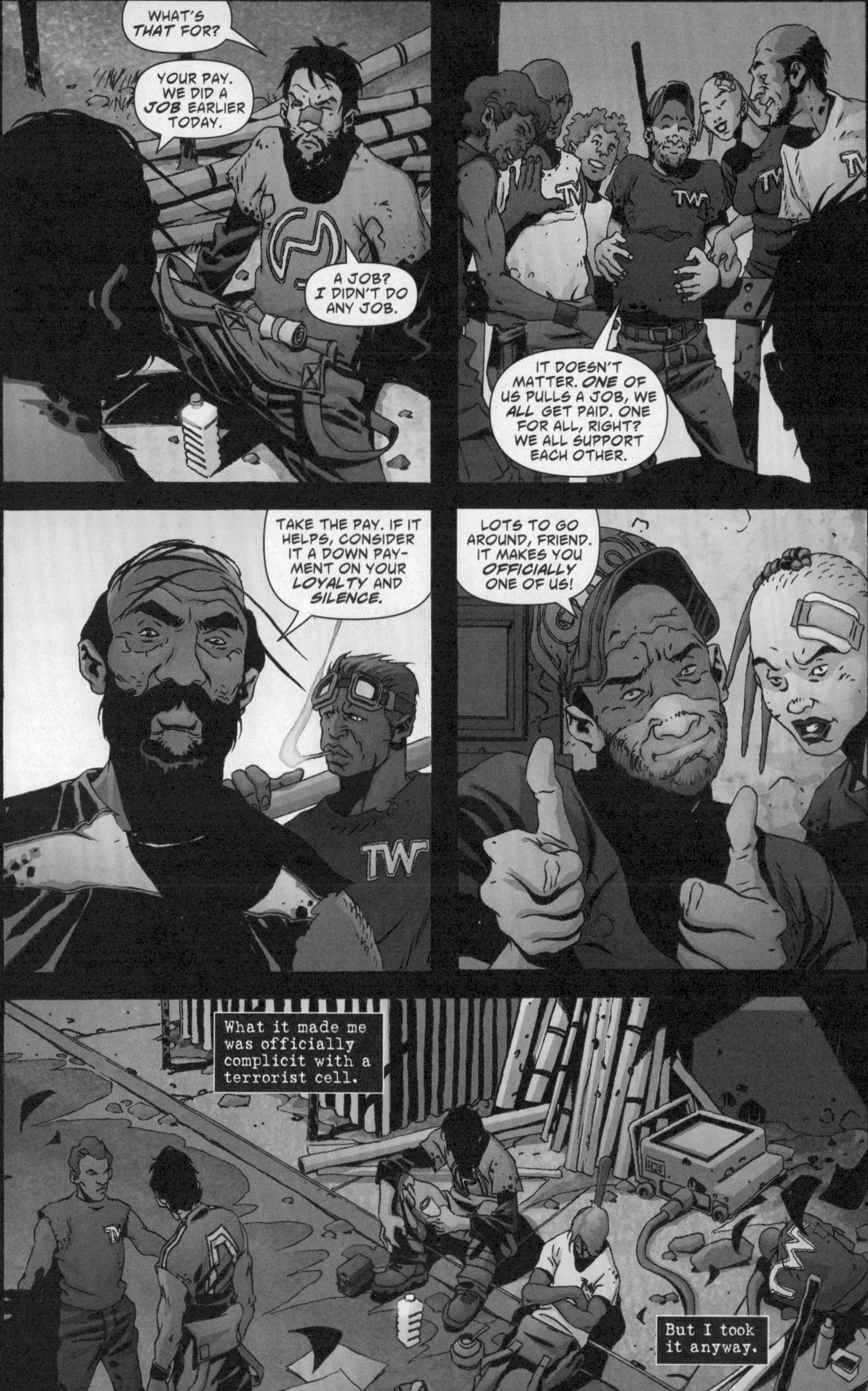
WHAT'S THAT FOR?
YOUR PAY. WE DID A JOB EARLIER TODAY.
A JOB? I DIDN'T DO ANY JOB.
IT DOESN'T MATTER. ONE OF US PULLS A JOB, WE ALL GET PAID. ONE FOR ALL, RIGHT? WE ALL SUPPORT EACH OTHER.
TAKE THE PAY. IF IT HELPS, CONSIDER IT A DOWN PAY-MENT ON YOUR LOYALTY AND SILENCE.
LOTS TO GO AROUND, FRIEND. IT MAKES YOU OFFICIALLY ONE OF US!
What it made me was officially complicit with a terrorist cell.
But I took it anyway.

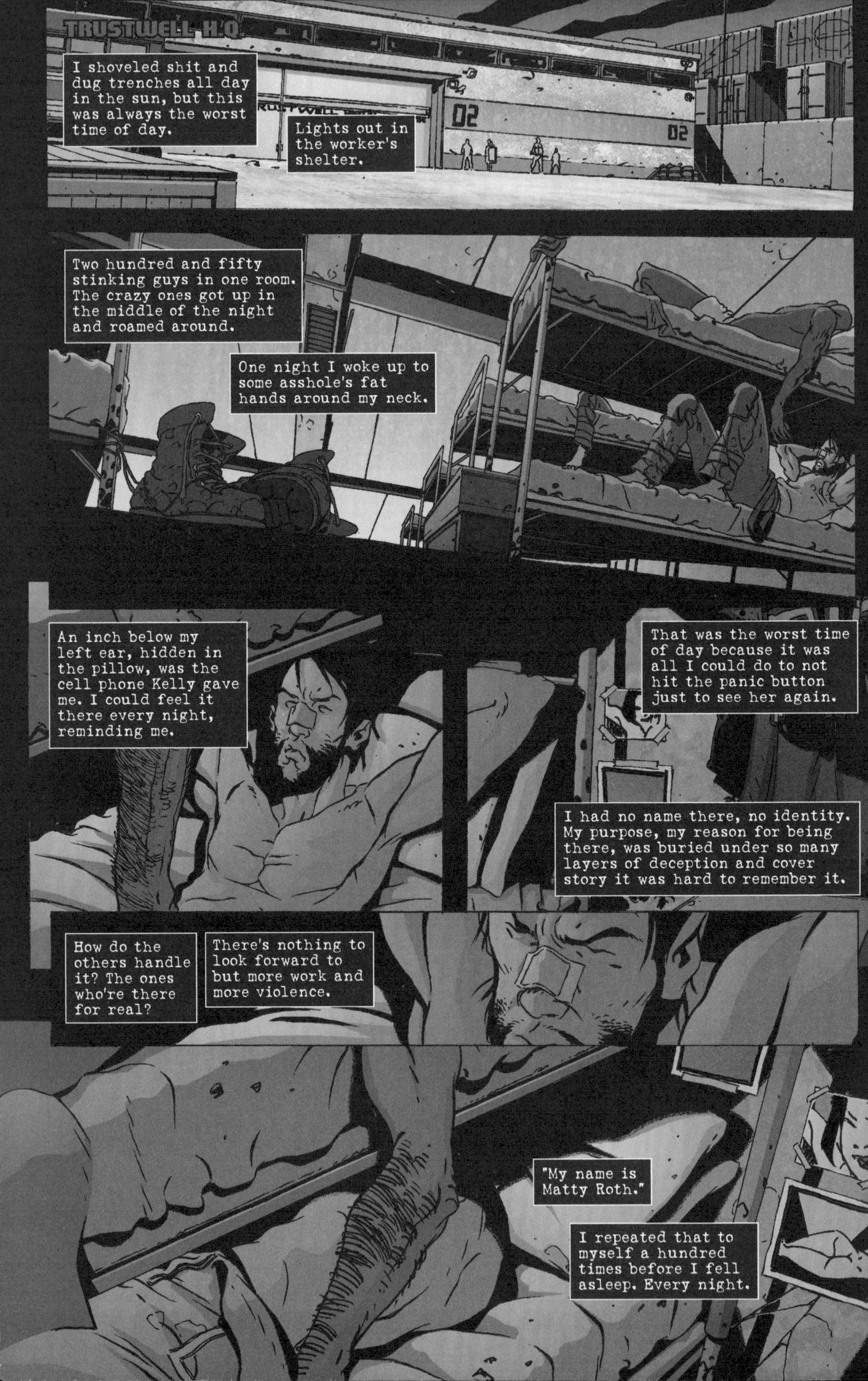
TRUSTWELL H.Q.
I shoveled shit and dug trenches all day in the sun, but this was always the worst time of day.
Lights out in the worker's shelter.
Two hundred and fifty stinking guys in one room. The crazy ones got up in the middle of the night and roamed around.
One night I woke up to some asshole's fat hands around my neck.
An inch below my left ear, hidden in the pillow, was the cell phone Kelly gave me. I could feel it there every night, reminding me.
That was the worst time of day because it was all I could do to not hit the panic button just to see her again.
I had no name there, no identity. My purpose, my reason for being there, was buried under so many layers of deception and cover story it was hard to remember it.
How do the others handle it? The ones who're there for real?
There's nothing to look forward to but more work and more violence.
"My name is Matty Roth."
I repeated that to myself a hundred times before I fell asleep. Every night.

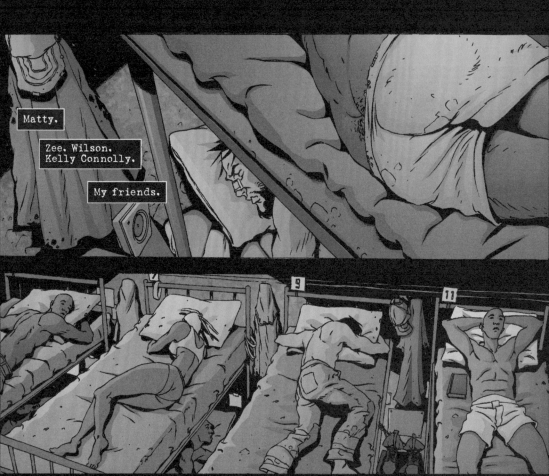

Matty.

Zee. Wilson.
Kelly Connolly.

My friends.

"...security tight this evening at the *Flatiron* checkpoints, in response to a massive car bomb that detonated just south of 23rd, on Sixth Avenue. Twelve people were killed, including the driver of the vehicle.

"Another sleepless night for the weary U.N. Peacekeepers charged with maintaining order in what can only be described as open hostility between belligerent Trustwell Security Forces and angry civilians.

"Dawn is only a few hours away, and one can't help but wonder with fear and helplessness just what the new day will bring."

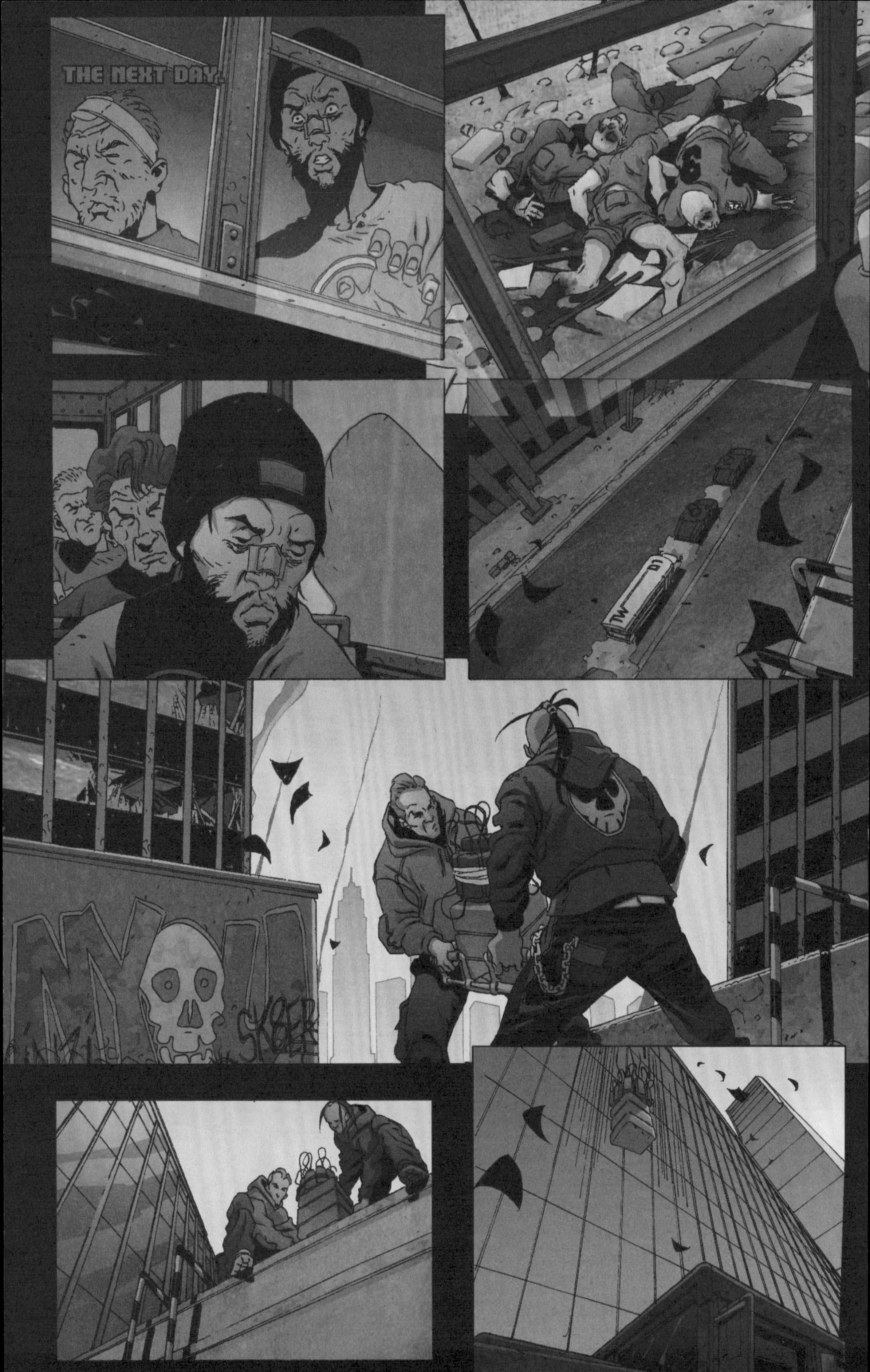
THE NEXT DAY...

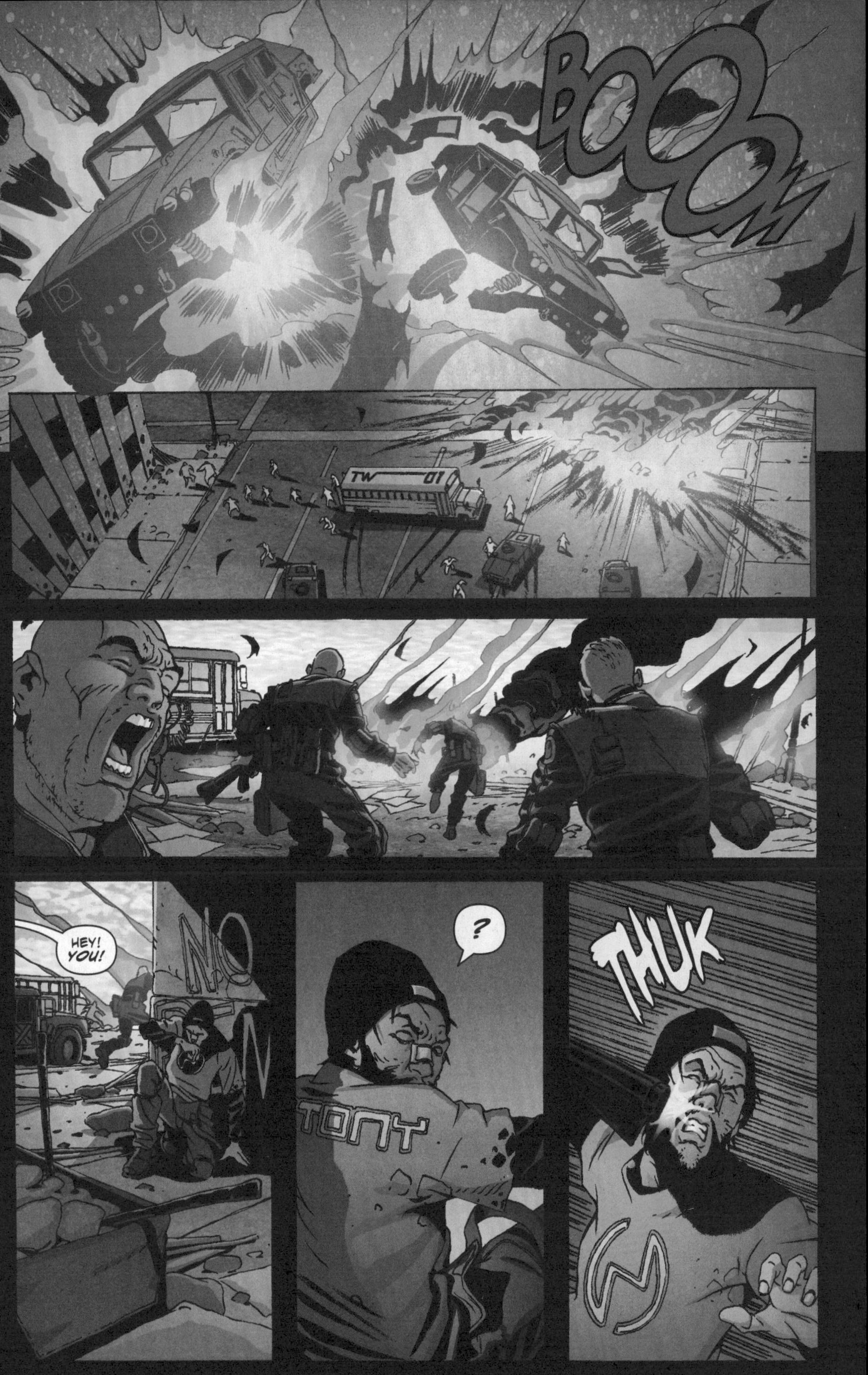
BOOOM
TW 01
HEY! YOU!
NO
?
TONY
THUK

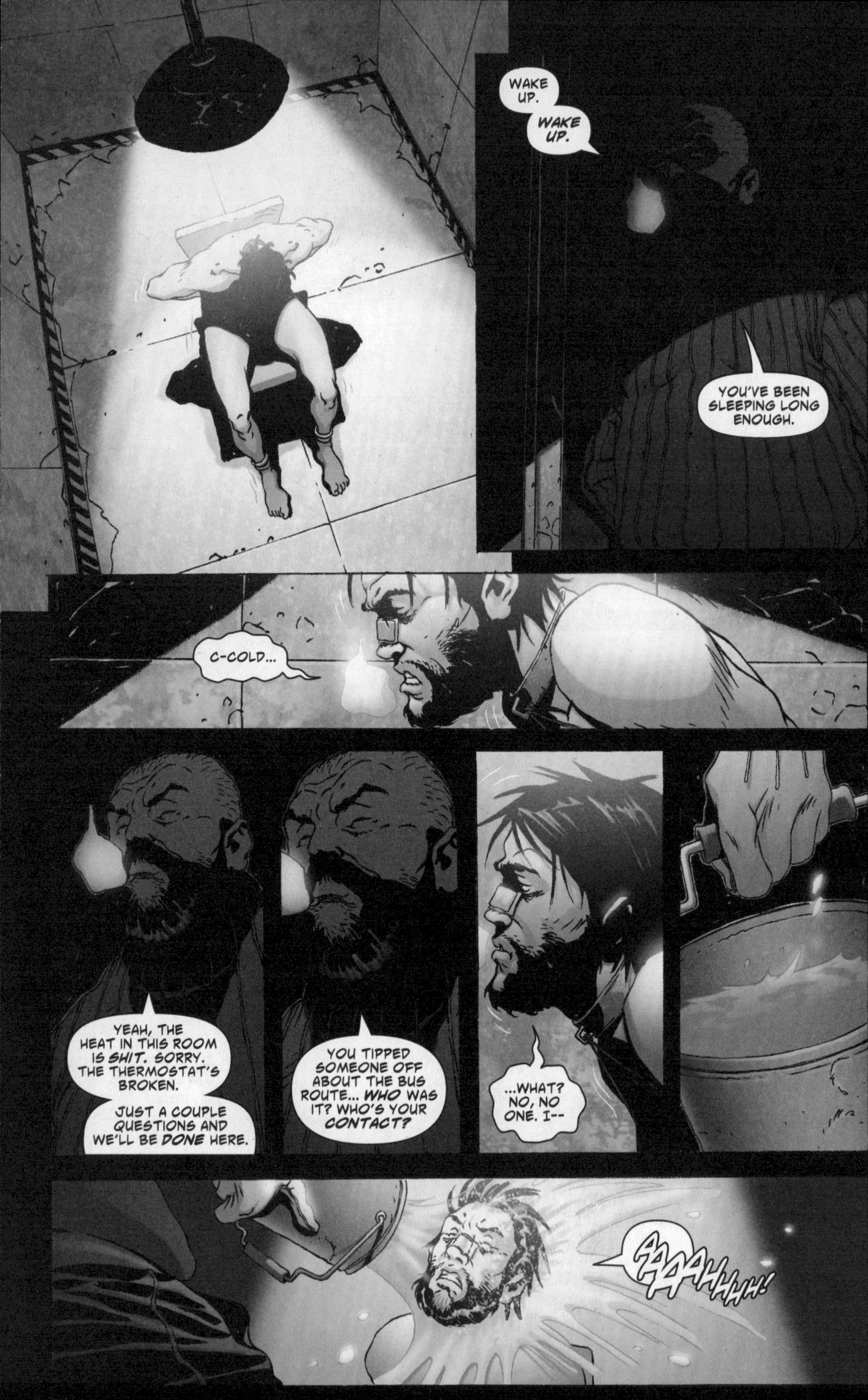
WAKE UP.
WAKE UP.
YOU'VE BEEN SLEEPING LONG ENOUGH.
C-COLD...
YEAH, THE HEAT IN THIS ROOM IS SHIT. SORRY. THE THERMOSTAT'S BROKEN.
JUST A COUPLE QUESTIONS AND WE'LL BE DONE HERE.
YOU TIPPED SOMEONE OFF ABOUT THE BUS ROUTE... WHO WAS IT? WHO'S YOUR CONTACT?
...WHAT? NO, NO ONE. I--
AAAAHHHHH!

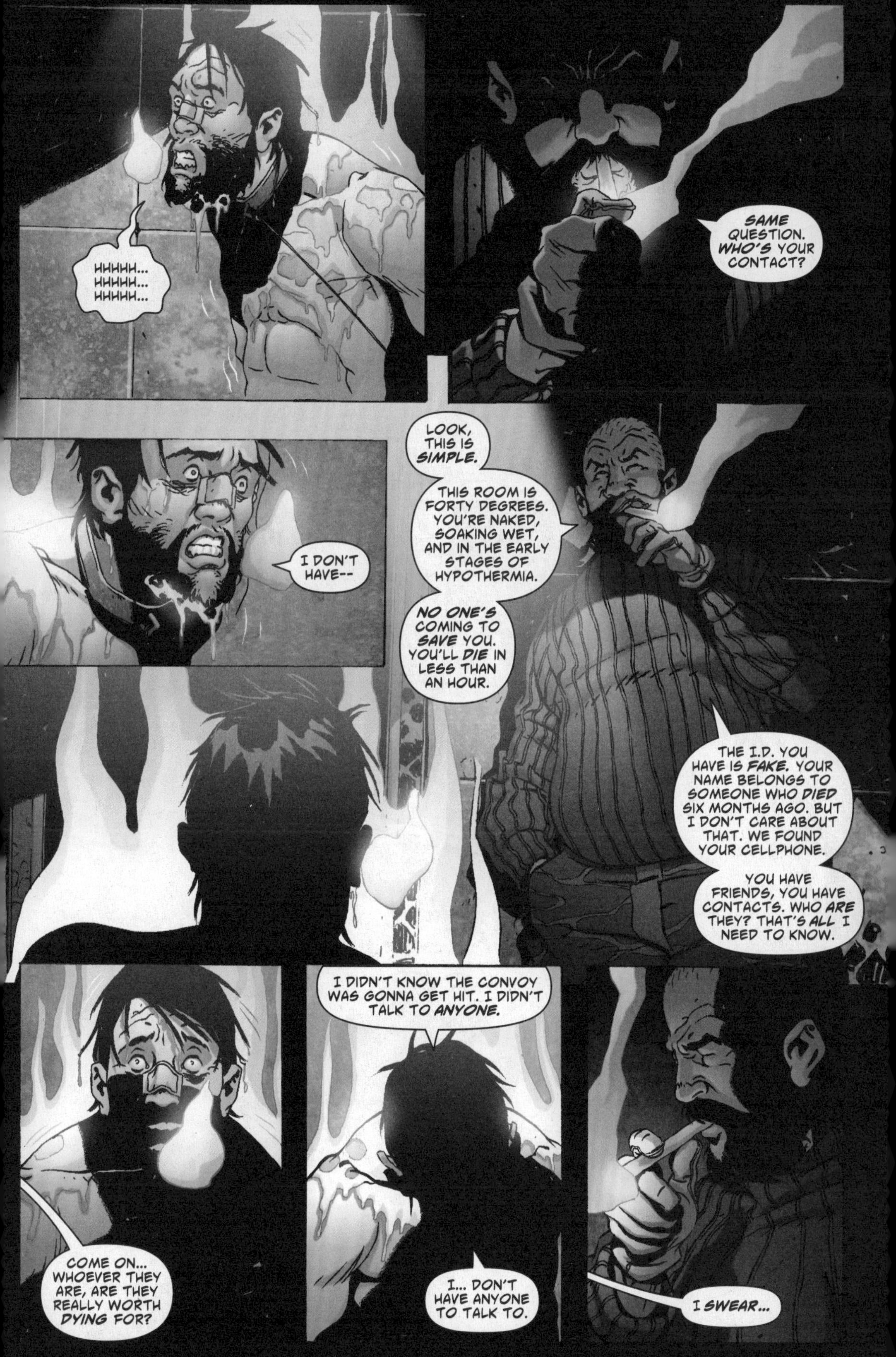
HHHHH... HHHHH... HHHHH...
SAME QUESTION. WHO'S YOUR CONTACT?
I DON'T HAVE--
LOOK, THIS IS SIMPLE.
THIS ROOM IS FORTY DEGREES. YOU'RE NAKED, SOAKING WET, AND IN THE EARLY STAGES OF HYPOTHERMIA.
NO ONE'S COMING TO SAVE YOU. YOU'LL DIE IN LESS THAN AN HOUR.
THE I.D. YOU HAVE IS FAKE. YOUR NAME BELONGS TO SOMEONE WHO DIED SIX MONTHS AGO. BUT I DON'T CARE ABOUT THAT. WE FOUND YOUR CELLPHONE.
YOU HAVE FRIENDS, YOU HAVE CONTACTS. WHO ARE THEY? THAT'S ALL I NEED TO KNOW.
COME ON... WHOEVER THEY ARE, ARE THEY REALLY WORTH DYING FOR?
I DIDN'T KNOW THE CONVOY WAS GONNA GET HIT. I DIDN'T TALK TO ANYONE.
I... DON'T HAVE ANYONE TO TALK TO.
I SWEAR...

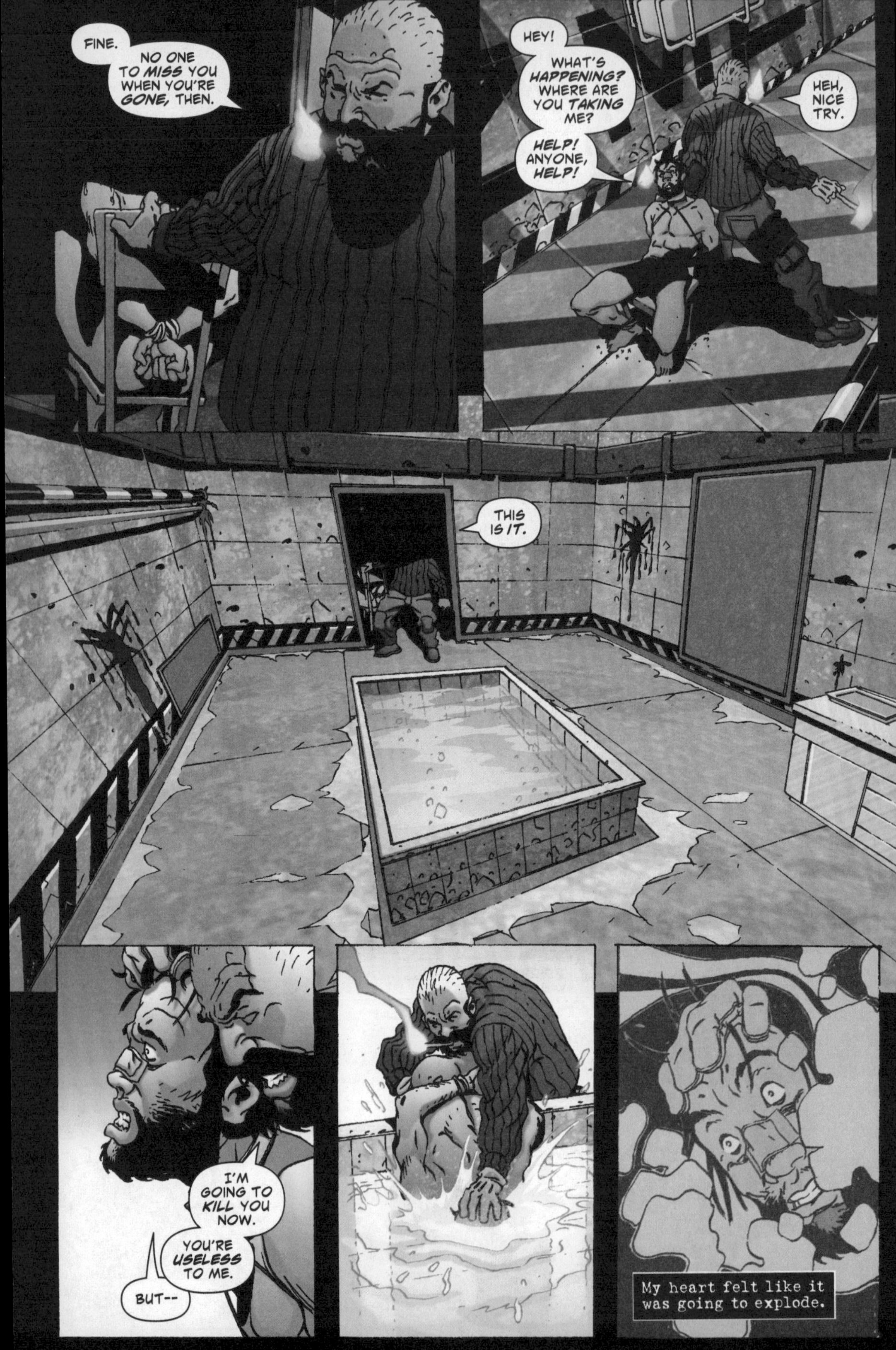
FINE.
NO ONE TO MISS YOU WHEN YOU'RE GONE, THEN.
HEY!
WHAT'S HAPPENING? WHERE ARE YOU TAKING ME?
HELP! ANYONE, HELP!
HEH, NICE TRY.
THIS IS IT.
I'M GOING TO KILL YOU NOW.
YOU'RE USELESS TO ME.
BUT--
My heart felt like it was going to explode.

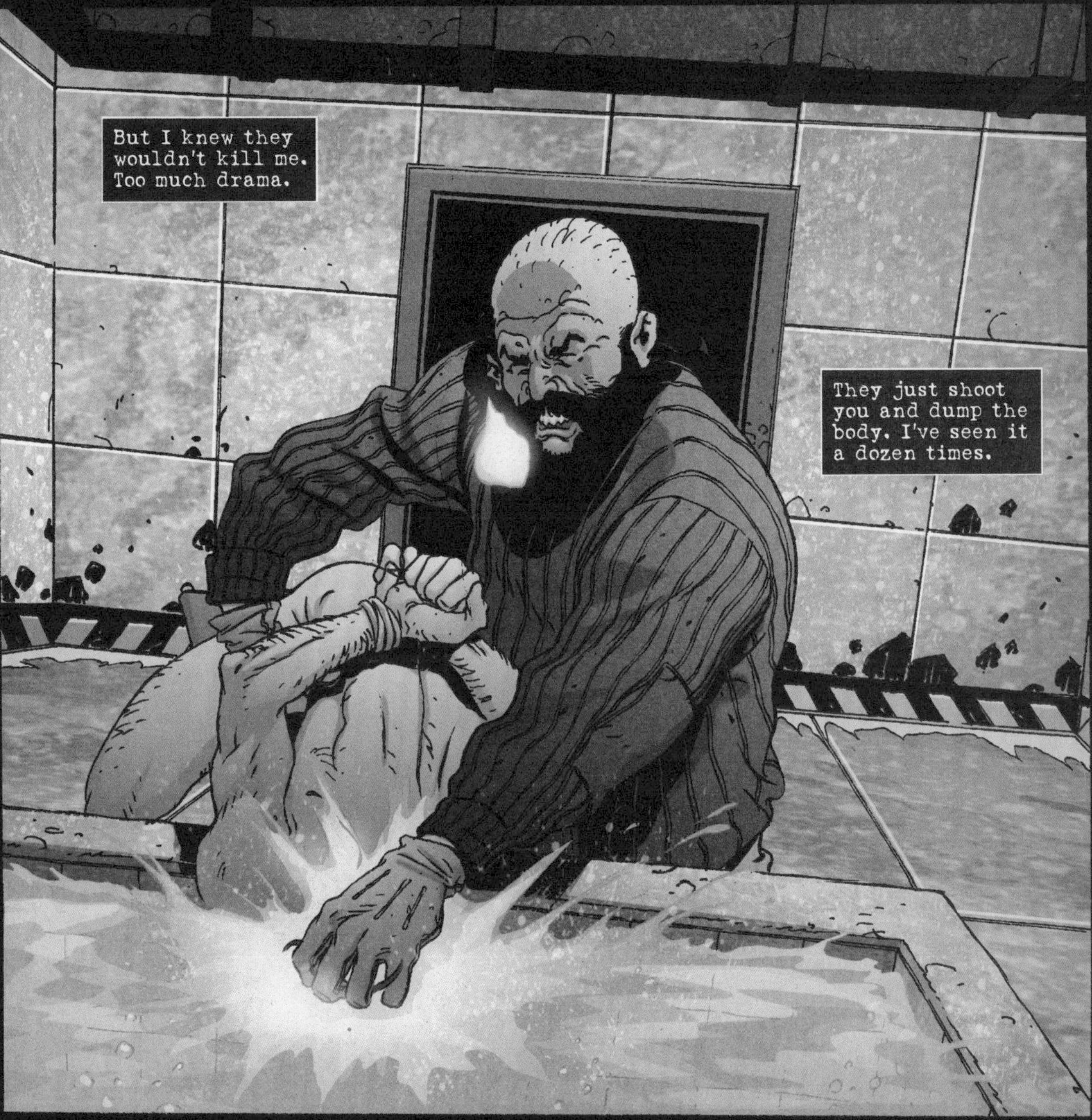
But I knew they wouldn't kill me. Too much drama.
They just shoot you and dump the body. I've seen it a dozen times.

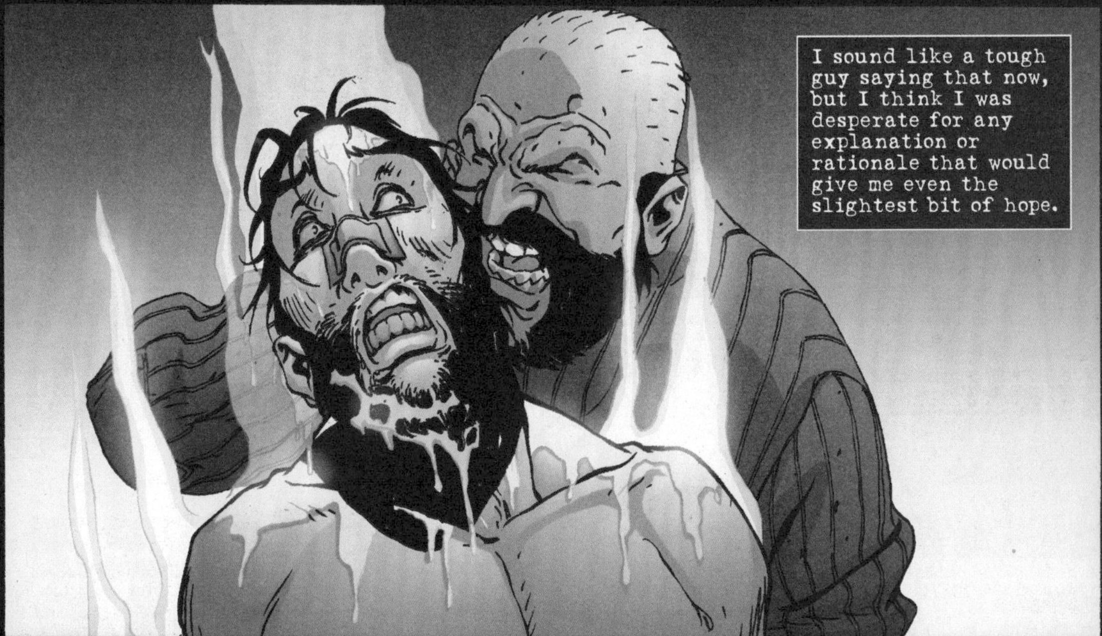
I sound like a tough guy saying that now, but I think I was desperate for any explanation or rationale that would give me even the slightest bit of hope.

The rest of the time was a blur to me then, and to me now.

No way to mark time. They didn't feed me much, so I couldn't even count meals.

They blasted me with cold, heat, and incredibly loud music that made my ears bleed.

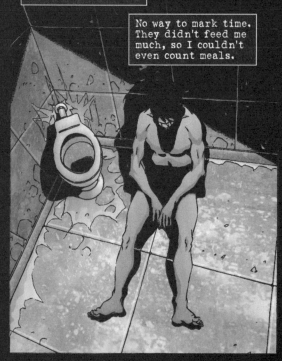

They questioned me a hundred different ways a hundred times over, making me so frustrated and bored I would often end up screaming.

The threats, the fear... I just thought about everything I've seen in the last year, tried to put it into perspective.

I thought about Zee and the bombs dropping on her home, living years and years in constant violence.

What would she say to me if I folded the minute some guy started getting tough with me?

I could deal with this.

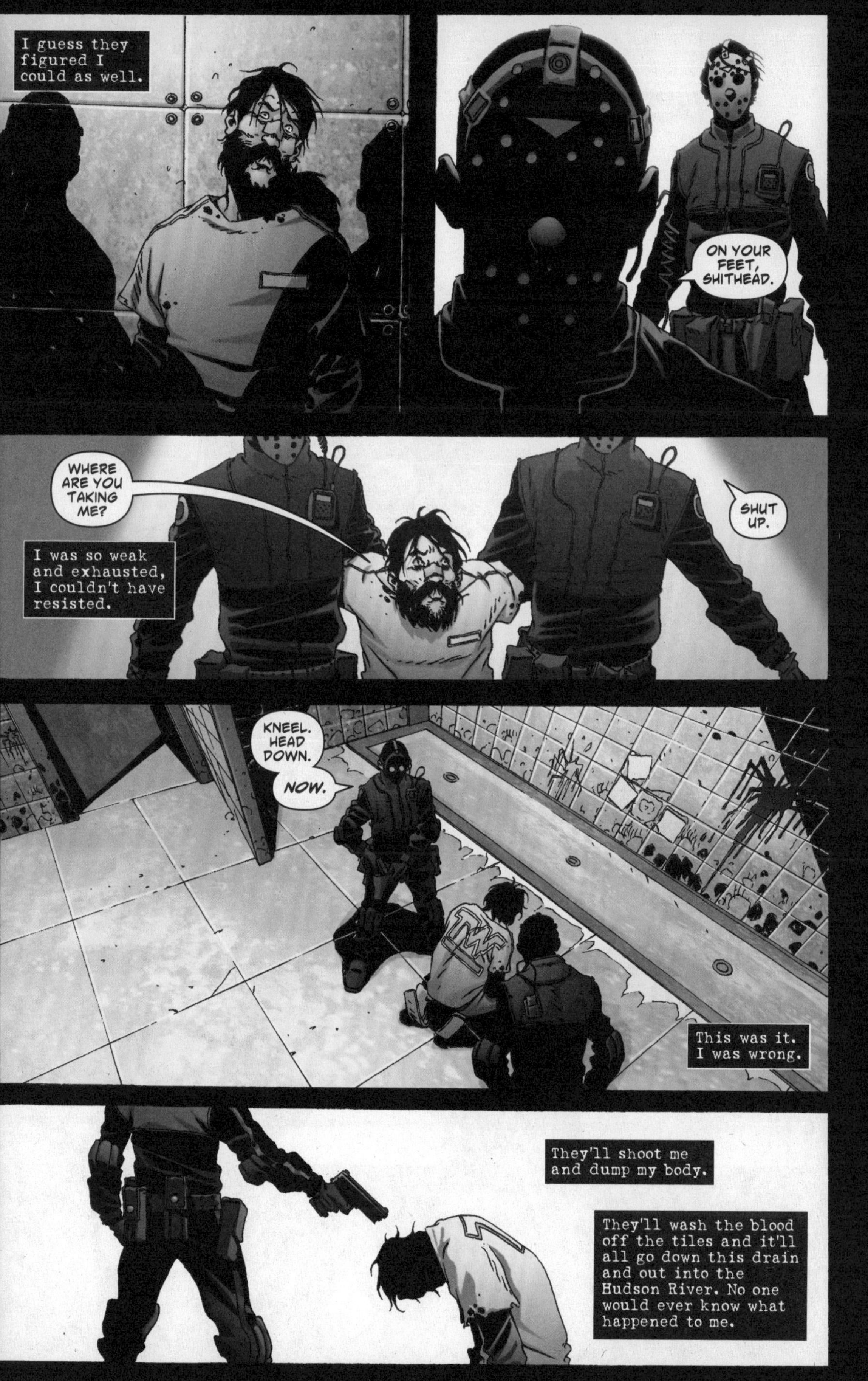
I guess they figured I could as well.
ON YOUR FEET, SHITHEAD.
WHERE ARE YOU TAKING ME?
I was so weak and exhausted, I couldn't have resisted.
SHUT UP.
KNEEL. HEAD DOWN.
NOW.
This was it. I was wrong.
They'll shoot me and dump my body.
They'll wash the blood off the tiles and it'll all go down this drain and out into the Hudson River. No one would ever know what happened to me.

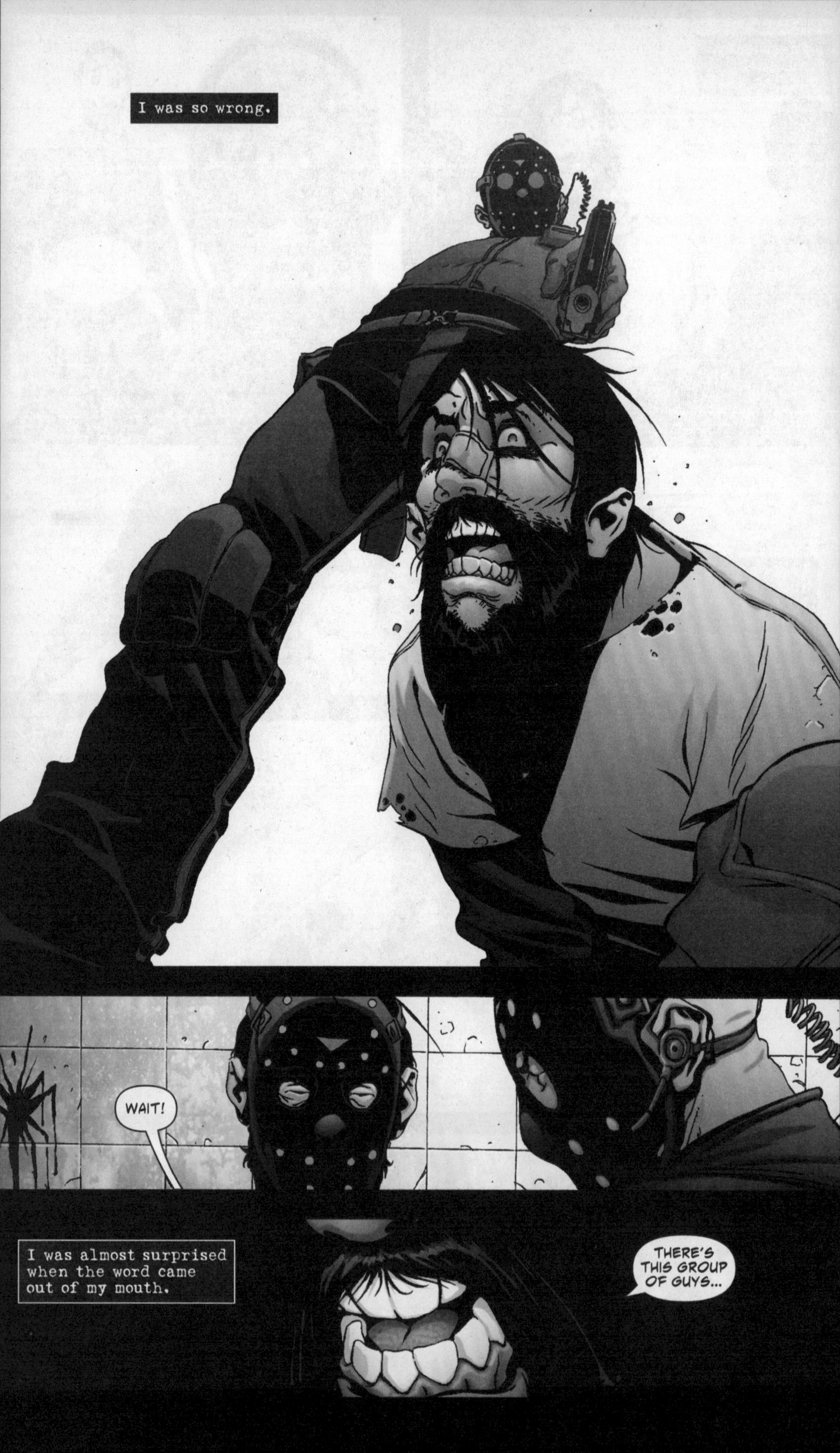
I was so wrong.
WAIT!
I was almost surprised when the word came out of my mouth.
THERE'S THIS GROUP OF GUYS...

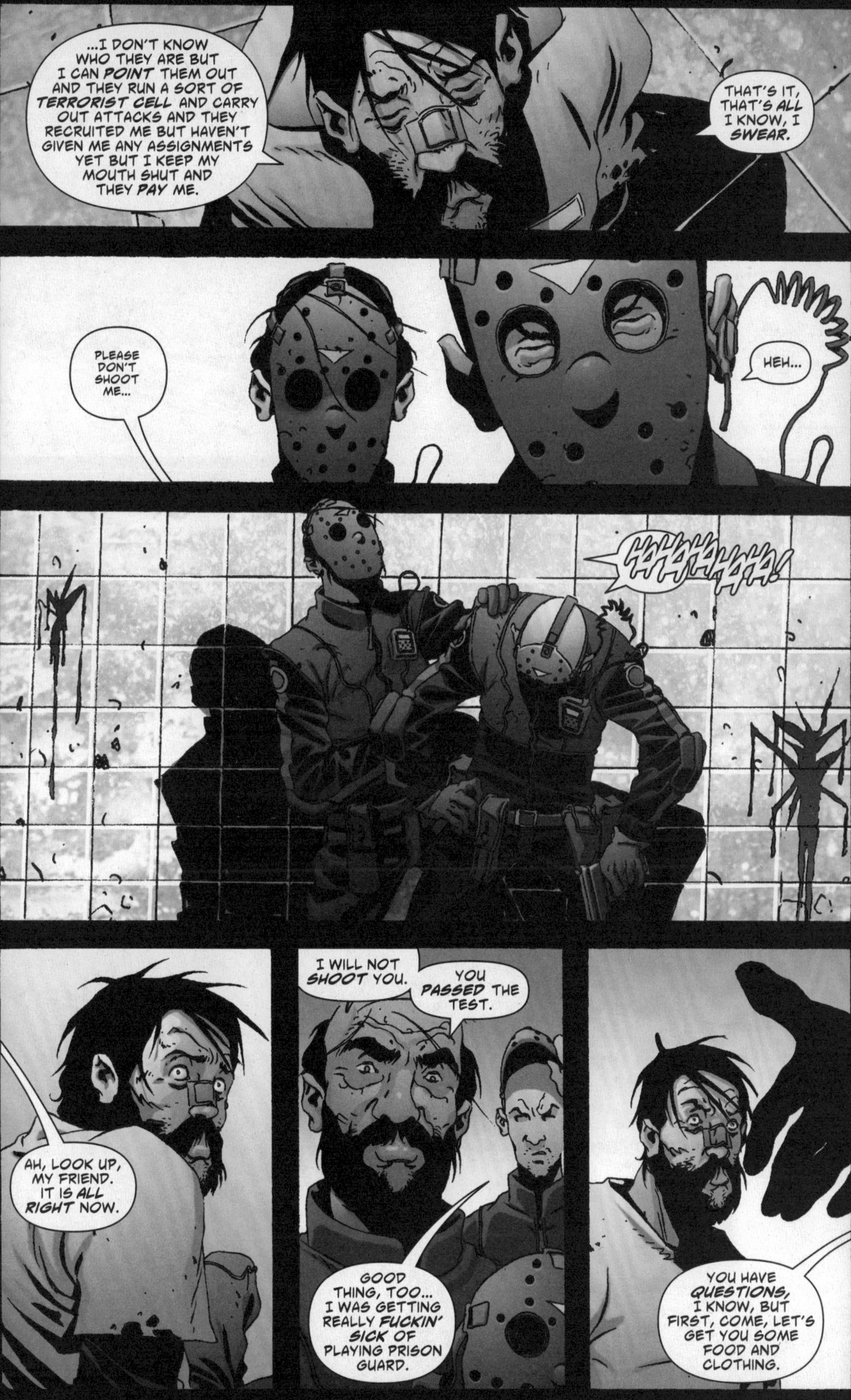
...I DON'T KNOW WHO THEY ARE BUT I CAN POINT THEM OUT AND THEY RUN A SORT OF TERRORIST CELL AND CARRY OUT ATTACKS AND THEY RECRUITED ME BUT HAVEN'T GIVEN ME ANY ASSIGNMENTS YET BUT I KEEP MY MOUTH SHUT AND THEY PAY ME.
THAT'S IT, THAT'S ALL I KNOW, I SWEAR.
PLEASE DON'T SHOOT ME...
HEH...
HAHAHAHAHA!
AH, LOOK UP, MY FRIEND. IT IS ALL RIGHT NOW.
I WILL NOT SHOOT YOU.
YOU PASSED THE TEST.
GOOD THING, TOO... I WAS GETTING REALLY FUCKIN' SICK OF PLAYING PRISON GUARD.
YOU HAVE QUESTIONS, I KNOW, BUT FIRST, COME, LET'S GET YOU SOME FOOD AND CLOTHING.

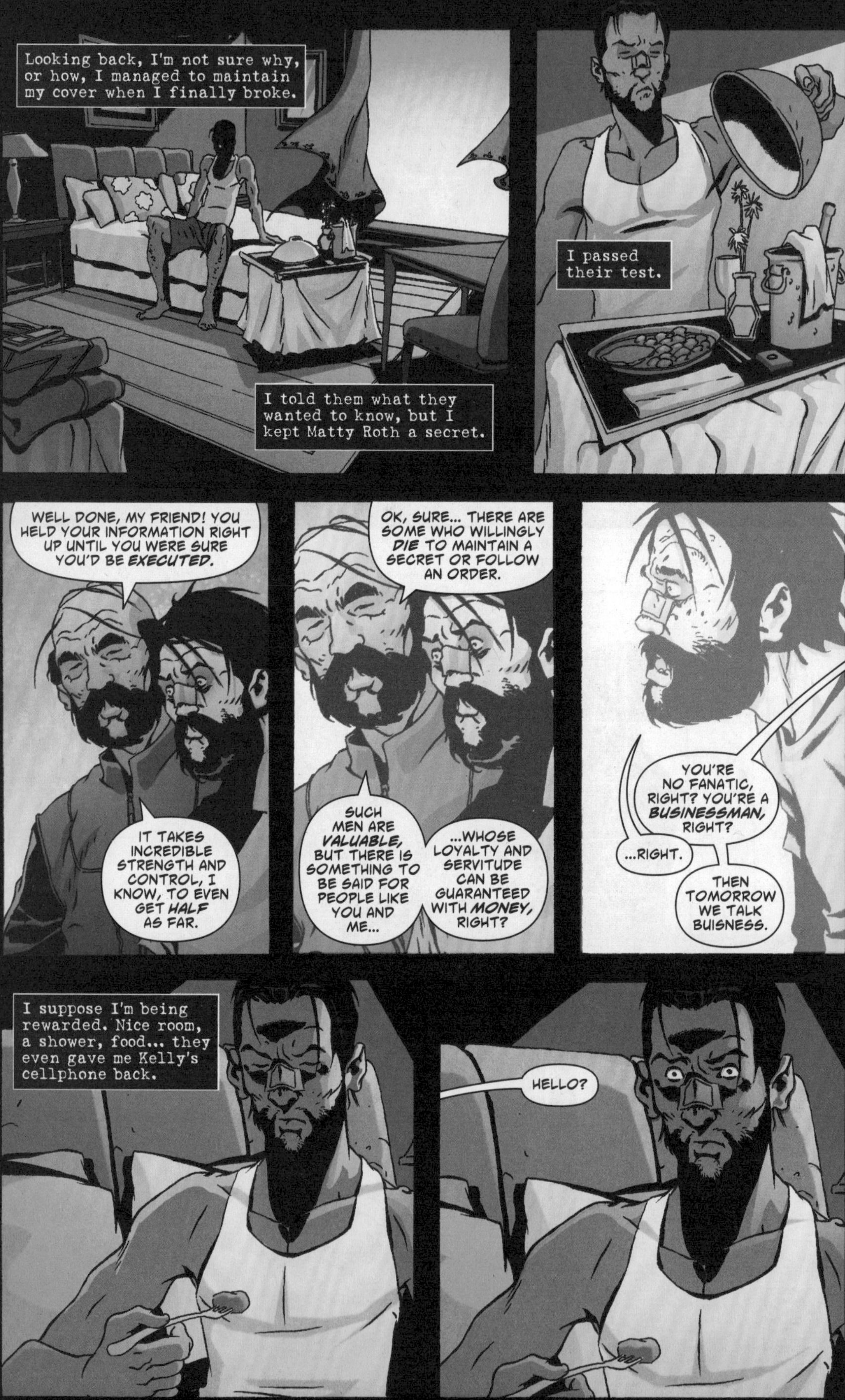

Looking back, I'm not sure why, or how, I managed to maintain my cover when I finally broke.
I told them what they wanted to know, but I kept Matty Roth a secret.
I passed their test.
WELL DONE, MY FRIEND! YOU HELD YOUR INFORMATION RIGHT UP UNTIL YOU WERE SURE YOU'D BE EXECUTED.
IT TAKES INCREDIBLE STRENGTH AND CONTROL, I KNOW, TO EVEN GET HALF AS FAR.
OK, SURE... THERE ARE SOME WHO WILLINGLY DIE TO MAINTAIN A SECRET OR FOLLOW AN ORDER.
SUCH MEN ARE VALUABLE, BUT THERE IS SOMETHING TO BE SAID FOR PEOPLE LIKE YOU AND ME...
...WHOSE LOYALTY AND SERVITUDE CAN BE GUARANTEED WITH MONEY, RIGHT?
YOU'RE NO FANATIC, RIGHT? YOU'RE A BUSINESSMAN, RIGHT?
...RIGHT.
THEN TOMORROW WE TALK BUISNESS.
I suppose I'm being rewarded. Nice room, a shower, food... they even gave me Kelly's cellphone back.
HELLO?

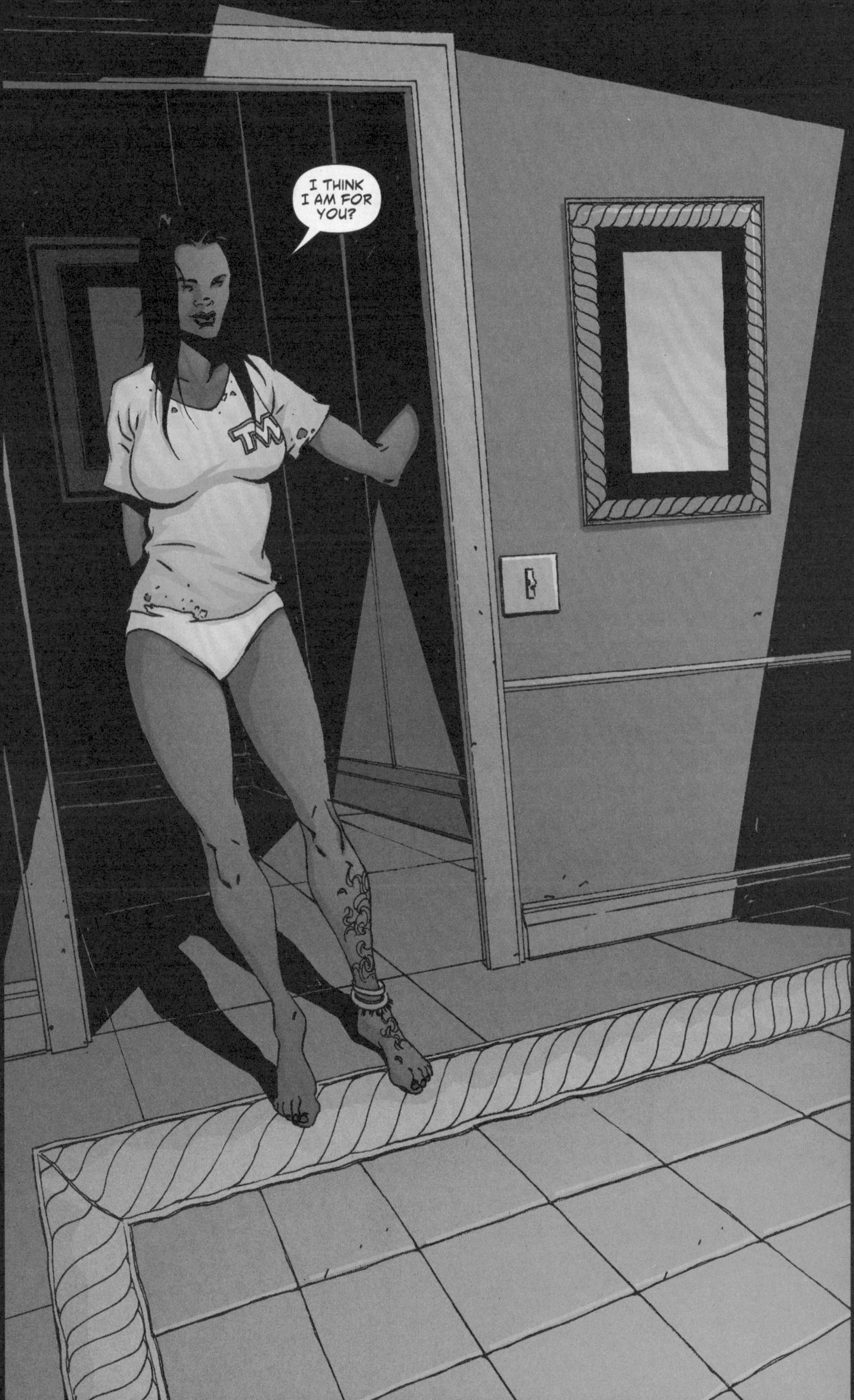
I THINK I AM FOR YOU?

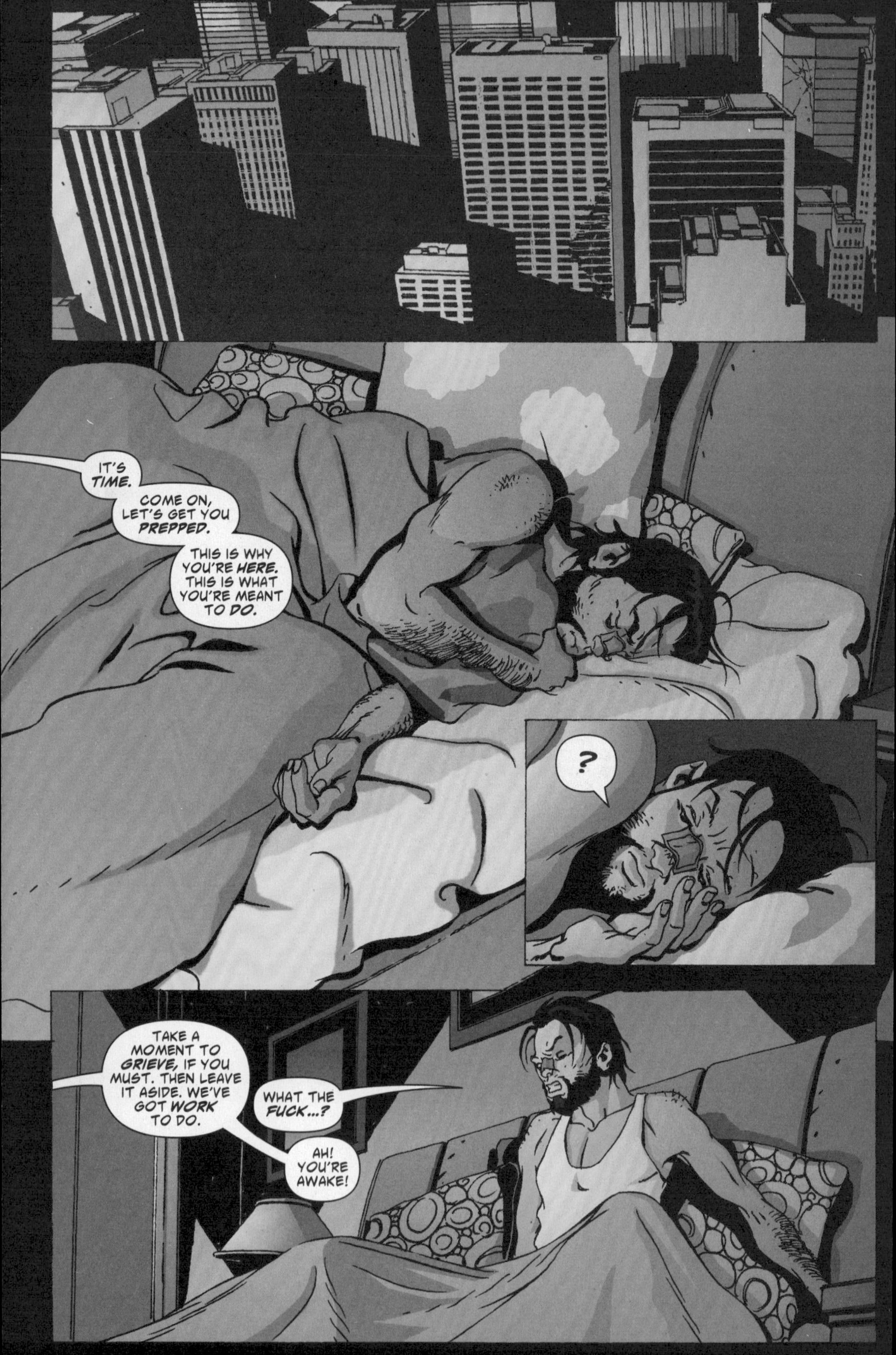

IT'S TIME.
COME ON, LET'S GET YOU PREPPED.
THIS IS WHY YOU'RE HERE. THIS IS WHAT YOU'RE MEANT TO DO.
?
TAKE A MOMENT TO GRIEVE, IF YOU MUST. THEN LEAVE IT ASIDE. WE'VE GOT WORK TO DO.
WHAT THE FUCK...?
AH! YOU'RE AWAKE!

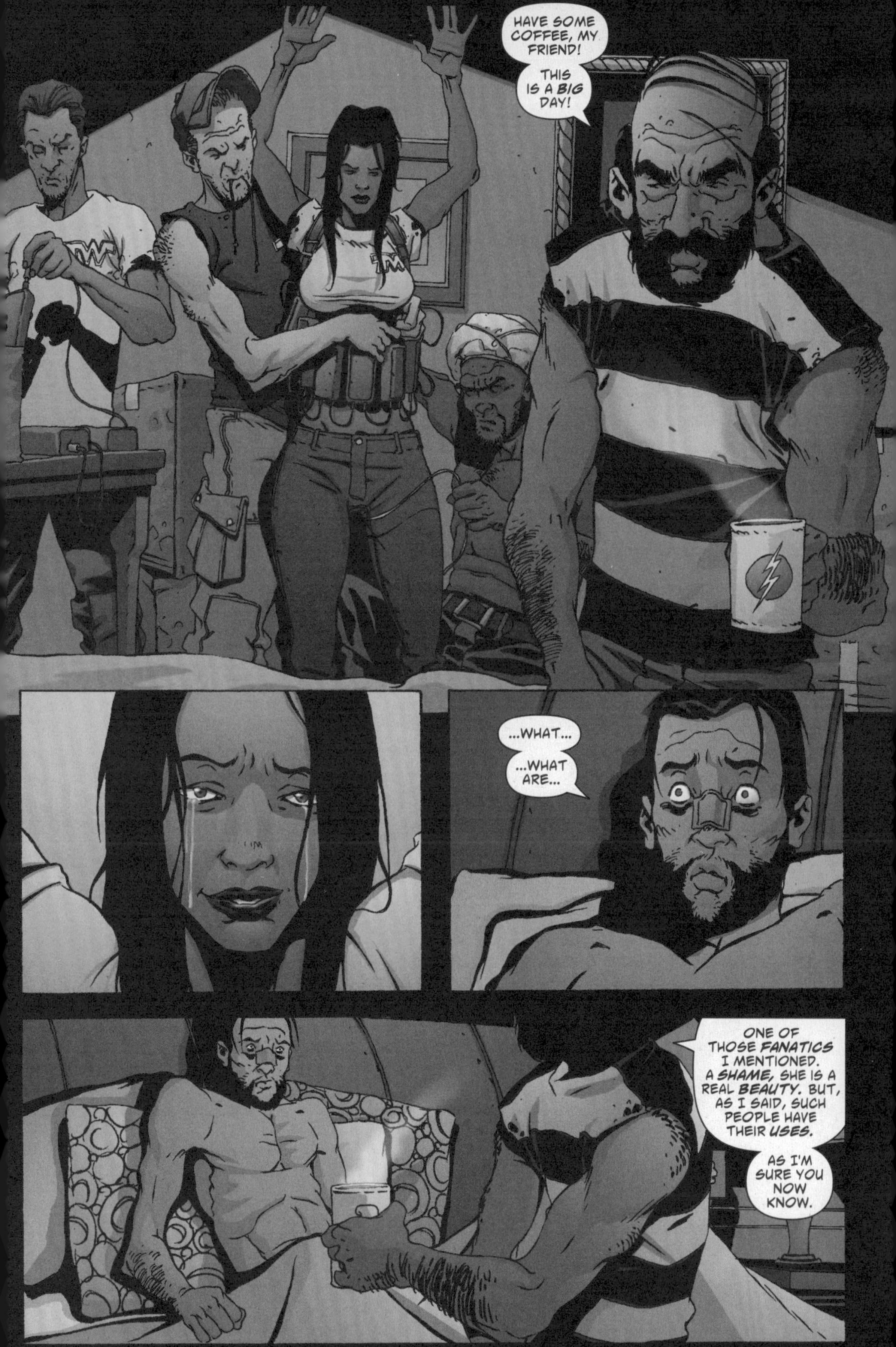
HAVE SOME COFFEE, MY FRIEND!
THIS IS A BIG DAY!
...WHAT...
...WHAT ARE...
ONE OF THOSE FANATICS I MENTIONED. A SHAME, SHE IS A REAL BEAUTY. BUT, AS I SAID, SUCH PEOPLE HAVE THEIR USES.
AS I'M SURE YOU NOW KNOW.

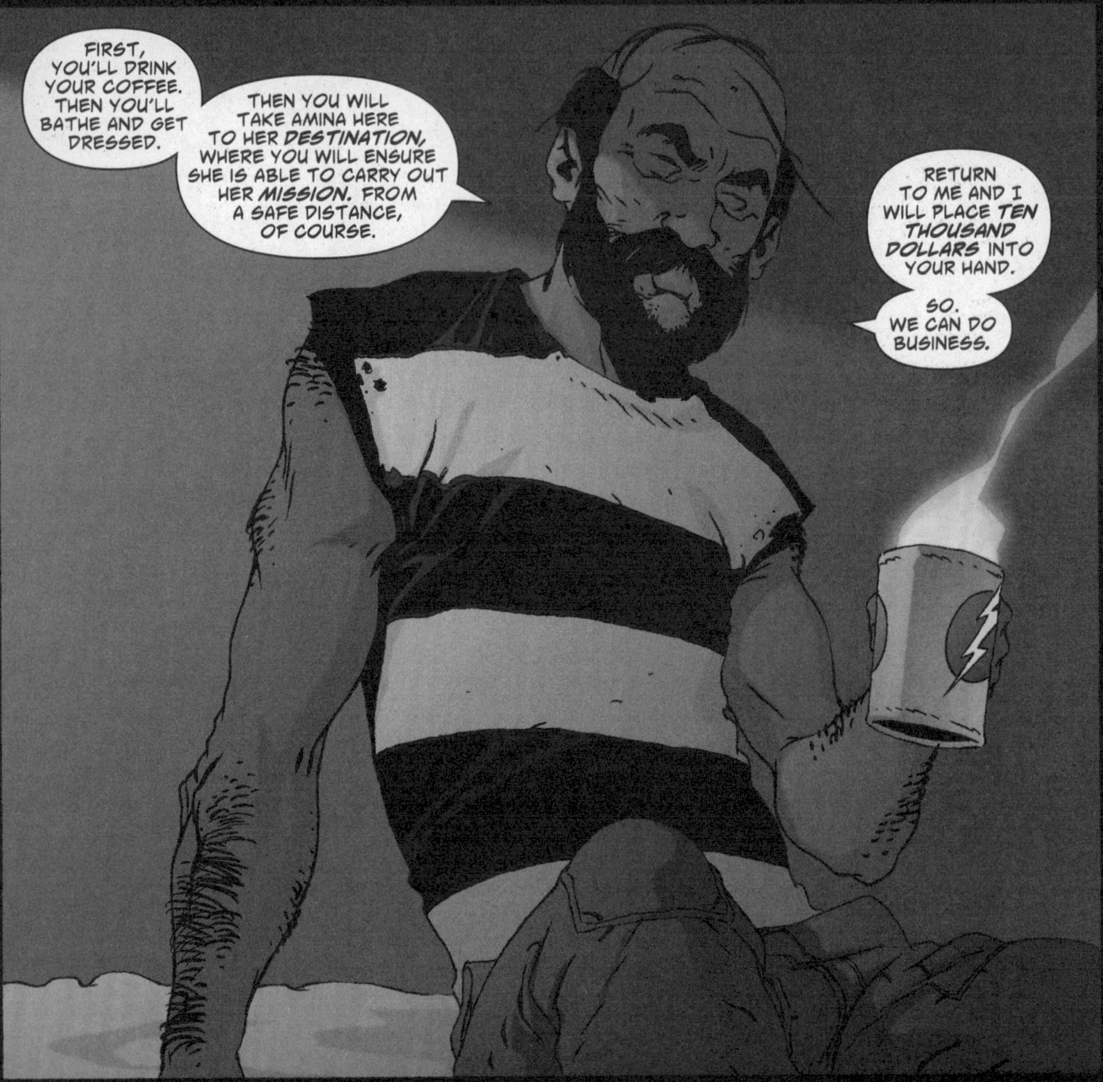
FIRST, YOU'LL DRINK YOUR COFFEE. THEN YOU'LL BATHE AND GET DRESSED.
THEN YOU WILL TAKE AMINA HERE TO HER *DESTINATION,* WHERE YOU WILL ENSURE SHE IS ABLE TO CARRY OUT HER *MISSION.* FROM A SAFE DISTANCE, OF COURSE.
RETURN TO ME AND I WILL PLACE *TEN THOUSAND DOLLARS* INTO YOUR HAND.
SO. WE CAN DO BUSINESS.

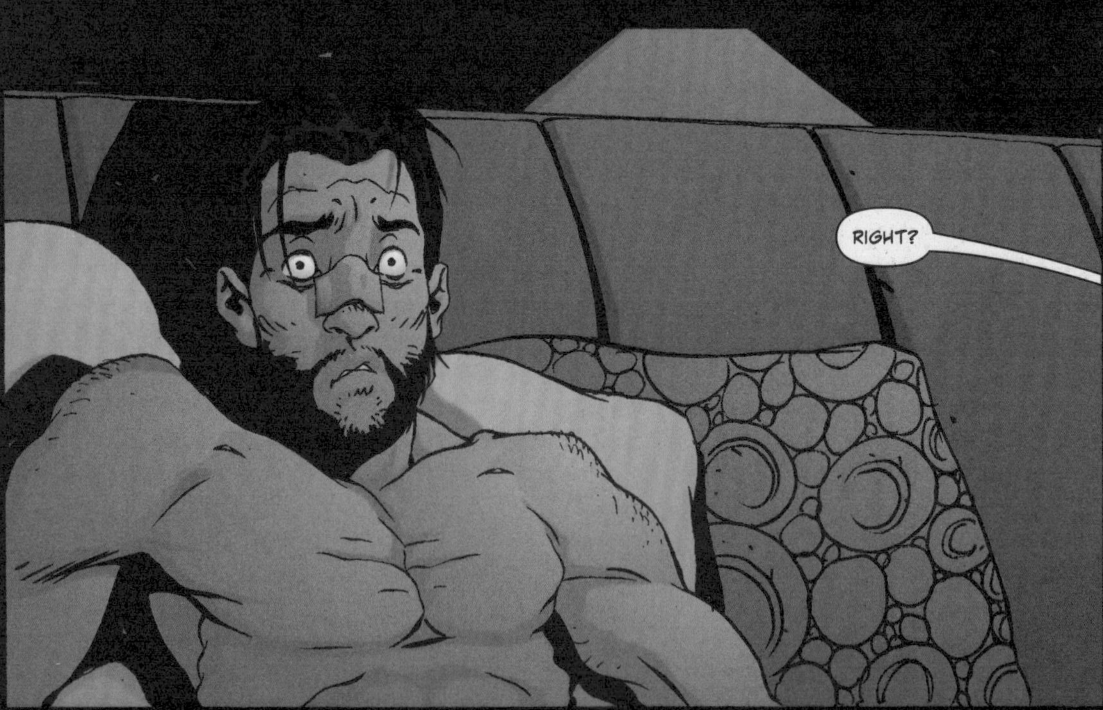
RIGHT?

# CHAPTER THREE

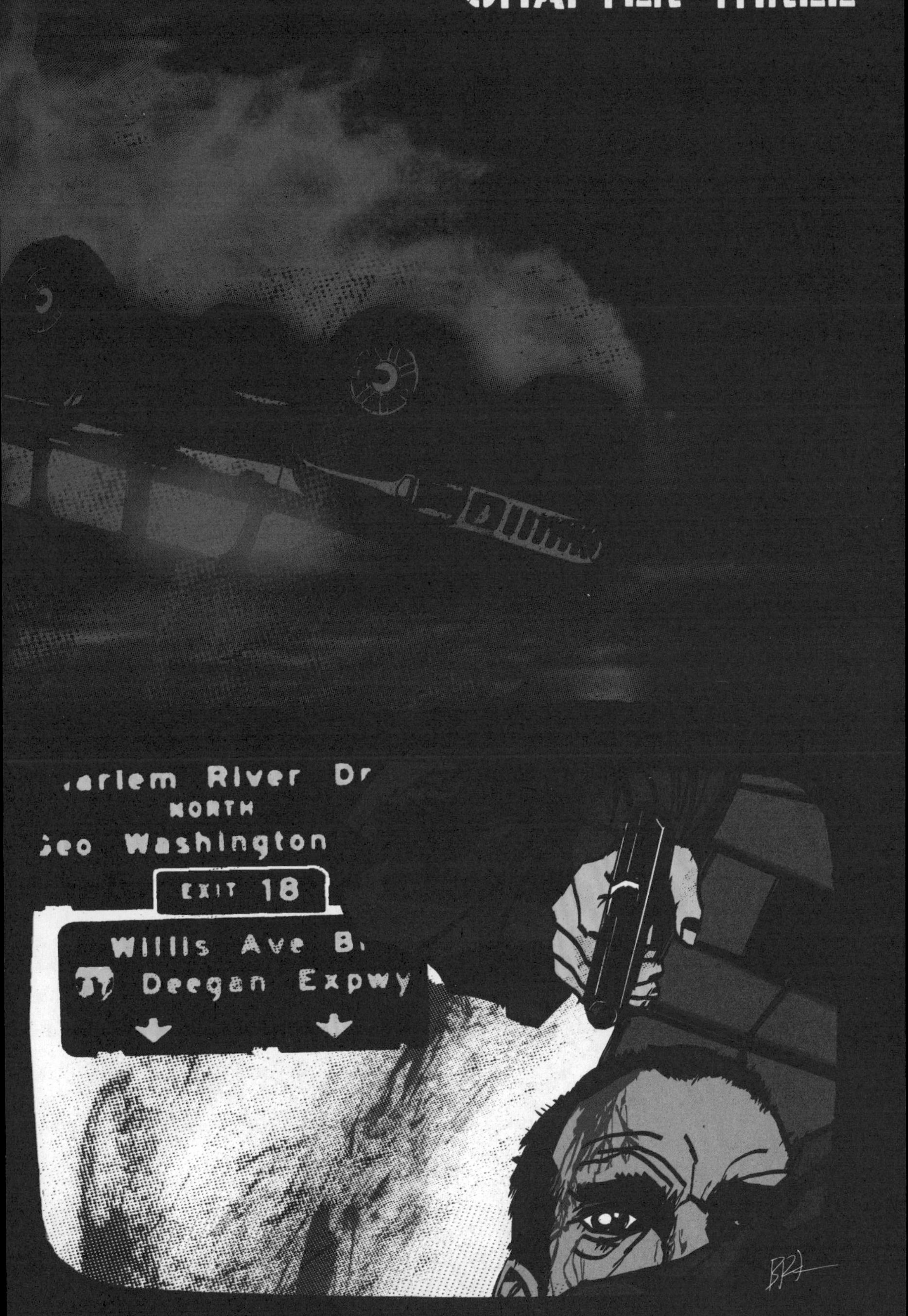
arlem River Dr
NORTH
eo Washington
EXIT 18
Willis Ave B
Deegan Expwy

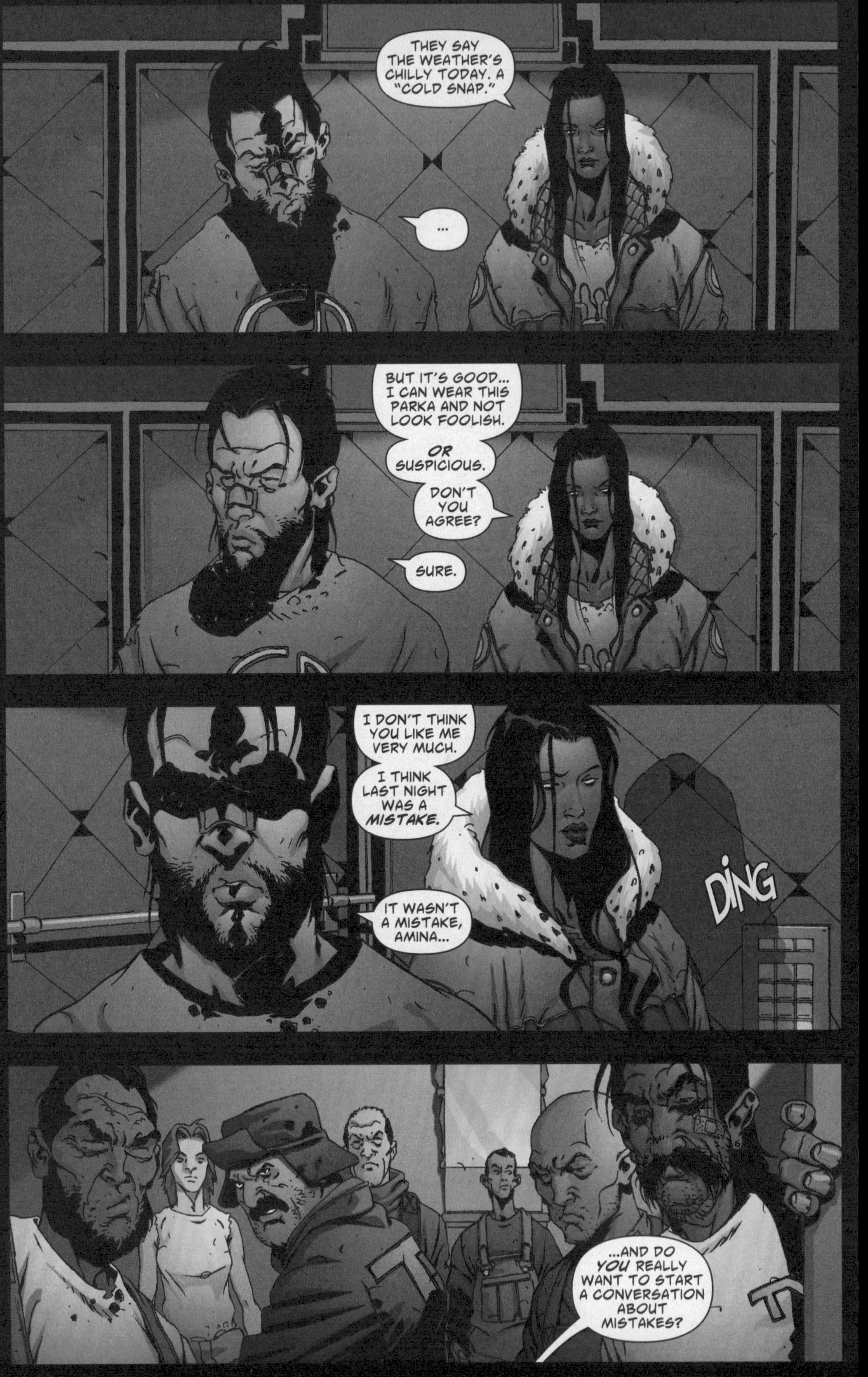
THEY SAY THE WEATHER'S CHILLY TODAY. A "COLD SNAP."
...
BUT IT'S GOOD... I CAN WEAR THIS PARKA AND NOT LOOK FOOLISH.
OR SUSPICIOUS.
DON'T YOU AGREE?
SURE.
I DON'T THINK YOU LIKE ME VERY MUCH.
I THINK LAST NIGHT WAS A MISTAKE.
IT WASN'T A MISTAKE, AMINA...
DING
...AND DO YOU REALLY WANT TO START A CONVERSATION ABOUT MISTAKES?

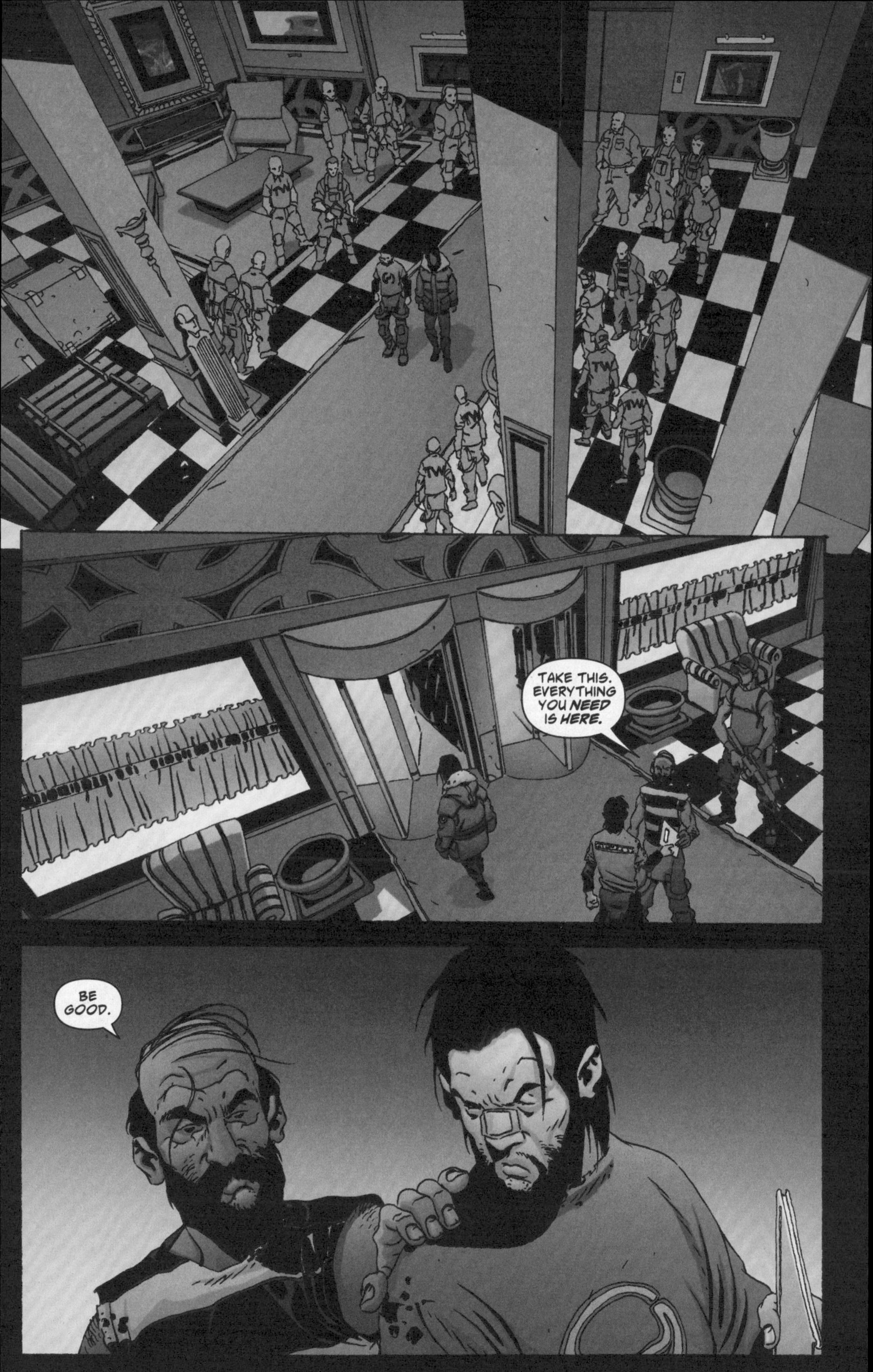
TAKE THIS. EVERYTHING YOU NEED IS HERE.
BE GOOD.

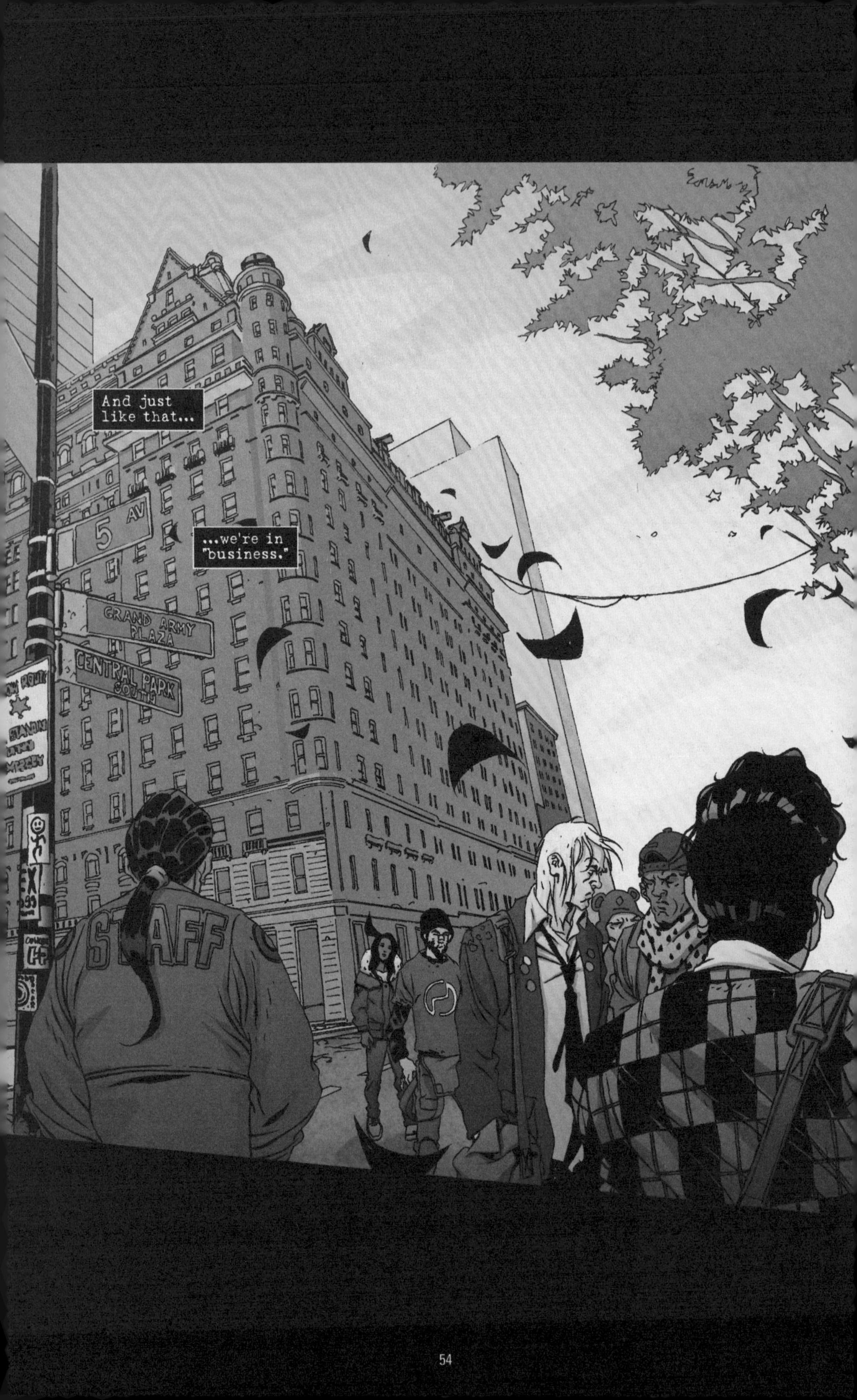
And just like that...
5 AV
...we're in "business."
GRAND ARMY PLAZA
CENTRAL PARK SOUTH
STAFF

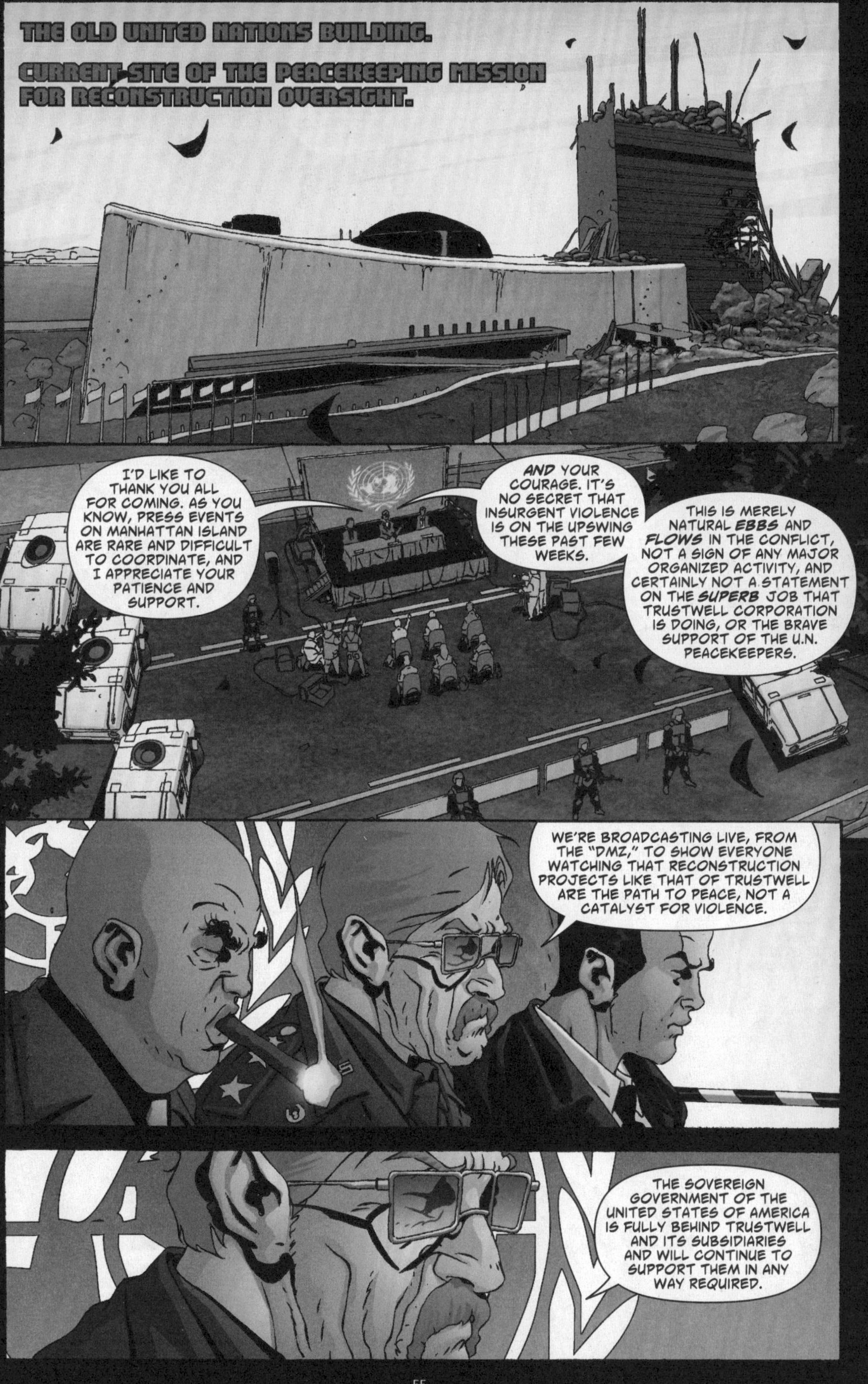
THE OLD UNITED NATIONS BUILDING.
CURRENT SITE OF THE PEACEKEEPING MISSION FOR RECONSTRUCTION OVERSIGHT.
I'D LIKE TO THANK YOU ALL FOR COMING. AS YOU KNOW, PRESS EVENTS ON MANHATTAN ISLAND ARE RARE AND DIFFICULT TO COORDINATE, AND I APPRECIATE YOUR PATIENCE AND SUPPORT.
AND YOUR COURAGE. IT'S NO SECRET THAT INSURGENT VIOLENCE IS ON THE UPSWING THESE PAST FEW WEEKS.
THIS IS MERELY NATURAL EBBS AND FLOWS IN THE CONFLICT, NOT A SIGN OF ANY MAJOR ORGANIZED ACTIVITY, AND CERTAINLY NOT A STATEMENT ON THE SUPERB JOB THAT TRUSTWELL CORPORATION IS DOING, OR THE BRAVE SUPPORT OF THE U.N. PEACEKEEPERS.
WE'RE BROADCASTING LIVE, FROM THE "DMZ," TO SHOW EVERYONE WATCHING THAT RECONSTRUCTION PROJECTS LIKE THAT OF TRUSTWELL ARE THE PATH TO PEACE, NOT A CATALYST FOR VIOLENCE.
THE SOVEREIGN GOVERNMENT OF THE UNITED STATES OF AMERICA IS FULLY BEHIND TRUSTWELL AND ITS SUBSIDIARIES AND WILL CONTINUE TO SUPPORT THEM IN ANY WAY REQUIRED.

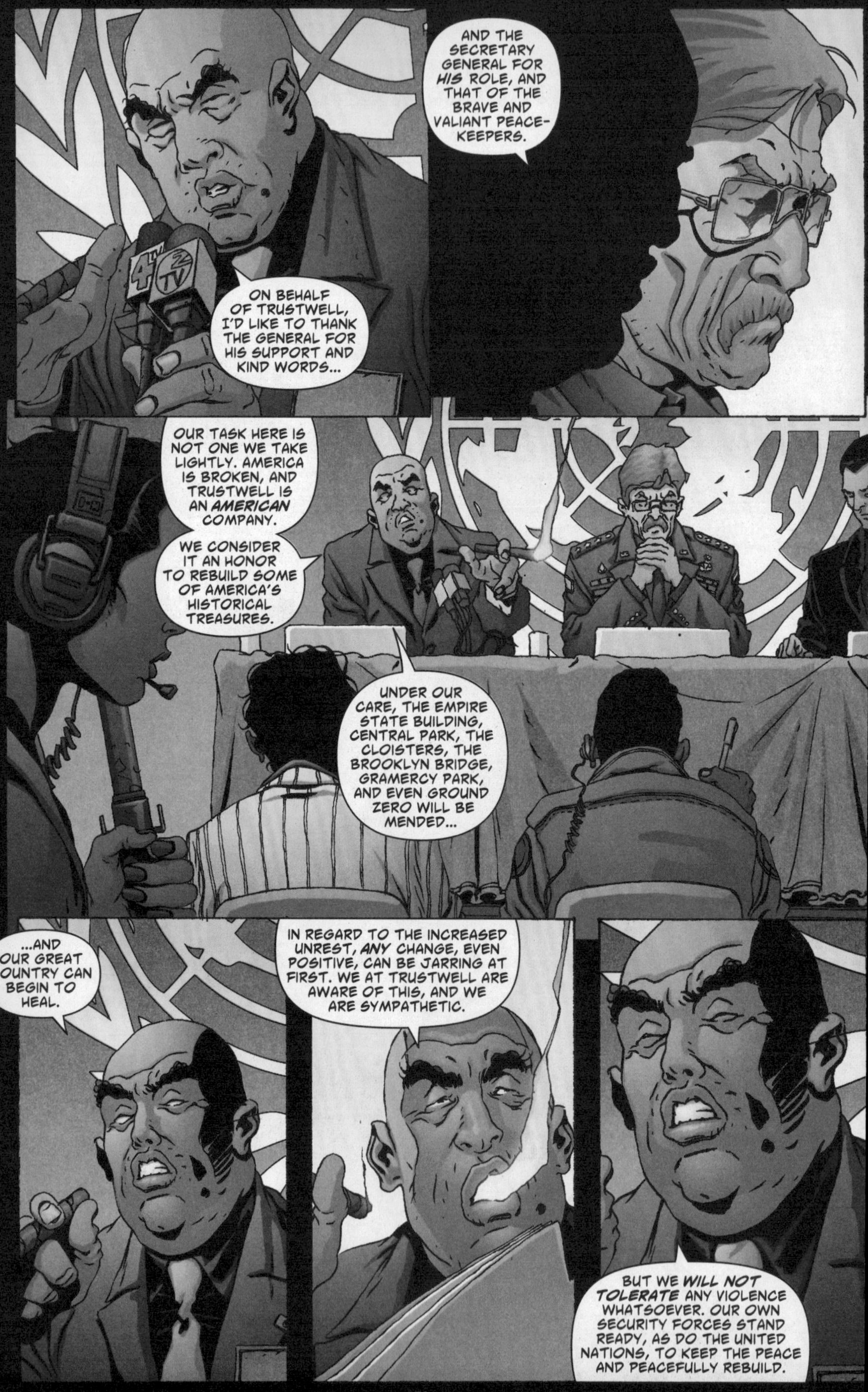
ON BEHALF OF TRUSTWELL, I'D LIKE TO THANK THE GENERAL FOR HIS SUPPORT AND KIND WORDS...
AND THE SECRETARY GENERAL FOR *HIS* ROLE, AND THAT OF THE BRAVE AND VALIANT PEACE-KEEPERS.
OUR TASK HERE IS NOT ONE WE TAKE LIGHTLY. AMERICA IS BROKEN, AND TRUSTWELL IS AN *AMERICAN* COMPANY.
WE CONSIDER IT AN HONOR TO REBUILD SOME OF AMERICA'S HISTORICAL TREASURES.
UNDER OUR CARE, THE EMPIRE STATE BUILDING, CENTRAL PARK, THE CLOISTERS, THE BROOKLYN BRIDGE, GRAMERCY PARK, AND EVEN GROUND ZERO WILL BE MENDED...
...AND OUR GREAT COUNTRY CAN BEGIN TO HEAL.
IN REGARD TO THE INCREASED UNREST, *ANY* CHANGE, EVEN POSITIVE, CAN BE JARRING AT FIRST. WE AT TRUSTWELL ARE AWARE OF THIS, AND WE ARE SYMPATHETIC.
BUT WE *WILL NOT TOLERATE* ANY VIOLENCE WHATSOEVER. OUR OWN SECURITY FORCES STAND READY, AS DO THE UNITED NATIONS, TO KEEP THE PEACE AND PEACEFULLY REBUILD.

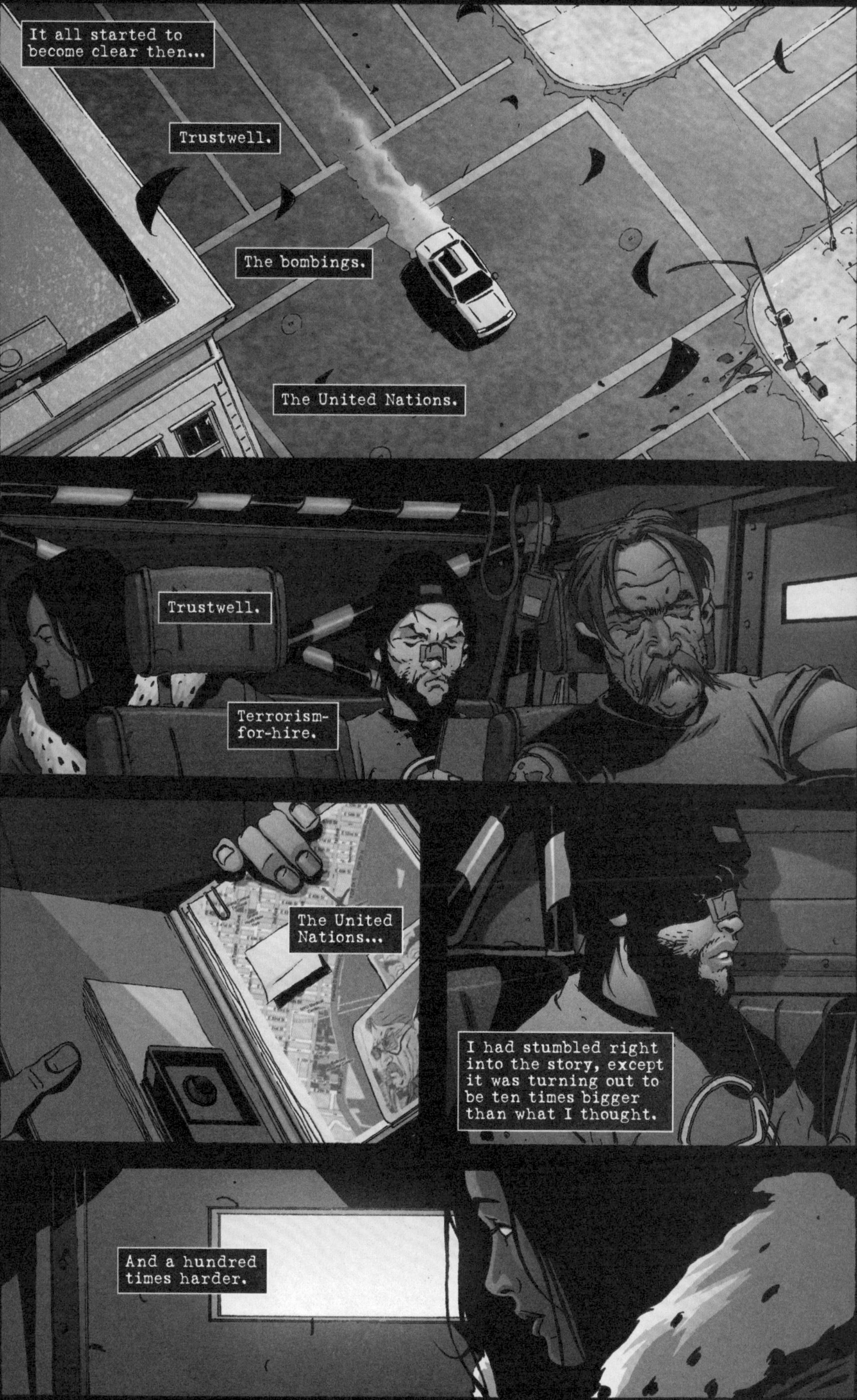
It all started to become clear then...
Trustwell.
The bombings.
The United Nations.
Trustwell.
Terrorism-for-hire.
The United Nations...
I had stumbled right into the story, except it was turning out to be ten times bigger than what I thought.
And a hundred times harder.

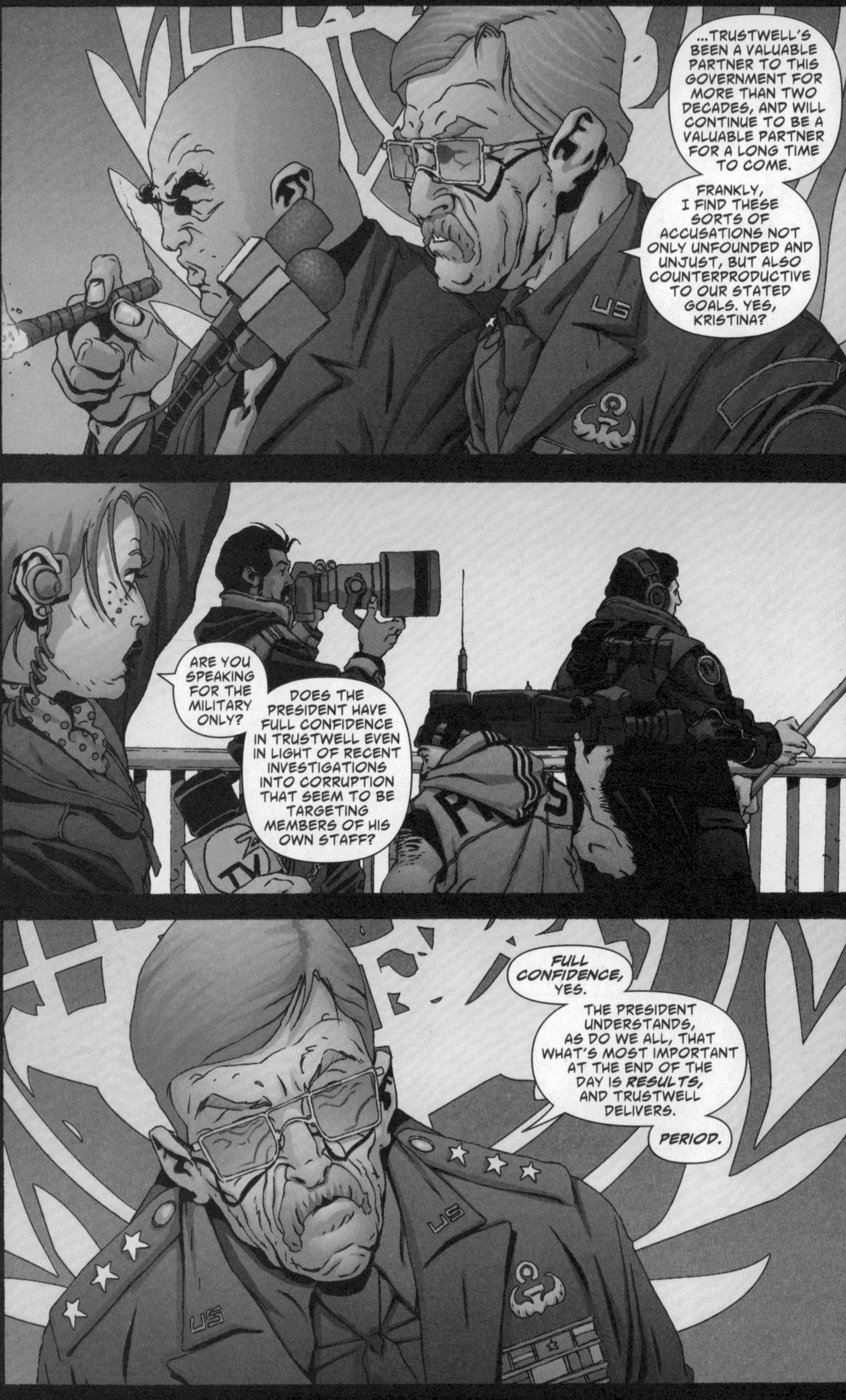
...TRUSTWELL'S BEEN A VALUABLE PARTNER TO THIS GOVERNMENT FOR MORE THAN TWO DECADES, AND WILL CONTINUE TO BE A VALUABLE PARTNER FOR A LONG TIME TO COME.
FRANKLY, I FIND THESE SORTS OF ACCUSATIONS NOT ONLY UNFOUNDED AND UNJUST, BUT ALSO COUNTERPRODUCTIVE TO OUR STATED GOALS. YES, KRISTINA?
ARE YOU SPEAKING FOR THE MILITARY ONLY?
DOES THE PRESIDENT HAVE FULL CONFIDENCE IN TRUSTWELL EVEN IN LIGHT OF RECENT INVESTIGATIONS INTO CORRUPTION THAT SEEM TO BE TARGETING MEMBERS OF HIS OWN STAFF?
*FULL CONFIDENCE,* YES.
THE PRESIDENT UNDERSTANDS, AS DO WE ALL, THAT WHAT'S MOST IMPORTANT AT THE END OF THE DAY IS *RESULTS,* AND TRUSTWELL DELIVERS.
*PERIOD.*

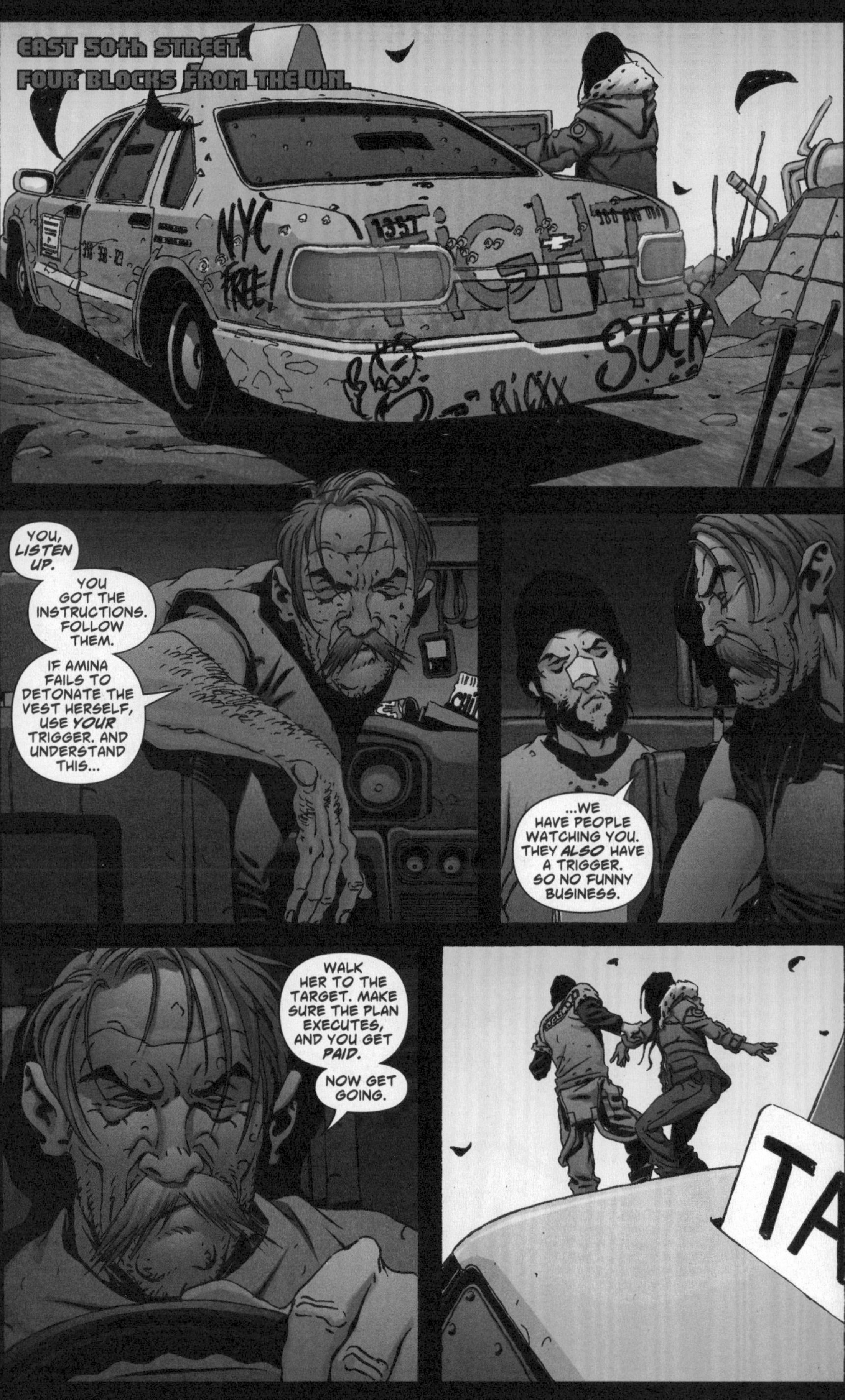
EAST 50th STREET.
FOUR BLOCKS FROM THE U.N.
NYC FREE!
SUCK
YOU, LISTEN UP.
YOU GOT THE INSTRUCTIONS. FOLLOW THEM.
IF AMINA FAILS TO DETONATE THE VEST HERSELF, USE YOUR TRIGGER. AND UNDERSTAND THIS...
...WE HAVE PEOPLE WATCHING YOU. THEY ALSO HAVE A TRIGGER. SO NO FUNNY BUSINESS.
WALK HER TO THE TARGET. MAKE SURE THE PLAN EXECUTES, AND YOU GET PAID.
NOW GET GOING.

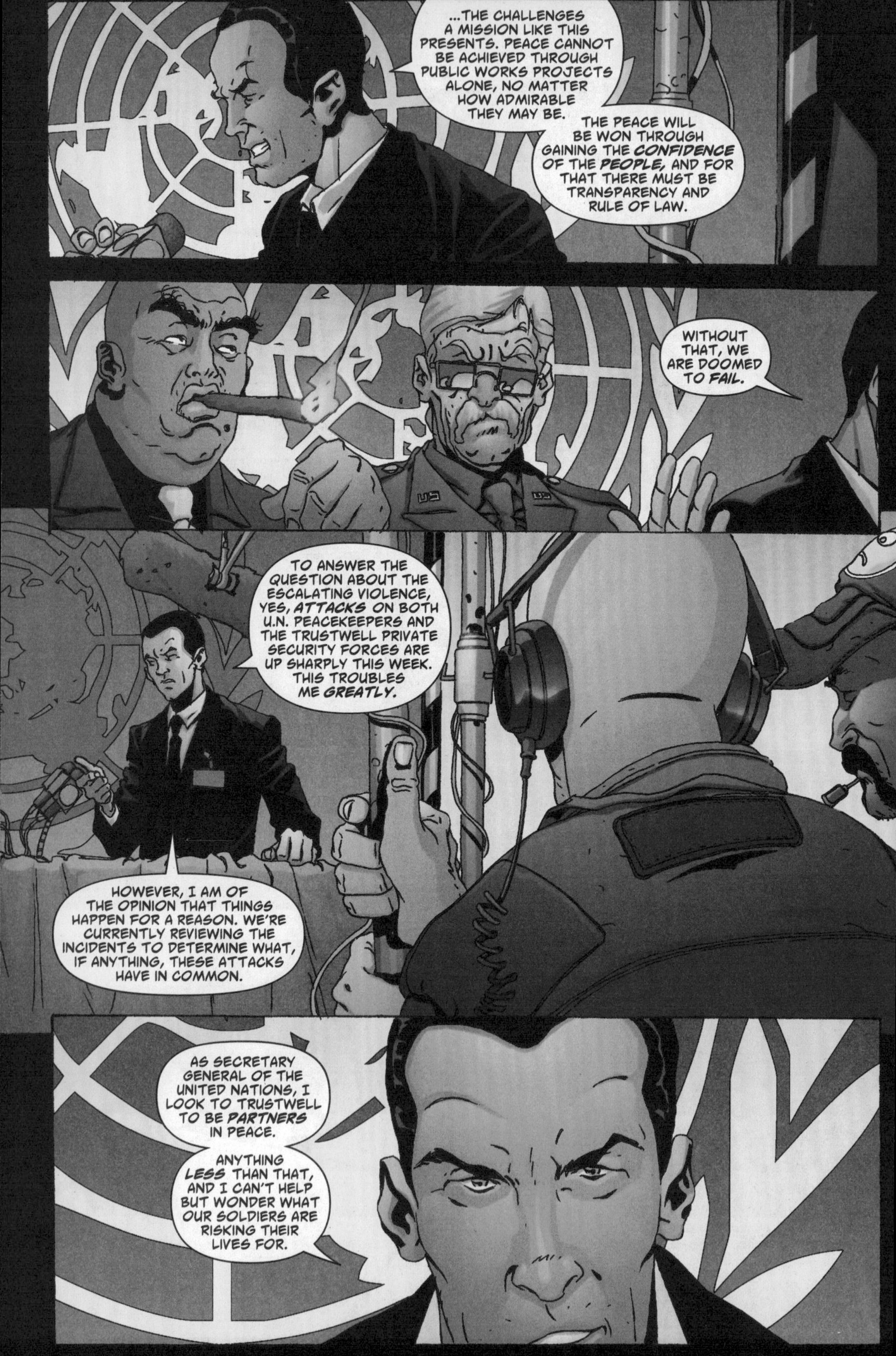
...THE CHALLENGES A MISSION LIKE THIS PRESENTS. PEACE CANNOT BE ACHIEVED THROUGH PUBLIC WORKS PROJECTS ALONE, NO MATTER HOW ADMIRABLE THEY MAY BE.
THE PEACE WILL BE WON THROUGH GAINING THE CONFIDENCE OF THE PEOPLE, AND FOR THAT THERE MUST BE TRANSPARENCY AND RULE OF LAW.
WITHOUT THAT, WE ARE DOOMED TO FAIL.
TO ANSWER THE QUESTION ABOUT THE ESCALATING VIOLENCE, YES, ATTACKS ON BOTH U.N. PEACEKEEPERS AND THE TRUSTWELL PRIVATE SECURITY FORCES ARE UP SHARPLY THIS WEEK. THIS TROUBLES ME GREATLY.
HOWEVER, I AM OF THE OPINION THAT THINGS HAPPEN FOR A REASON. WE'RE CURRENTLY REVIEWING THE INCIDENTS TO DETERMINE WHAT, IF ANYTHING, THESE ATTACKS HAVE IN COMMON.
AS SECRETARY GENERAL OF THE UNITED NATIONS, I LOOK TO TRUSTWELL TO BE PARTNERS IN PEACE.
ANYTHING LESS THAN THAT, AND I CAN'T HELP BUT WONDER WHAT OUR SOLDIERS ARE RISKING THEIR LIVES FOR.

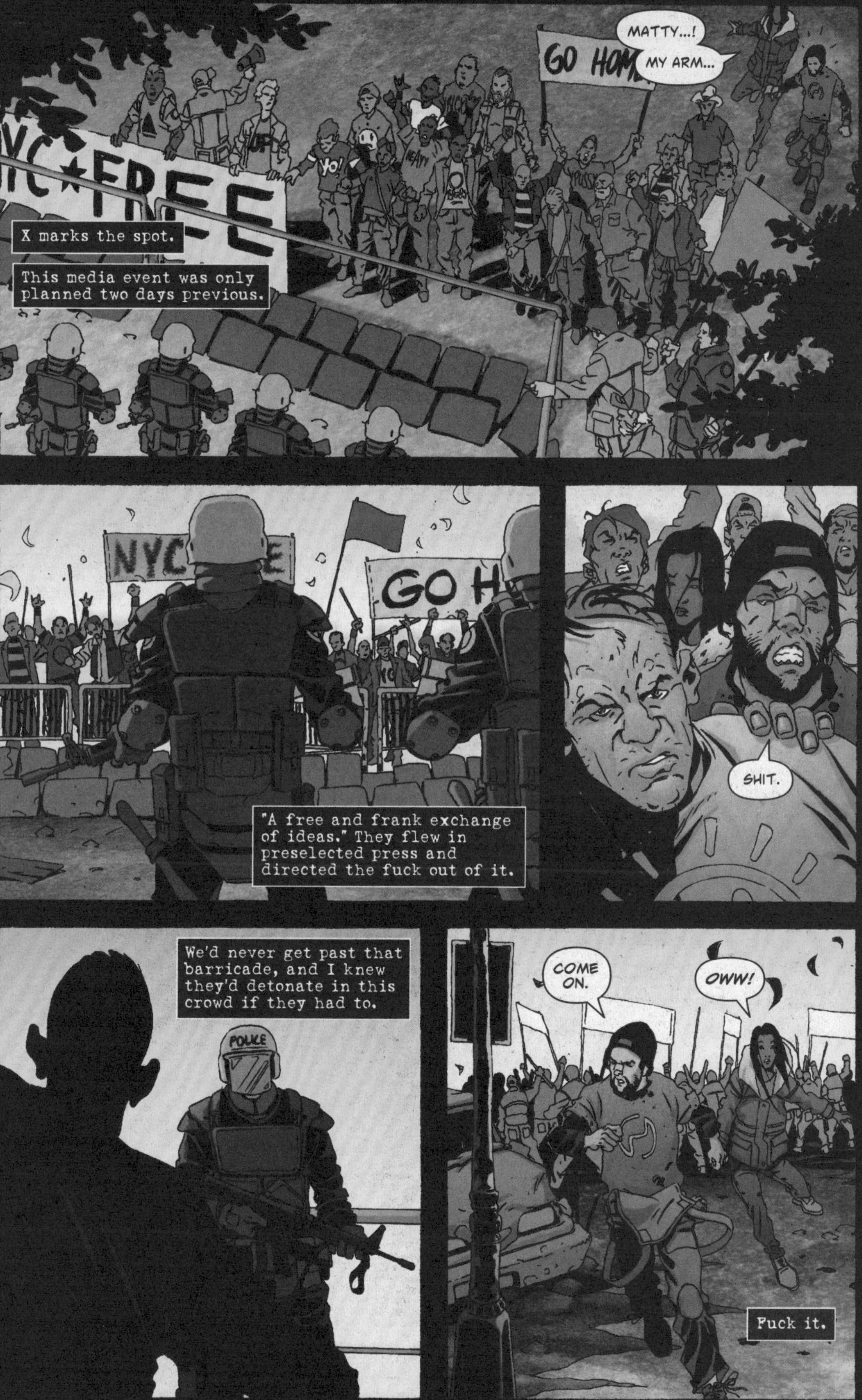

GO HOM
MATTY...!
MY ARM...
NYC★FREE
YO!
HEAVY
X marks the spot.
This media event was only planned two days previous.
NYC
GO H
"A free and frank exchange of ideas." They flew in preselected press and directed the fuck out of it.
SHIT.
We'd never get past that barricade, and I knew they'd detonate in this crowd if they had to.
POLICE
COME ON.
OWW!
Fuck it.

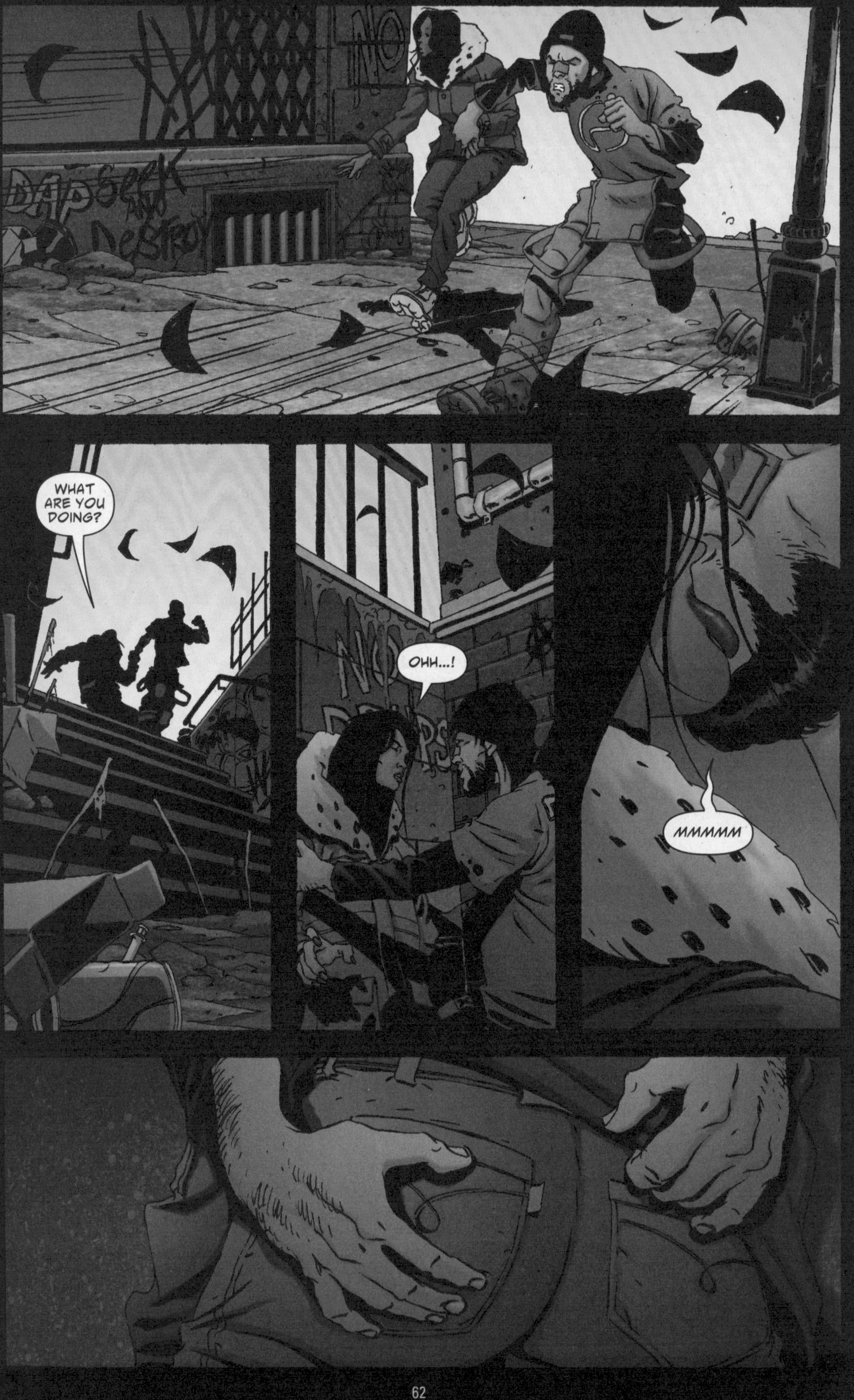
WHAT ARE YOU DOING?
OHH...!
MMMMM

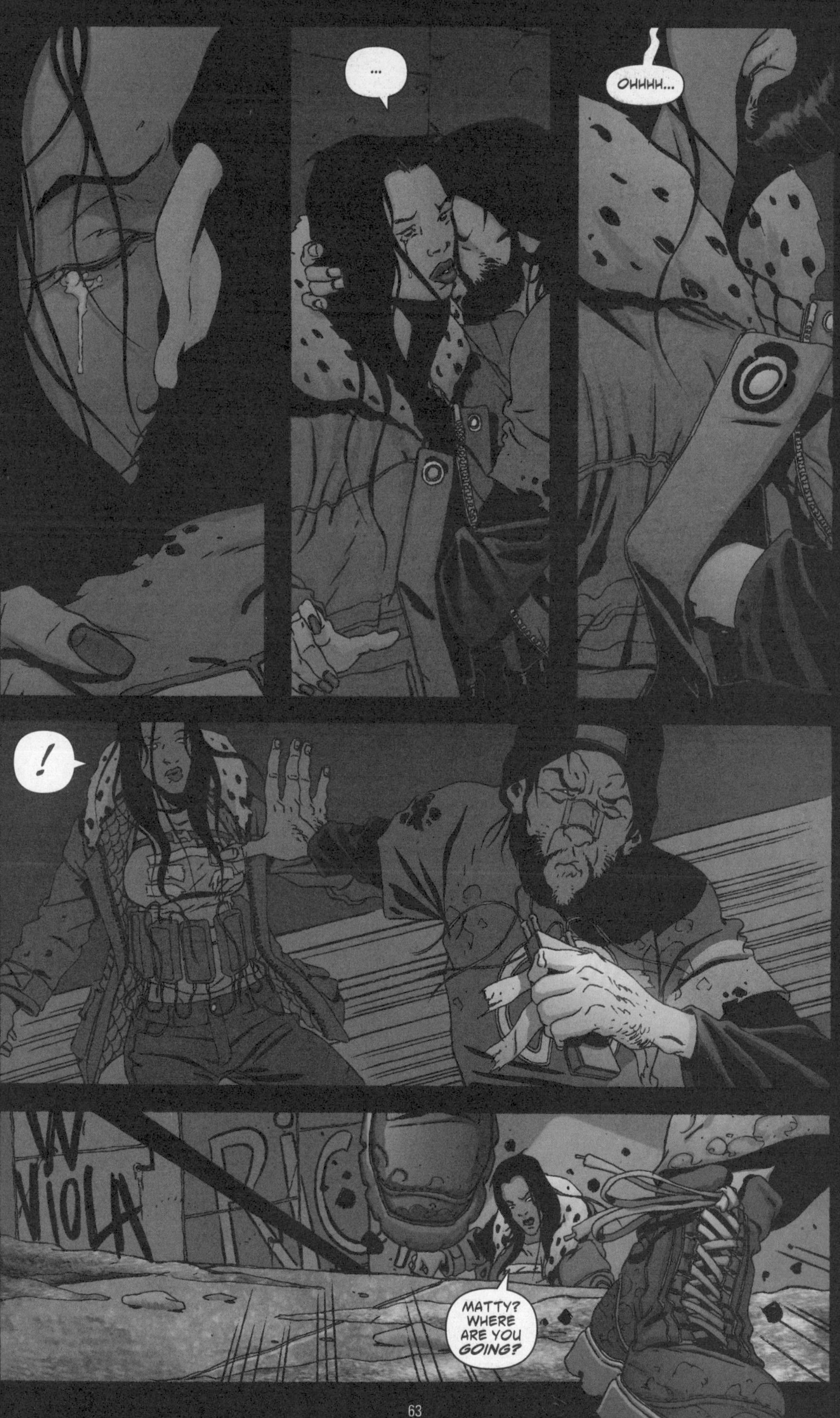
...
OHHHH...
!
VIVA
VIOLA
MATTY? WHERE ARE YOU GOING?

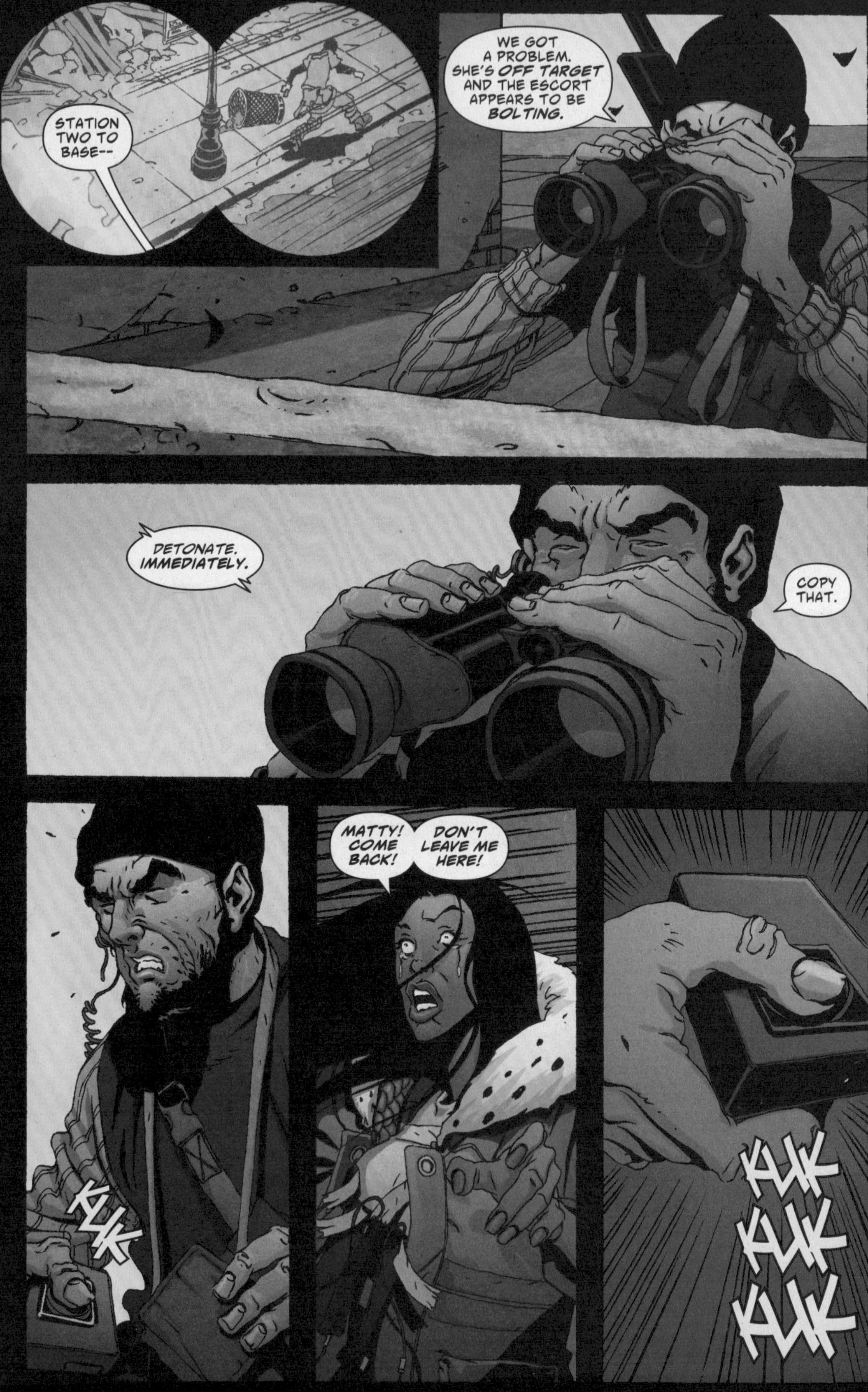
STATION TWO TO BASE--
WE GOT A PROBLEM. SHE'S OFF TARGET AND THE ESCORT APPEARS TO BE BOLTING.
DETONATE. IMMEDIATELY.
COPY THAT.
MATTY! COME BACK!
DON'T LEAVE ME HERE!
KLIK
KLIK
KLIK
KLIK

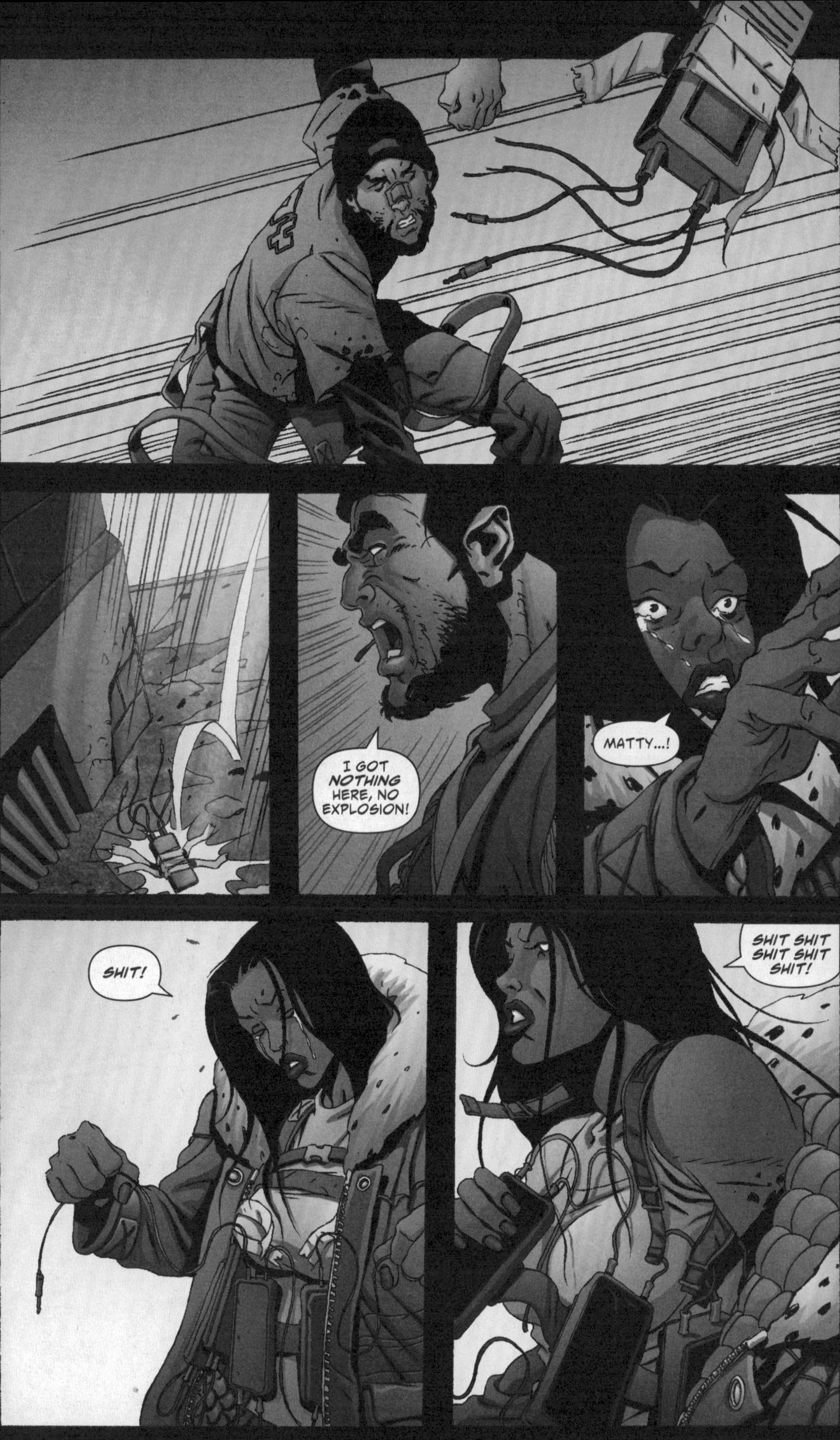
I GOT NOTHING HERE, NO EXPLOSION!
MATTY...!
SHIT!
SHIT SHIT SHIT SHIT SHIT!

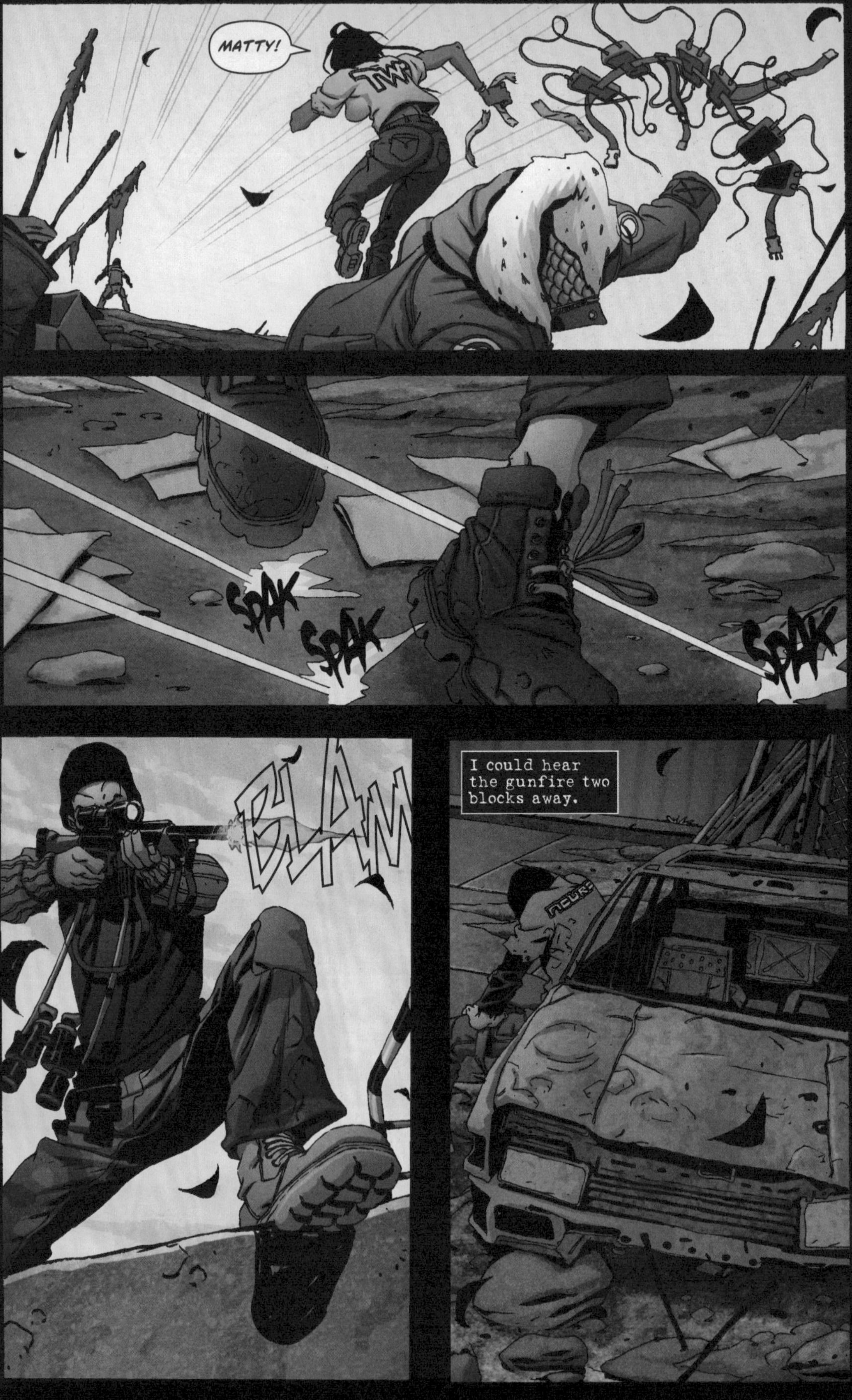
MATTY!
SPAK
SPAK
SPAK
BLAM
I could hear the gunfire two blocks away.

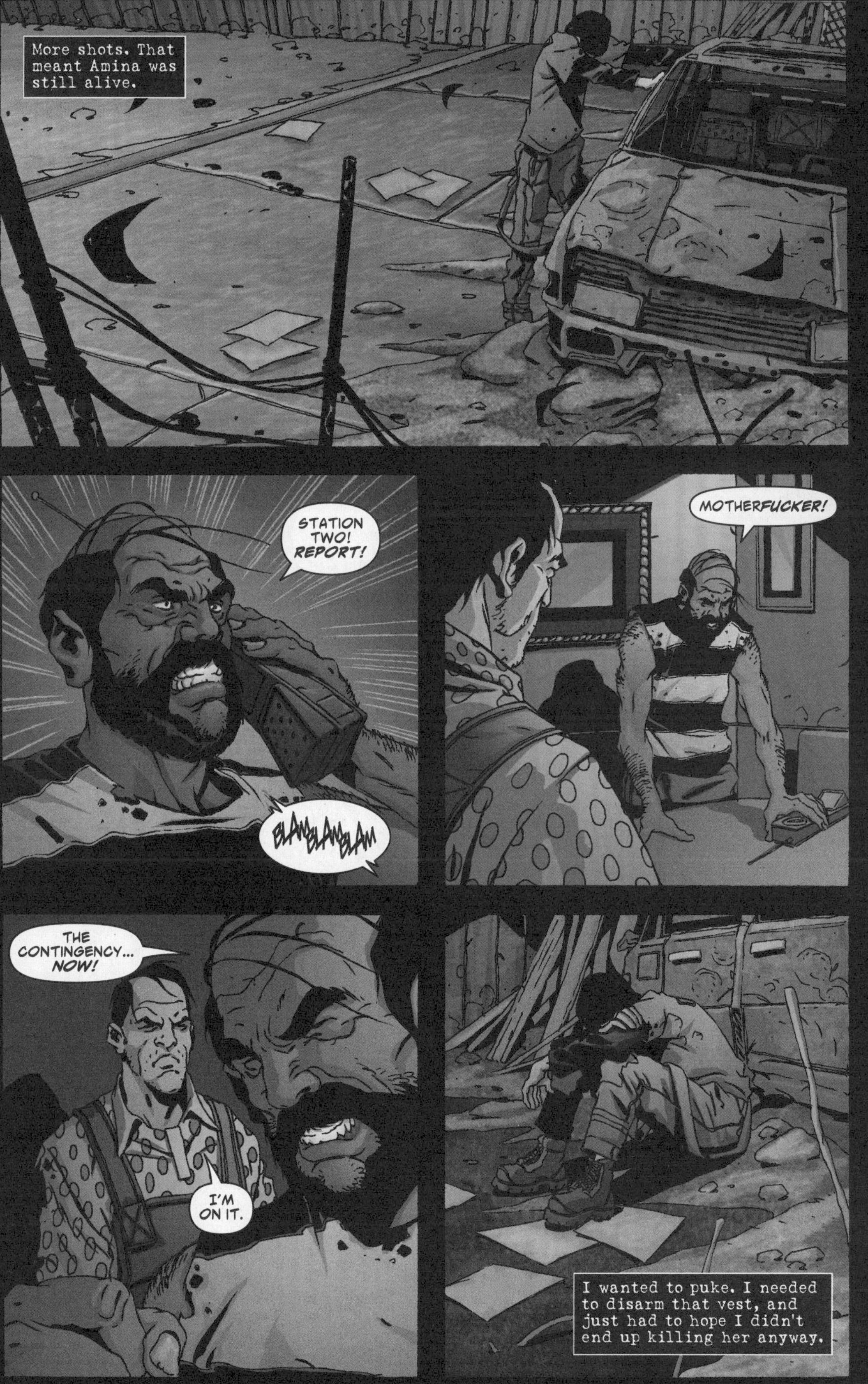
More shots. That meant Amina was still alive.
STATION TWO! REPORT!
BLAMBLAMBLAM
MOTHERFUCKER!
THE CONTINGENCY... NOW!
I'M ON IT.
I wanted to puke. I needed to disarm that vest, and just had to hope I didn't end up killing her anyway.

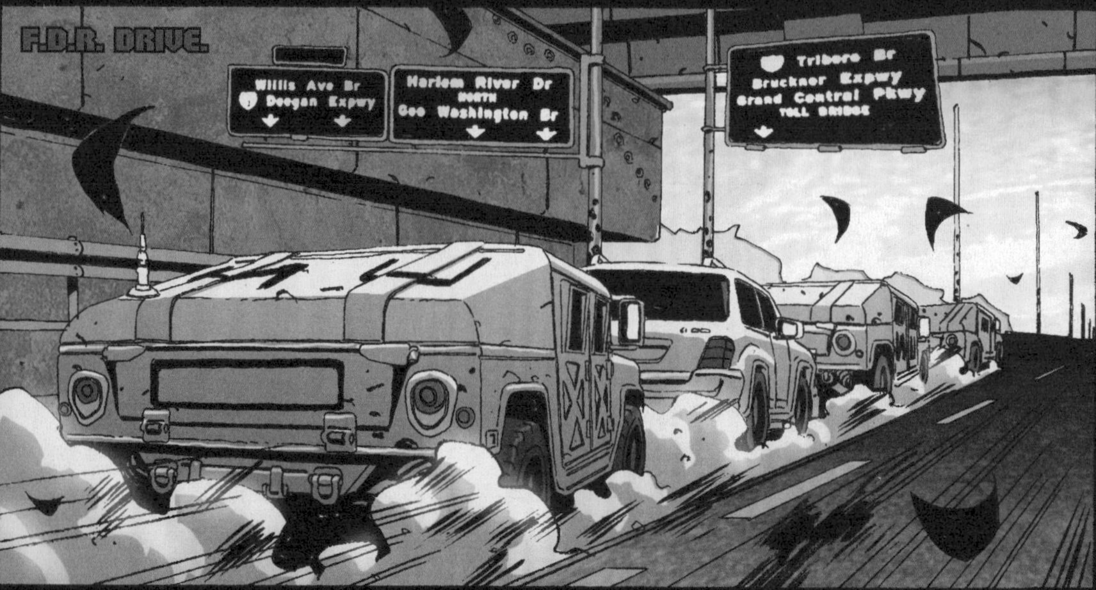
F.D.R. DRIVE.
Willis Ave Br
Deegan Expwy
Harlem River Dr
NORTH
Geo Washington Br
Triboro Br
Bruckner Expwy
Grand Central Pkwy

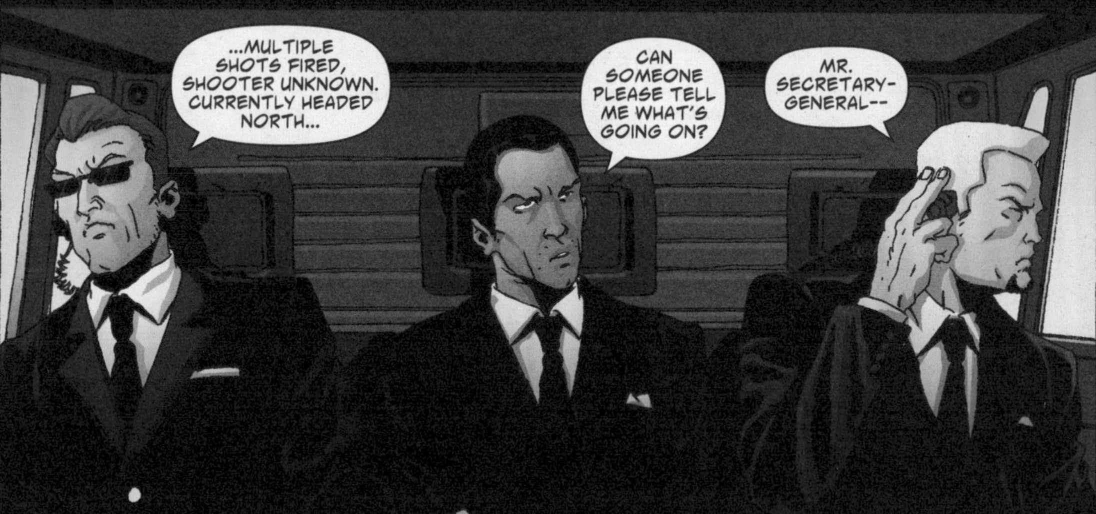
...MULTIPLE SHOTS FIRED, SHOOTER UNKNOWN. CURRENTLY HEADED NORTH...
CAN SOMEONE PLEASE TELL ME WHAT'S GOING ON?
MR. SECRETARY-GENERAL--

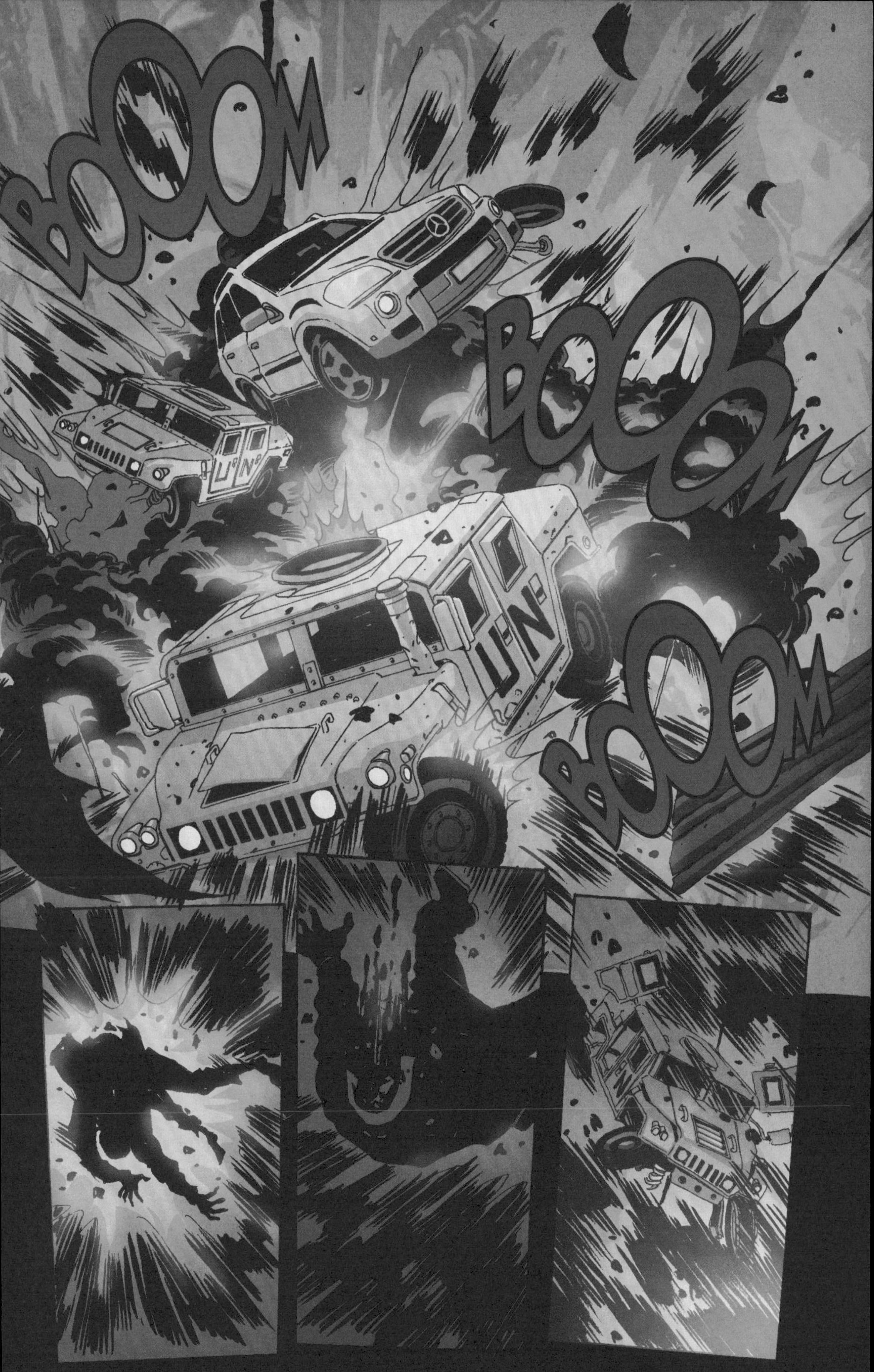
BOOOM
BOOOM
BOOOM

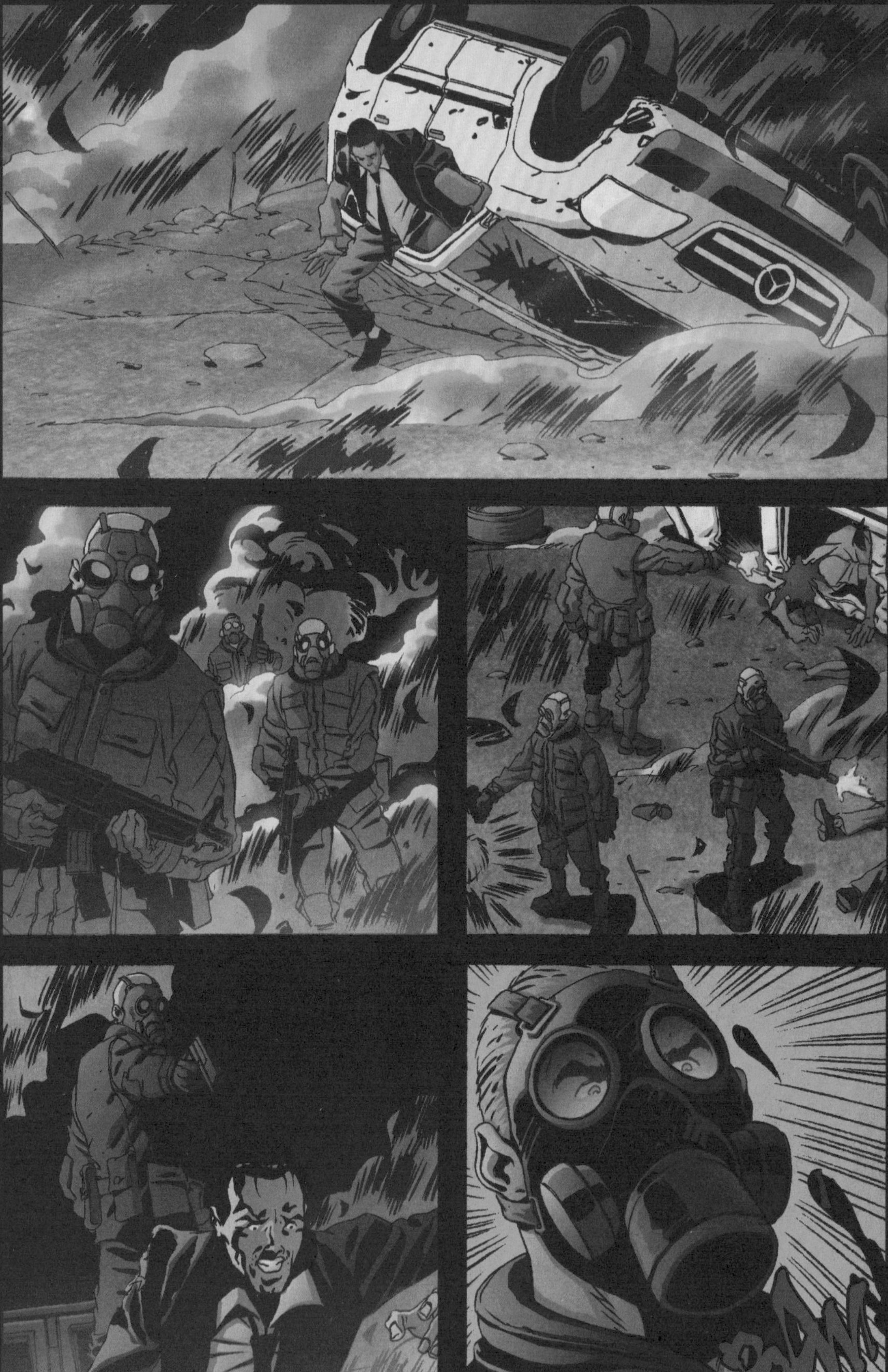

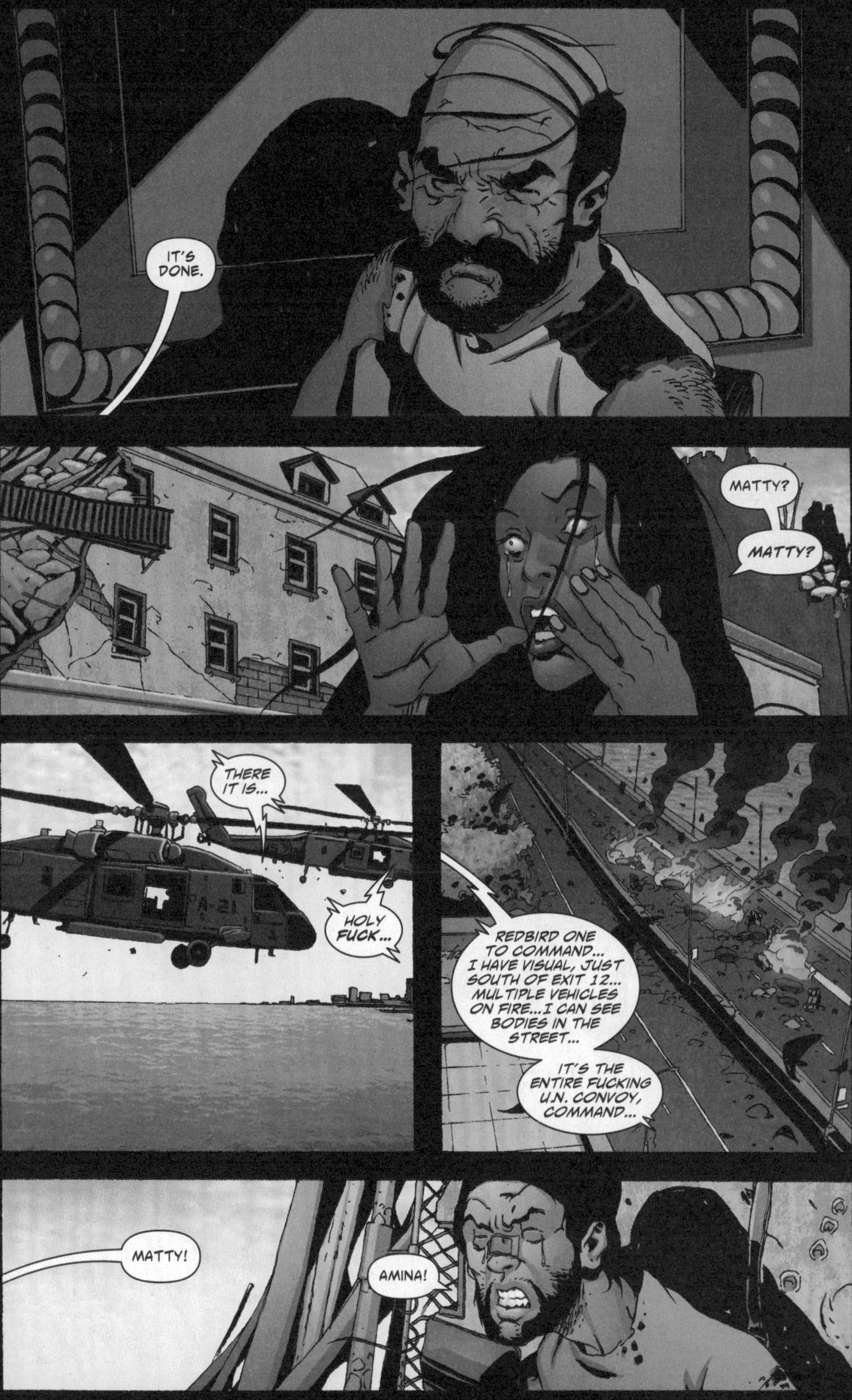
IT'S DONE.
MATTY?
MATTY?
THERE IT IS...
HOLY FUCK...
REDBIRD ONE TO COMMAND... I HAVE VISUAL, JUST SOUTH OF EXIT 12... MULTIPLE VEHICLES ON FIRE...I CAN SEE BODIES IN THE STREET...
IT'S THE ENTIRE FUCKING U.N. CONVOY, COMMAND...
MATTY!
AMINA!

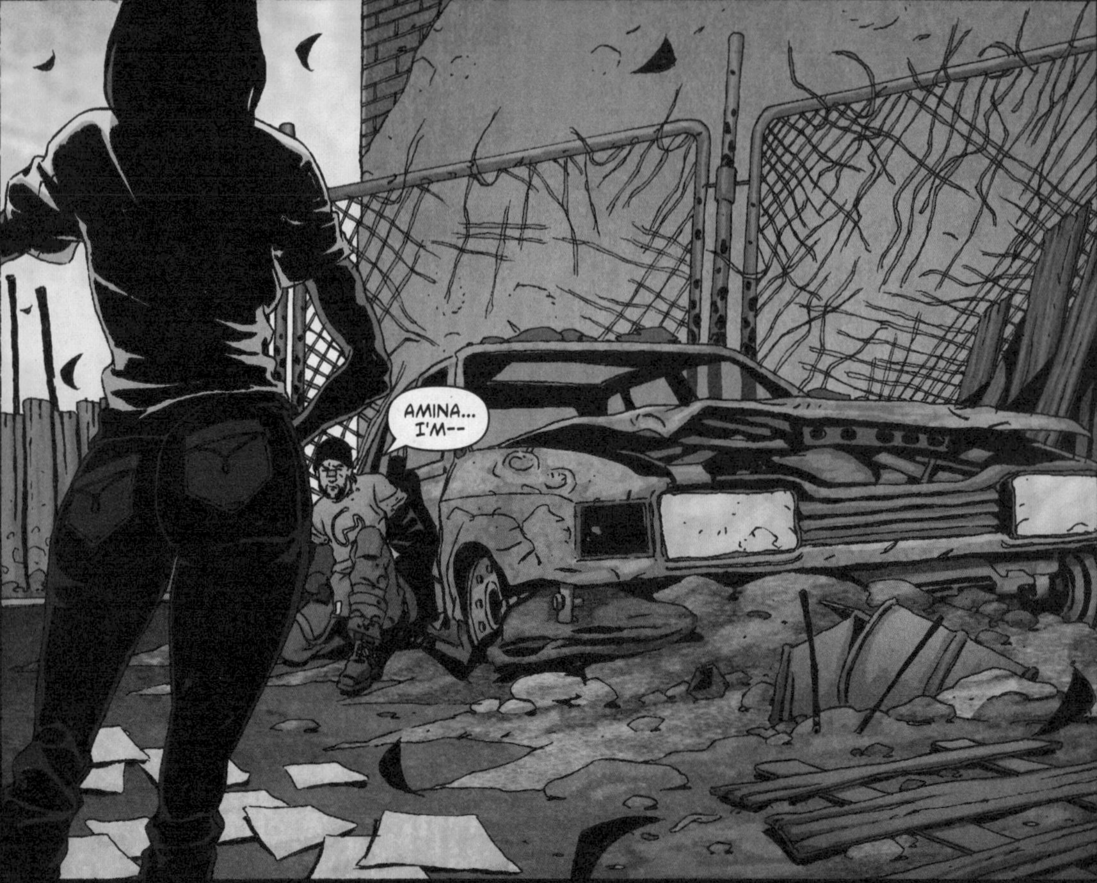
AMINA... I'M--

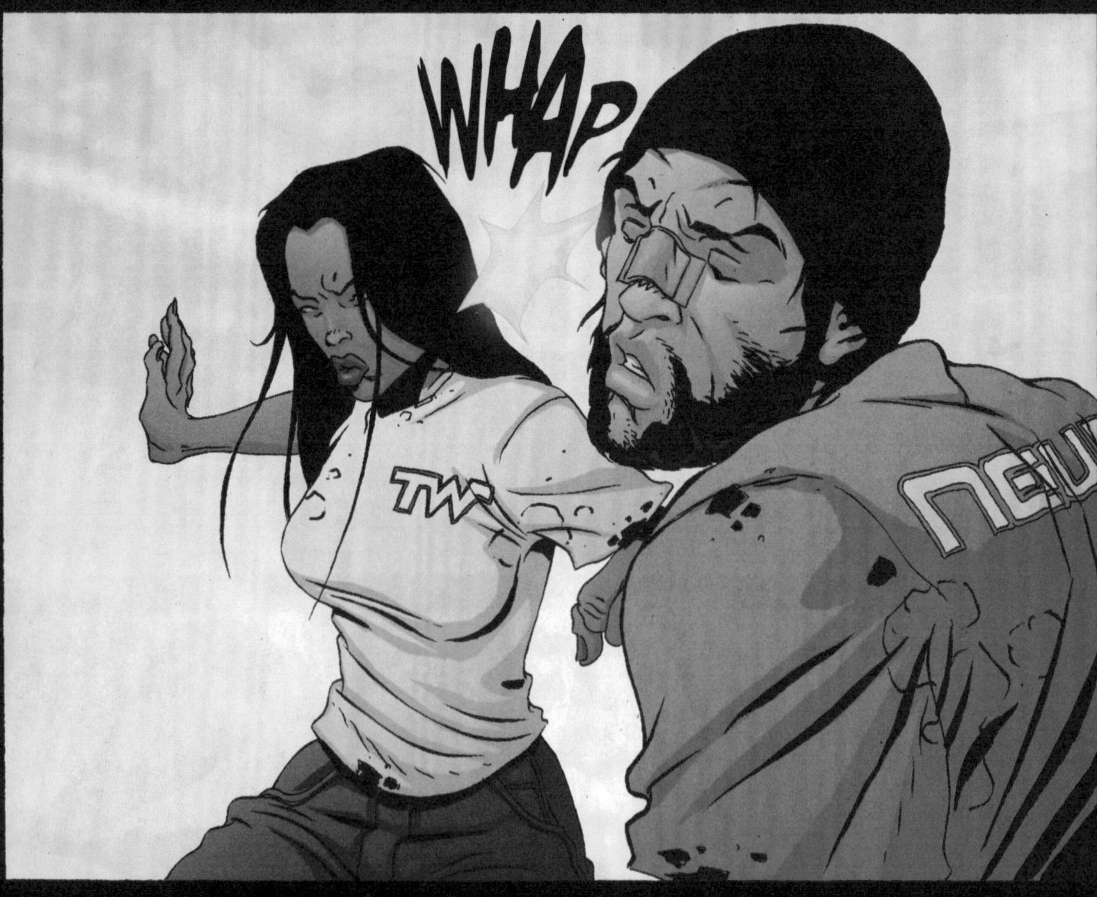
WHAP

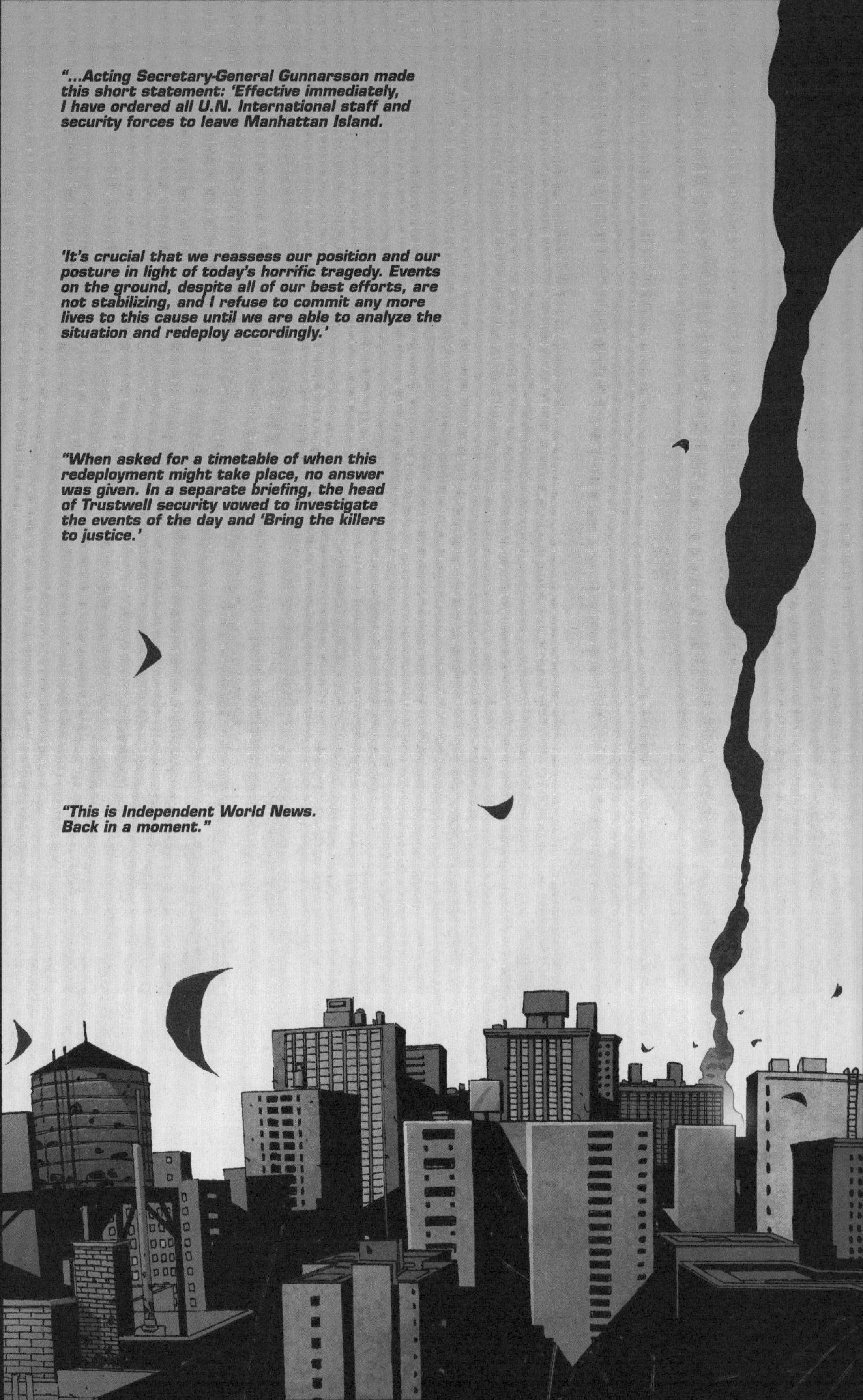
"...Acting Secretary-General Gunnarsson made this short statement: 'Effective immediately, I have ordered all U.N. International staff and security forces to leave Manhattan Island.
'It's crucial that we reassess our position and our posture in light of today's horrific tragedy. Events on the ground, despite all of our best efforts, are not stabilizing, and I refuse to commit any more lives to this cause until we are able to analyze the situation and redeploy accordingly.'
"When asked for a timetable of when this redeployment might take place, no answer was given. In a separate briefing, the head of Trustwell security vowed to investigate the events of the day and 'Bring the killers to justice.'
"This is Independent World News. Back in a moment."

# CHAPTER FOUR

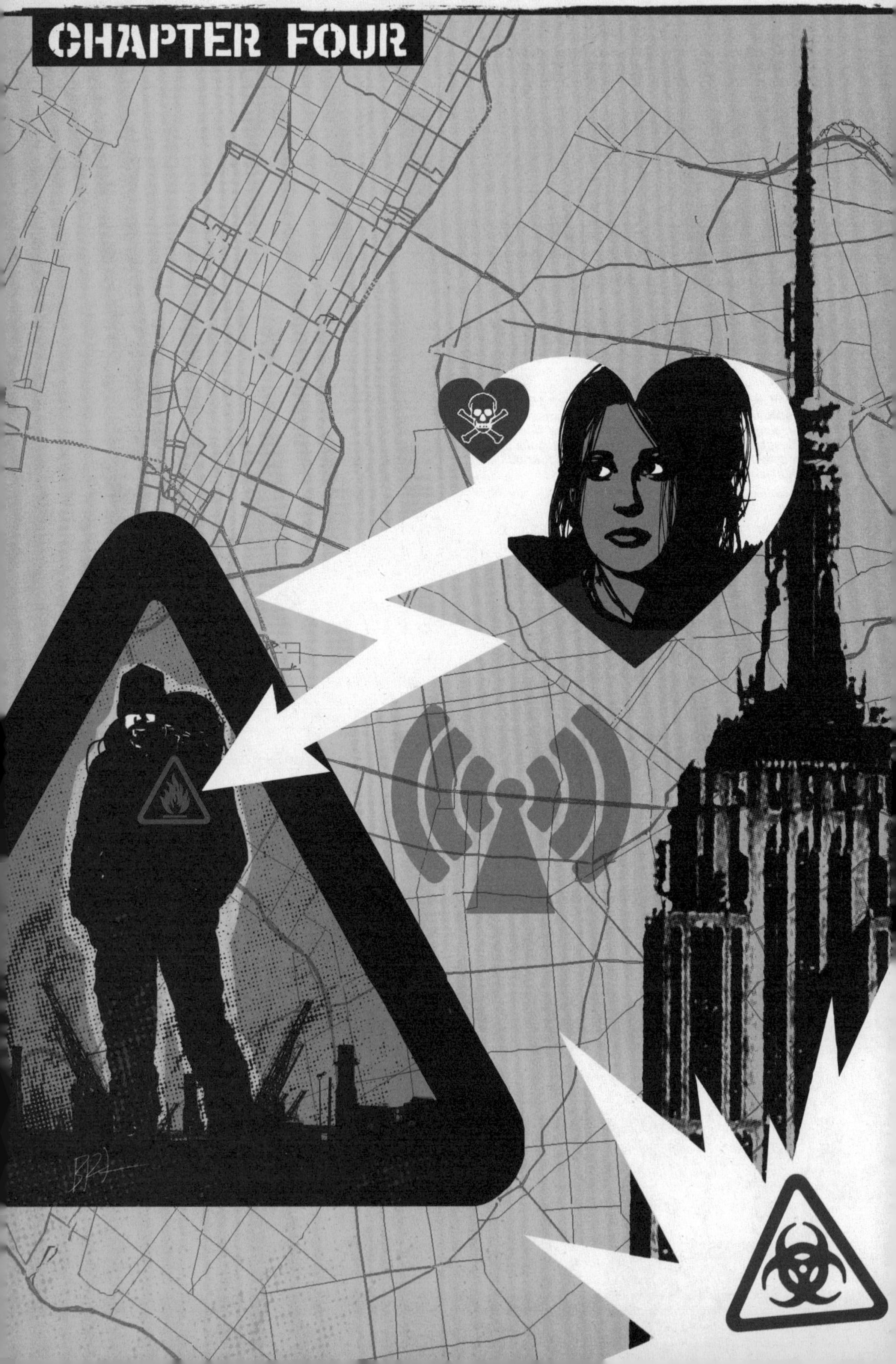

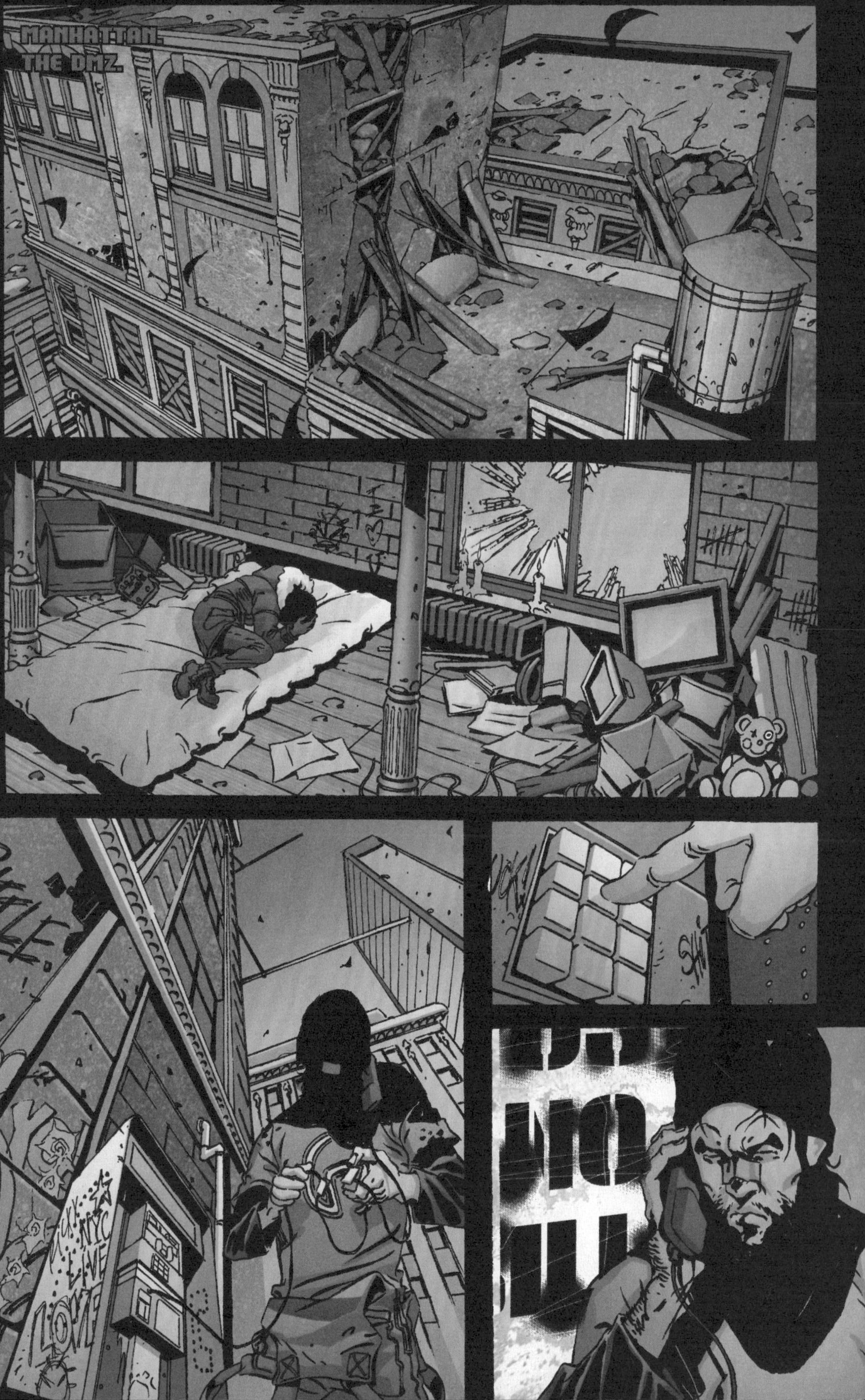
MANHATTAN.
THE DMZ.

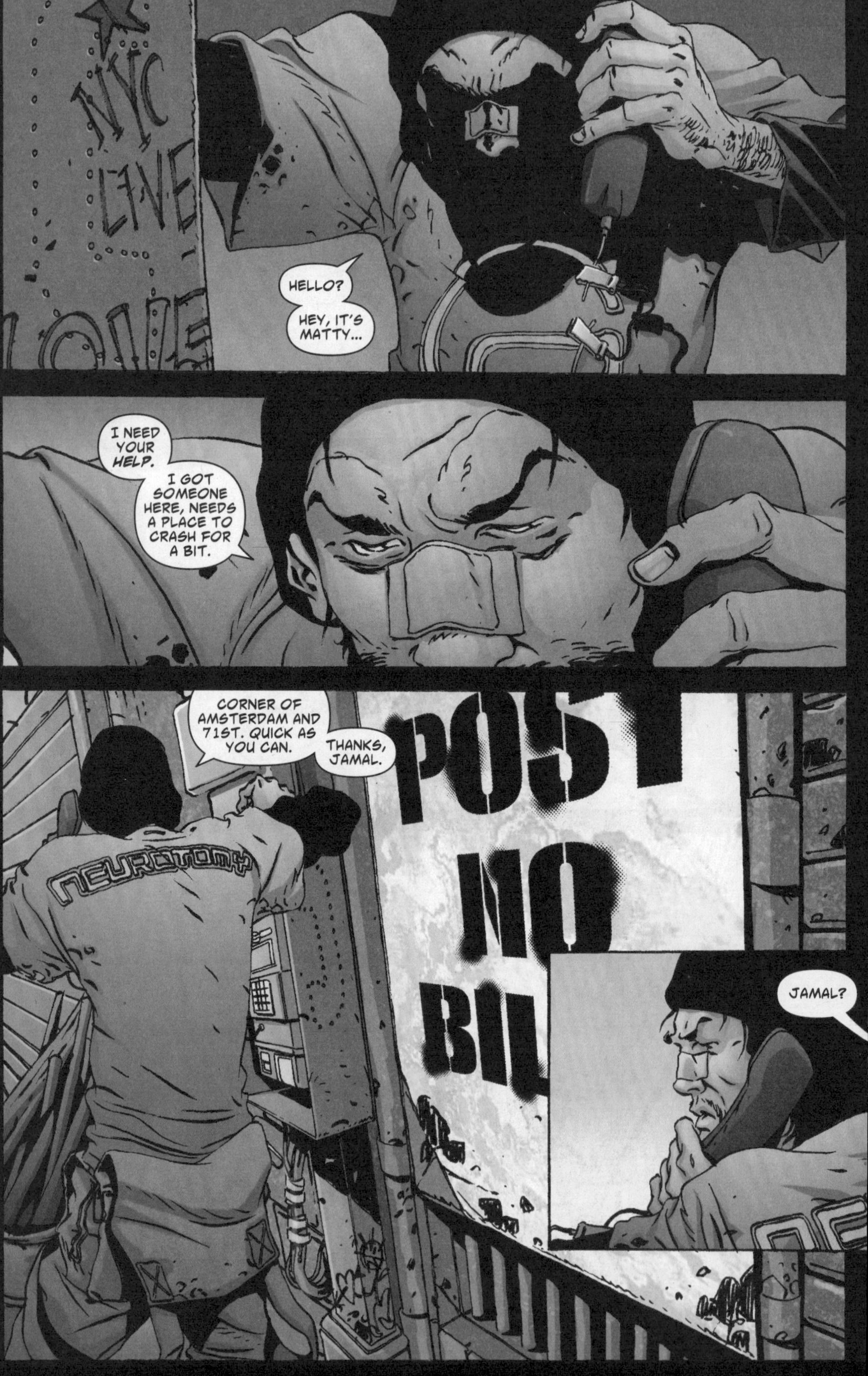
NYC
LIVE
LOVE
HELLO?
HEY, IT'S MATTY...
I NEED YOUR HELP.
I GOT SOMEONE HERE, NEEDS A PLACE TO CRASH FOR A BIT.
CORNER OF AMSTERDAM AND 71ST. QUICK AS YOU CAN.
THANKS, JAMAL.
NEUROTOMY
POST
NO
BILL
JAMAL?

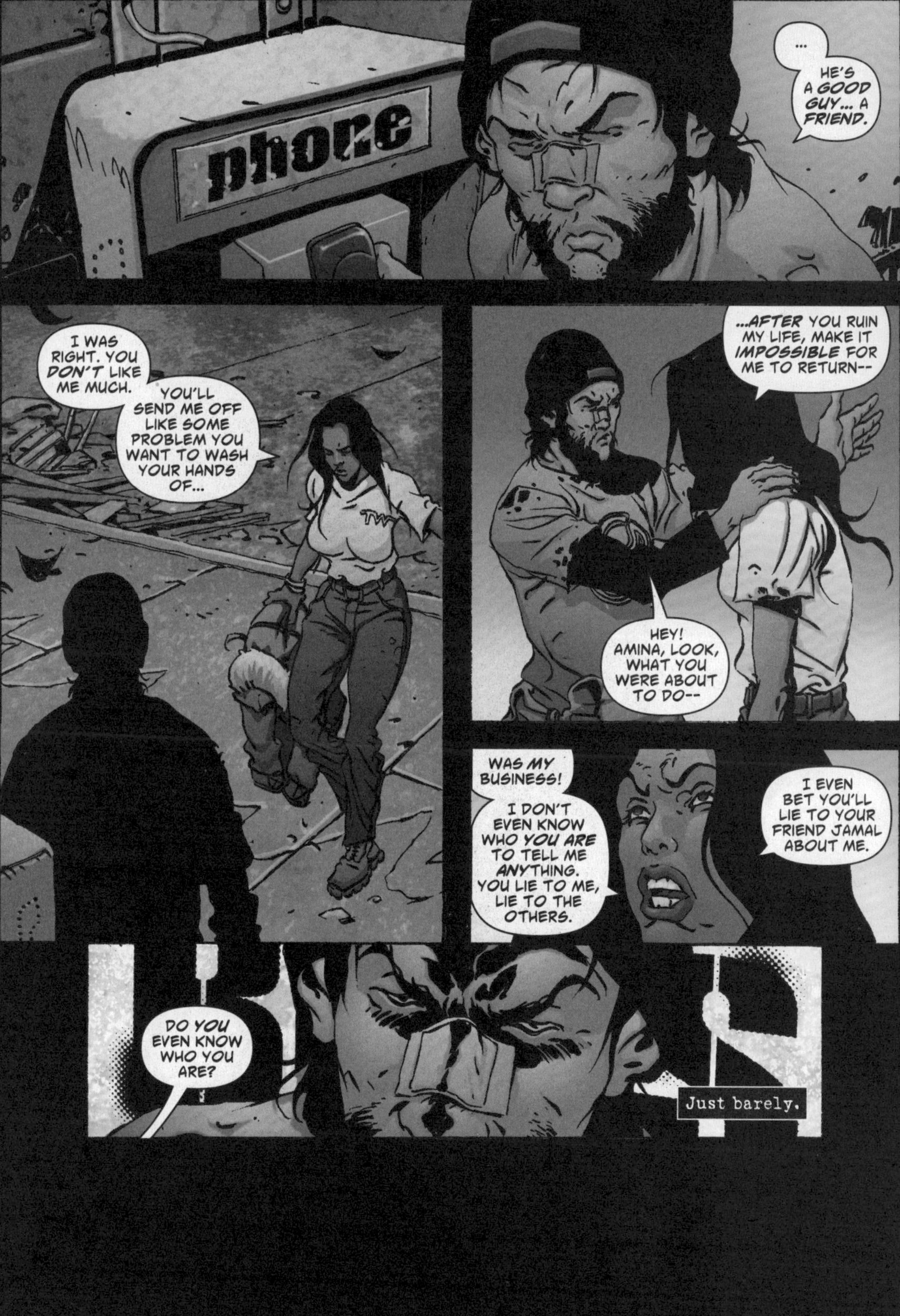
phone
...
HE'S A GOOD GUY... A FRIEND.
I WAS RIGHT. YOU DON'T LIKE ME MUCH.
YOU'LL SEND ME OFF LIKE SOME PROBLEM YOU WANT TO WASH YOUR HANDS OF...
...AFTER YOU RUIN MY LIFE, MAKE IT IMPOSSIBLE FOR ME TO RETURN--
HEY! AMINA, LOOK, WHAT YOU WERE ABOUT TO DO--
WAS MY BUSINESS!
I DON'T EVEN KNOW WHO YOU ARE TO TELL ME ANYTHING. YOU LIE TO ME, LIE TO THE OTHERS.
I EVEN BET YOU'LL LIE TO YOUR FRIEND JAMAL ABOUT ME.
DO YOU EVEN KNOW WHO YOU ARE?
Just barely.

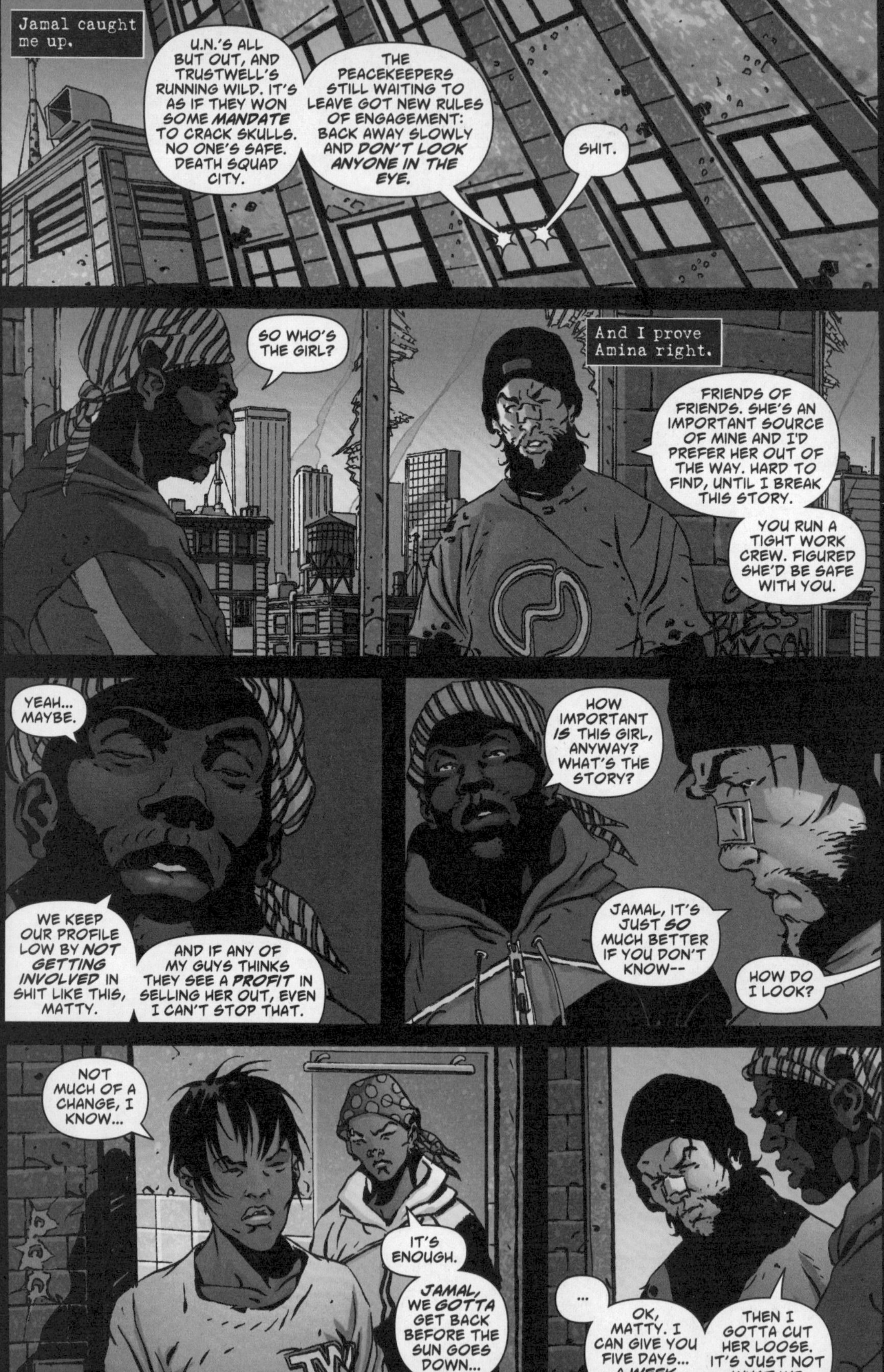
Jamal caught me up.
U.N.'S ALL BUT OUT, AND TRUSTWELL'S RUNNING WILD. IT'S AS IF THEY WON SOME MANDATE TO CRACK SKULLS. NO ONE'S SAFE. DEATH SQUAD CITY.
THE PEACEKEEPERS STILL WAITING TO LEAVE GOT NEW RULES OF ENGAGEMENT: BACK AWAY SLOWLY AND DON'T LOOK ANYONE IN THE EYE.
SHIT.
SO WHO'S THE GIRL?
And I prove Amina right.
FRIENDS OF FRIENDS. SHE'S AN IMPORTANT SOURCE OF MINE AND I'D PREFER HER OUT OF THE WAY. HARD TO FIND, UNTIL I BREAK THIS STORY.
YOU RUN A TIGHT WORK CREW. FIGURED SHE'D BE SAFE WITH YOU.
YEAH... MAYBE.
WE KEEP OUR PROFILE LOW BY NOT GETTING INVOLVED IN SHIT LIKE THIS, MATTY.
AND IF ANY OF MY GUYS THINKS THEY SEE A PROFIT IN SELLING HER OUT, EVEN I CAN'T STOP THAT.
HOW IMPORTANT IS THIS GIRL, ANYWAY? WHAT'S THE STORY?
JAMAL, IT'S JUST SO MUCH BETTER IF YOU DON'T KNOW--
HOW DO I LOOK?
NOT MUCH OF A CHANGE, I KNOW...
IT'S ENOUGH.
JAMAL, WE GOTTA GET BACK BEFORE THE SUN GOES DOWN...
...
OK, MATTY. I CAN GIVE YOU FIVE DAYS... A WEEK TOPS.
THEN I GOTTA CUT HER LOOSE. IT'S JUST NOT WHAT WE DO, MAN.

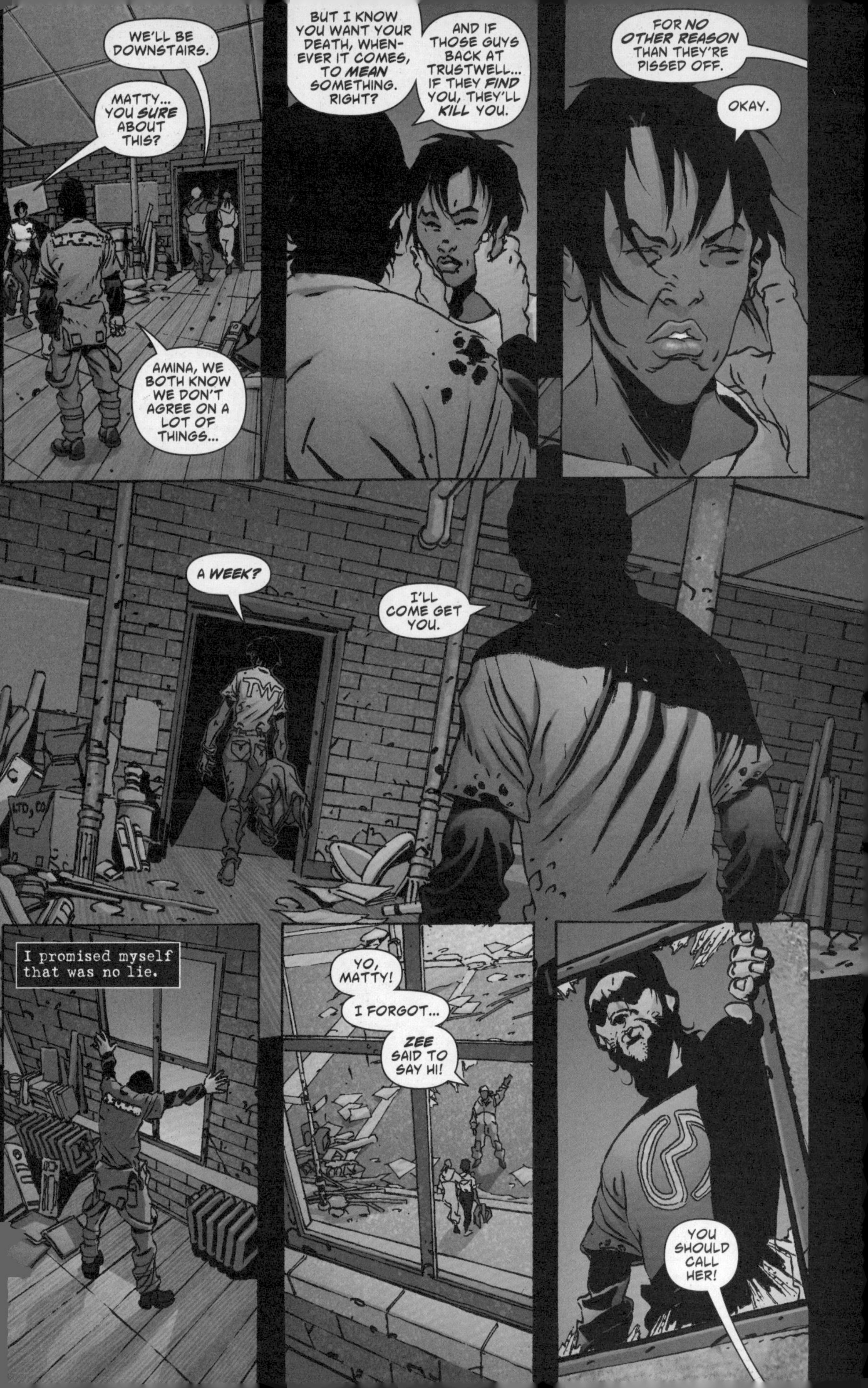

WE'LL BE DOWNSTAIRS.
MATTY... YOU SURE ABOUT THIS?
AMINA, WE BOTH KNOW WE DON'T AGREE ON A LOT OF THINGS...
BUT I KNOW YOU WANT YOUR DEATH, WHENEVER IT COMES, TO MEAN SOMETHING. RIGHT?
AND IF THOSE GUYS BACK AT TRUSTWELL... IF THEY FIND YOU, THEY'LL KILL YOU.
FOR NO OTHER REASON THAN THEY'RE PISSED OFF.
OKAY.
A WEEK?
I'LL COME GET YOU.
I promised myself that was no lie.
YO, MATTY!
I FORGOT...
ZEE SAID TO SAY HI!
YOU SHOULD CALL HER!

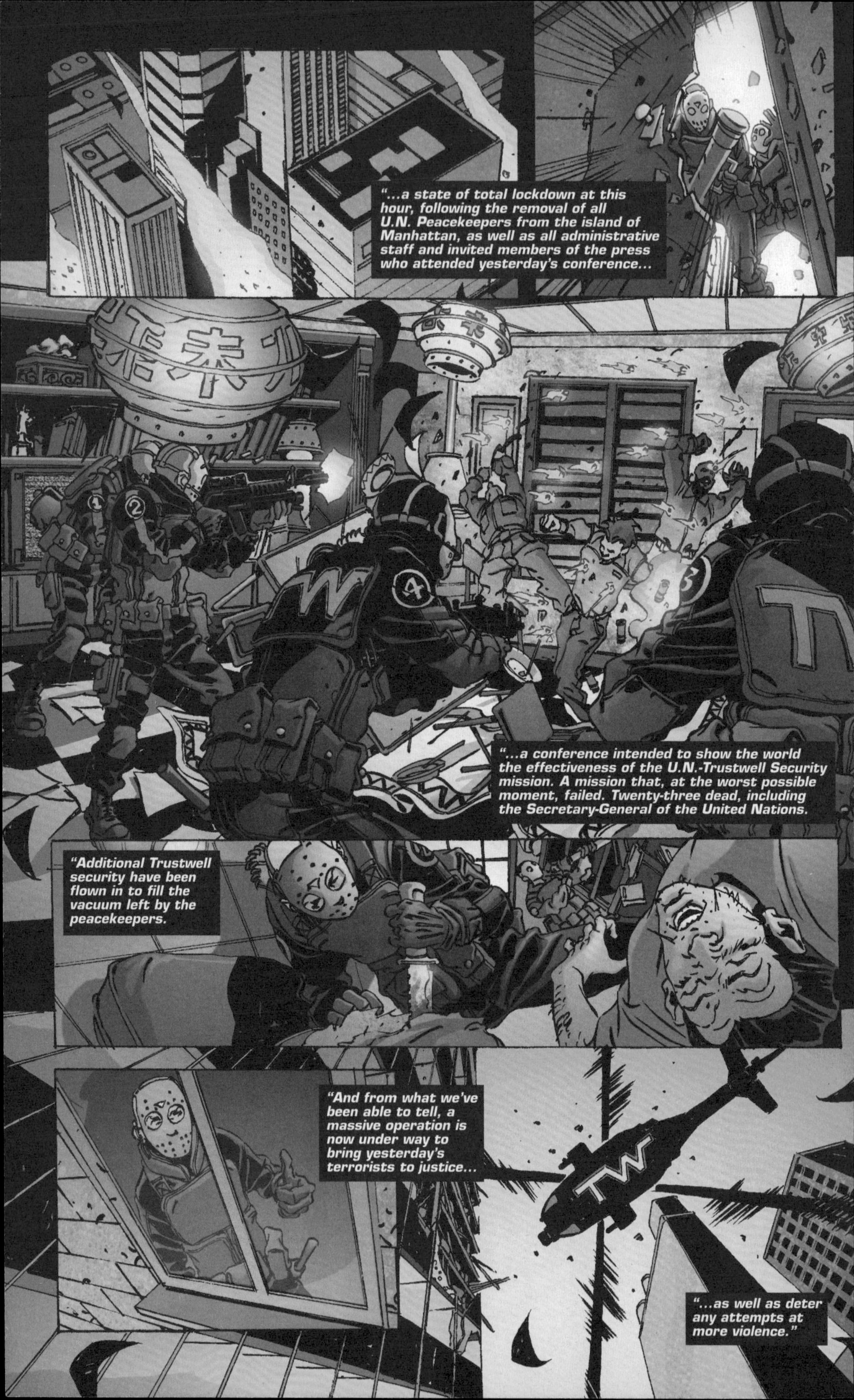
"...a state of total lockdown at this hour, following the removal of all U.N. Peacekeepers from the island of Manhattan, as well as all administrative staff and invited members of the press who attended yesterday's conference...
"...a conference intended to show the world the effectiveness of the U.N.-Trustwell Security mission. A mission that, at the worst possible moment, failed. Twenty-three dead, including the Secretary-General of the United Nations.
"Additional Trustwell security have been flown in to fill the vacuum left by the peacekeepers.
"And from what we've been able to tell, a massive operation is now under way to bring yesterday's terrorists to justice...
"...as well as deter any attempts at more violence."

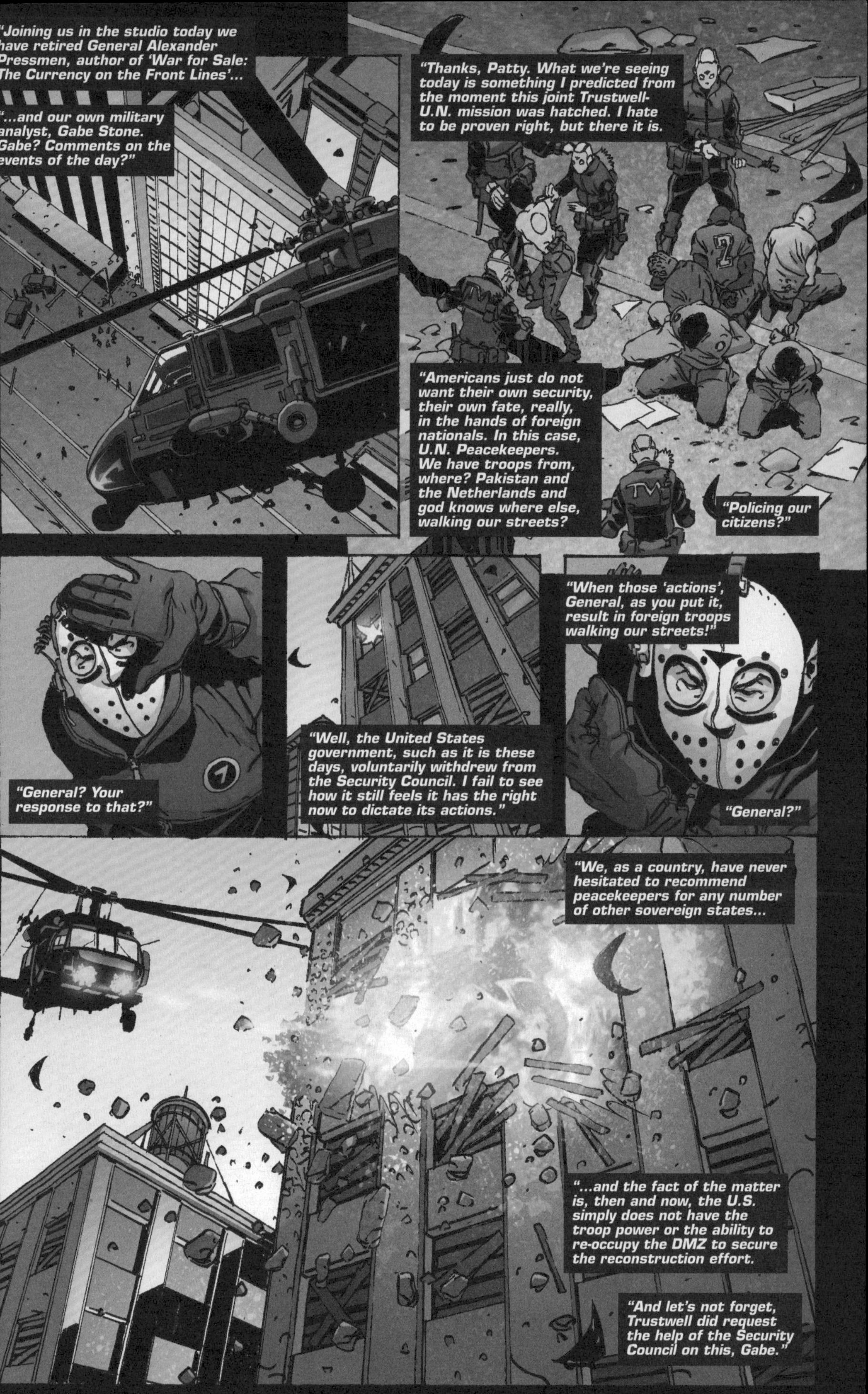
"Joining us in the studio today we have retired General Alexander Pressmen, author of 'War for Sale: The Currency on the Front Lines'...
"...and our own military analyst, Gabe Stone. Gabe? Comments on the events of the day?"
"Thanks, Patty. What we're seeing today is something I predicted from the moment this joint Trustwell-U.N. mission was hatched. I hate to be proven right, but there it is.
"Americans just do not want their own security, their own fate, really, in the hands of foreign nationals. In this case, U.N. Peacekeepers. We have troops from, where? Pakistan and the Netherlands and god knows where else, walking our streets?
"Policing our citizens?"
"General? Your response to that?"
"Well, the United States government, such as it is these days, voluntarily withdrew from the Security Council. I fail to see how it still feels it has the right now to dictate its actions."
"When those 'actions', General, as you put it, result in foreign troops walking our streets!"
"General?"
"We, as a country, have never hesitated to recommend peacekeepers for any number of other sovereign states...
"...and the fact of the matter is, then and now, the U.S. simply does not have the troop power or the ability to re-occupy the DMZ to secure the reconstruction effort.
"And let's not forget, Trustwell did request the help of the Security Council on this, Gabe."

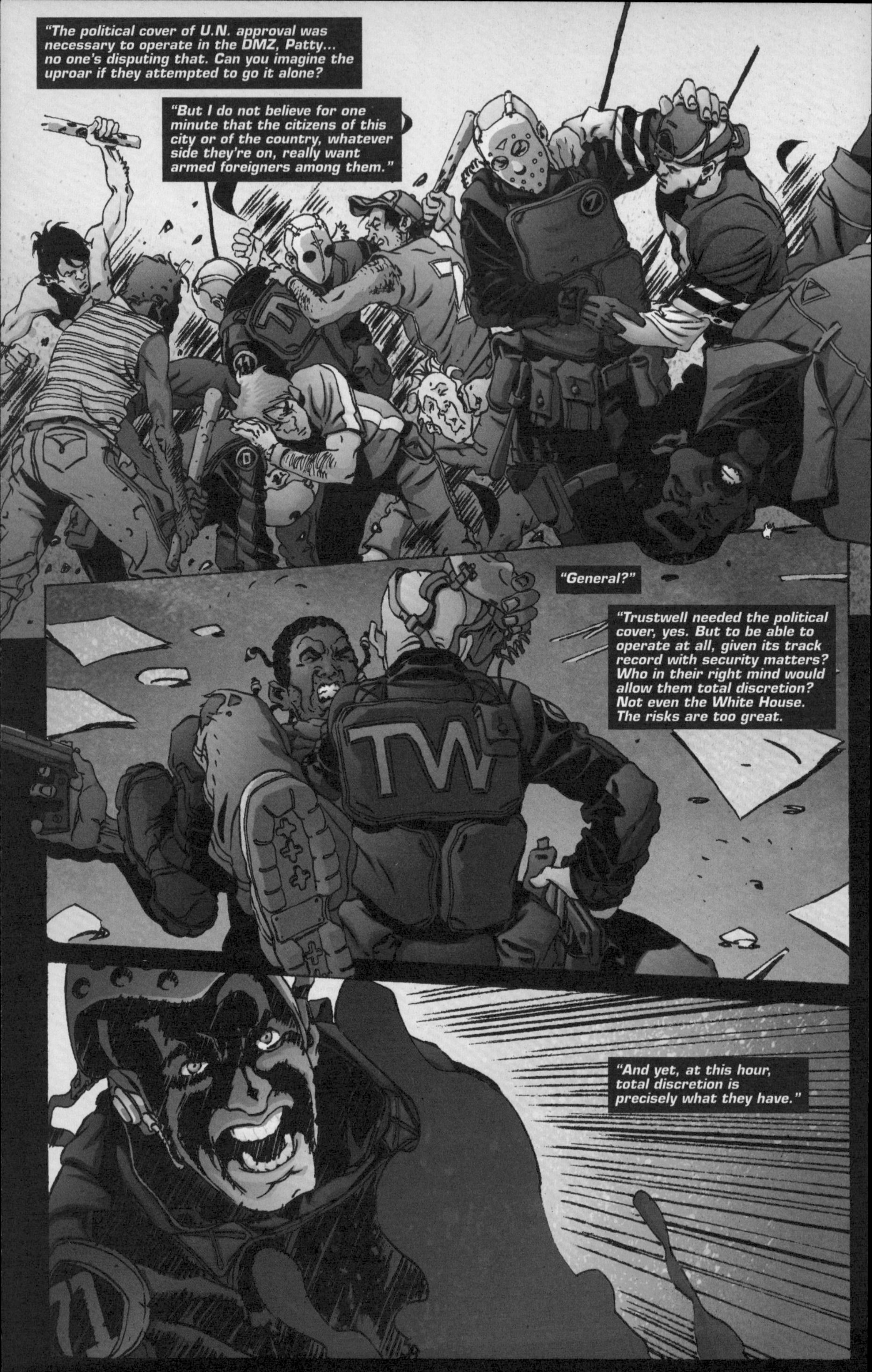
"The political cover of U.N. approval was necessary to operate in the DMZ, Patty... no one's disputing that. Can you imagine the uproar if they attempted to go it alone?
"But I do not believe for one minute that the citizens of this city or of the country, whatever side they're on, really want armed foreigners among them."
"General?"
"Trustwell needed the political cover, yes. But to be able to operate at all, given its track record with security matters? Who in their right mind would allow them total discretion? Not even the White House. The risks are too great.
TW
"And yet, at this hour, total discretion is precisely what they have."

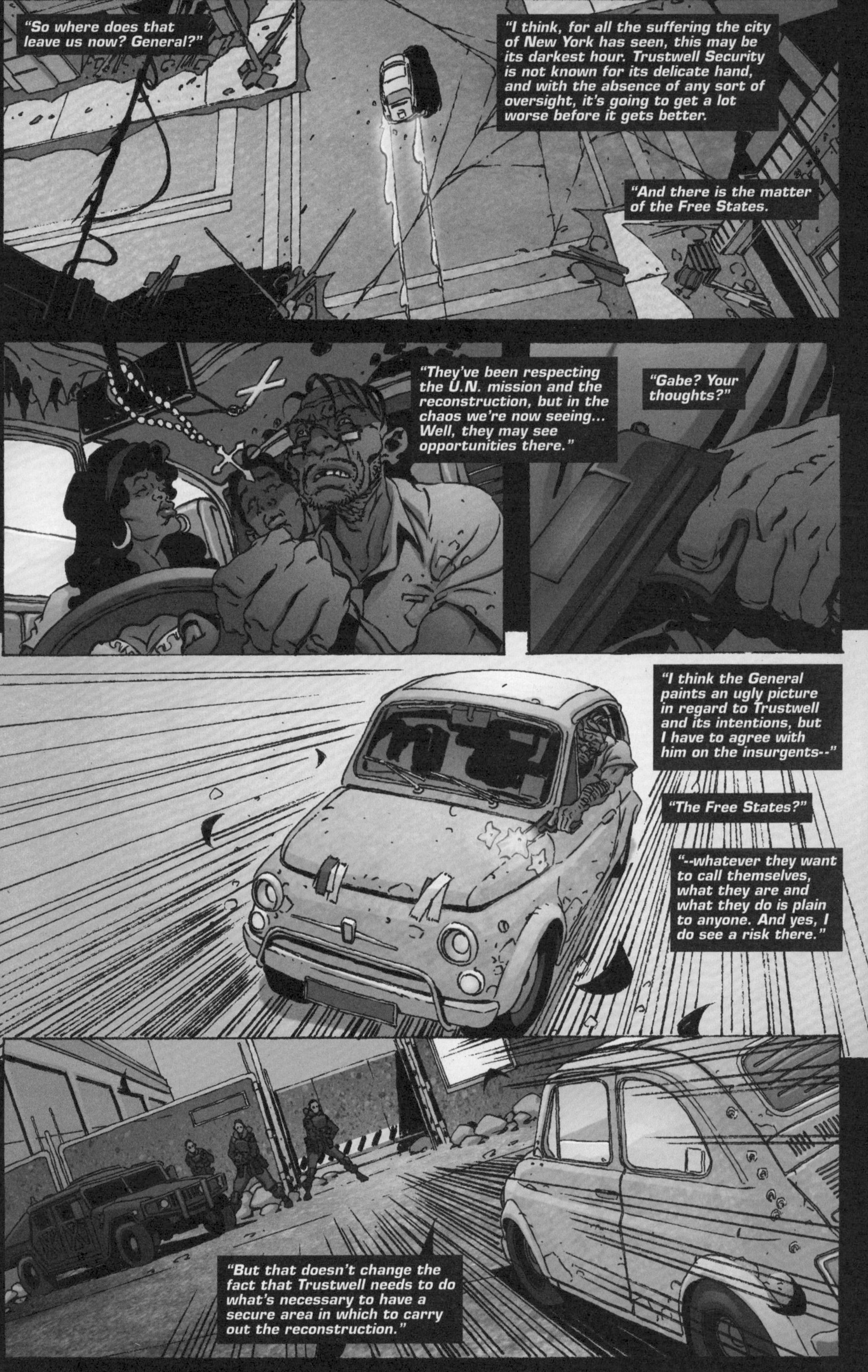
"So where does that leave us now? General?"
"I think, for all the suffering the city of New York has seen, this may be its darkest hour. Trustwell Security is not known for its delicate hand, and with the absence of any sort of oversight, it's going to get a lot worse before it gets better.
"And there is the matter of the Free States.
"They've been respecting the U.N. mission and the reconstruction, but in the chaos we're now seeing... Well, they may see opportunities there."
"Gabe? Your thoughts?"
"I think the General paints an ugly picture in regard to Trustwell and its intentions, but I have to agree with him on the insurgents--"
"The Free States?"
"--whatever they want to call themselves, what they are and what they do is plain to anyone. And yes, I do see a risk there."
"But that doesn't change the fact that Trustwell needs to do what's necessary to have a secure area in which to carry out the reconstruction."

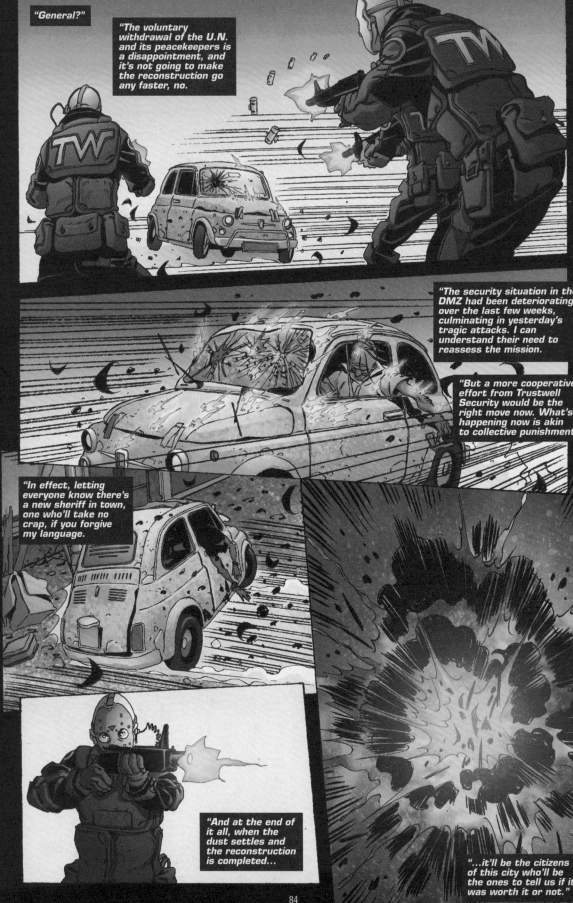

"General?"

"The voluntary withdrawal of the U.N. and its peacekeepers is a disappointment, and it's not going to make the reconstruction go any faster, no.

"The security situation in the DMZ had been deteriorating over the last few weeks, culminating in yesterday's tragic attacks. I can understand their need to reassess the mission.

"But a more cooperative effort from Trustwell Security would be the right move now. What's happening now is akin to collective punishment.

"In effect, letting everyone know there's a new sheriff in town, one who'll take no crap, if you forgive my language.

"And at the end of it all, when the dust settles and the reconstruction is completed...

"...it'll be the citizens of this city who'll be the ones to tell us if it was worth it or not."

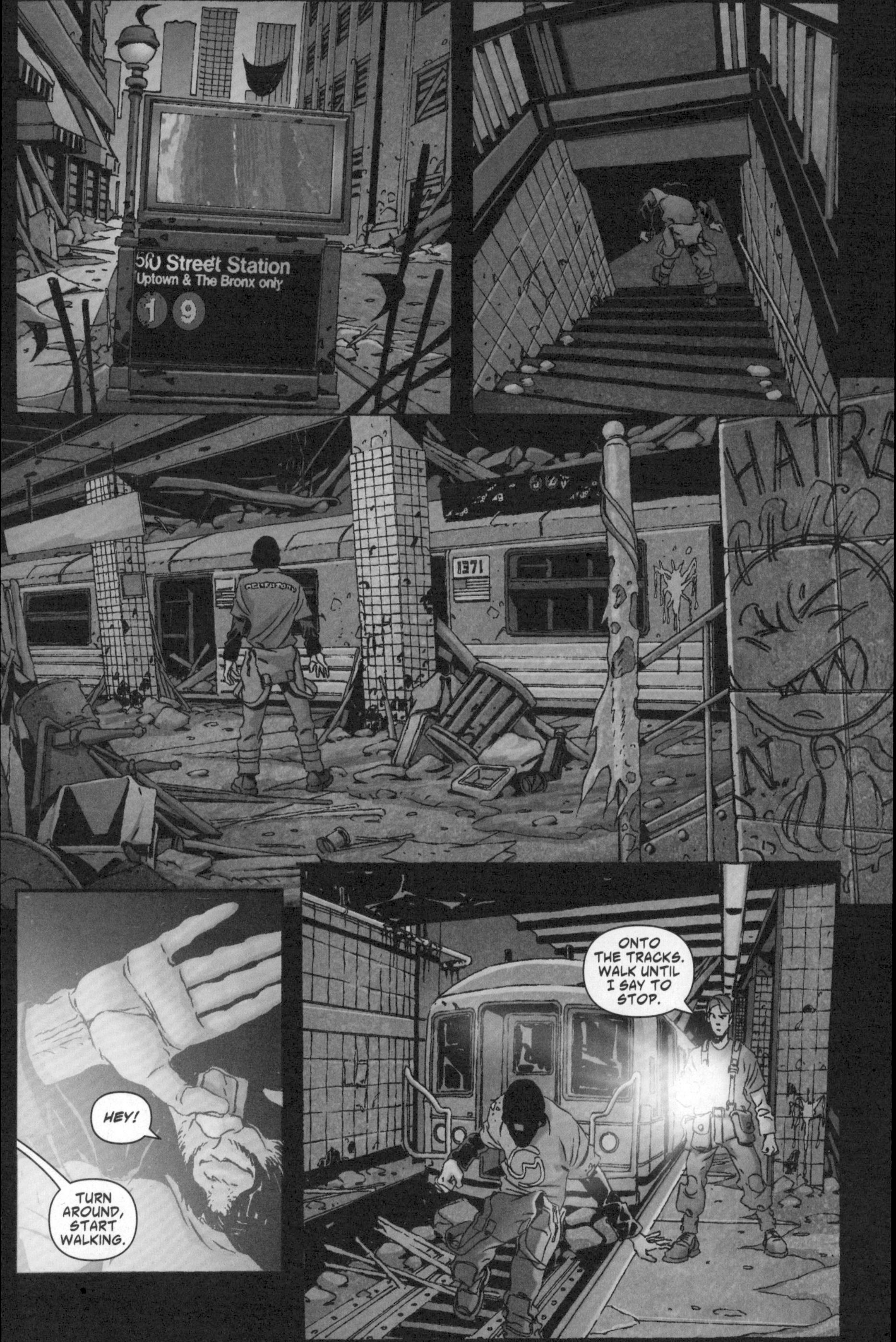
50 Street Station
Uptown & The Bronx only
1 9
1371
HEY!
TURN AROUND, START WALKING.
ONTO THE TRACKS. WALK UNTIL I SAY TO STOP.

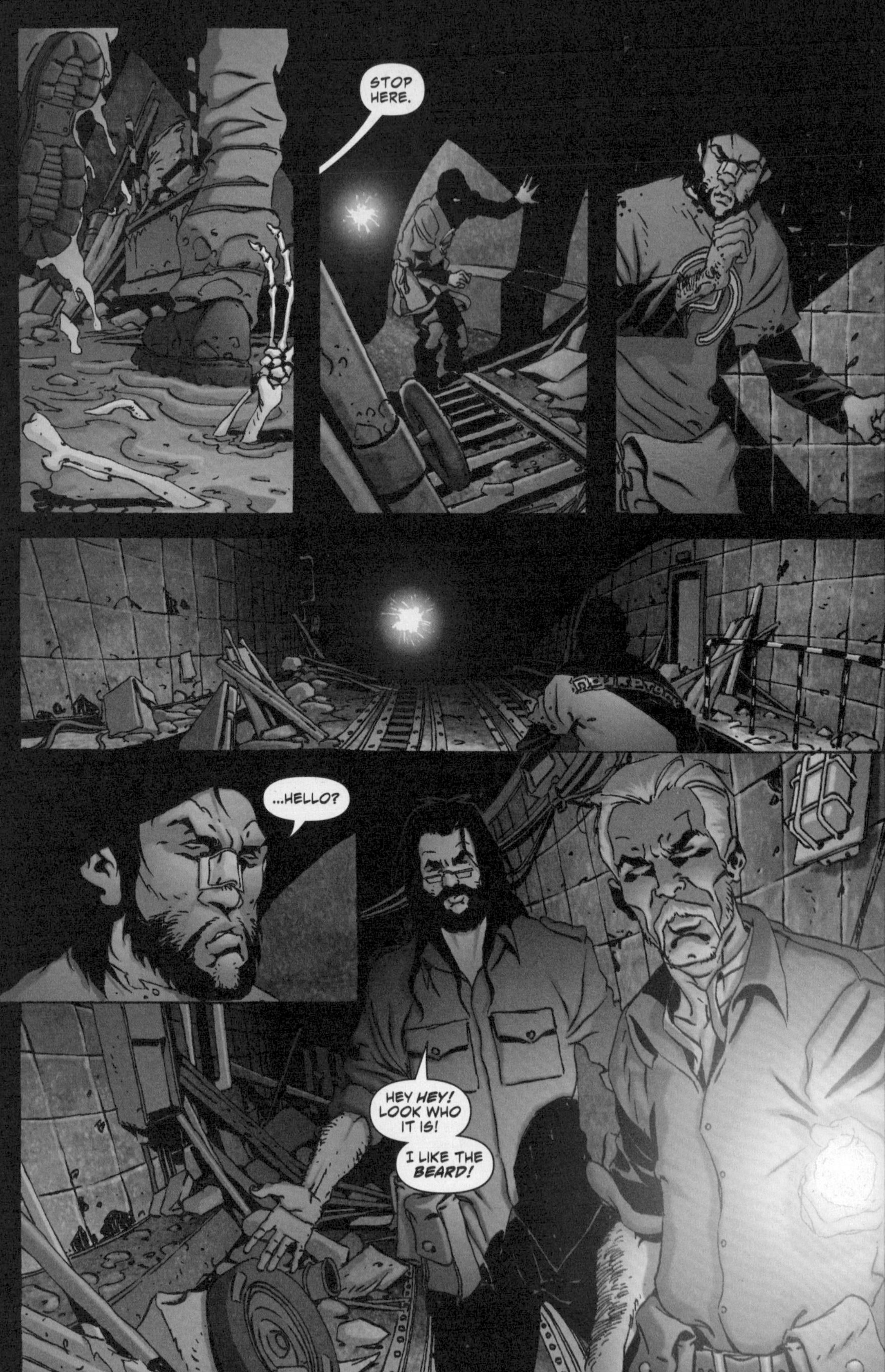
STOP HERE.
...HELLO?
HEY HEY! LOOK WHO IT IS!
I LIKE THE BEARD!

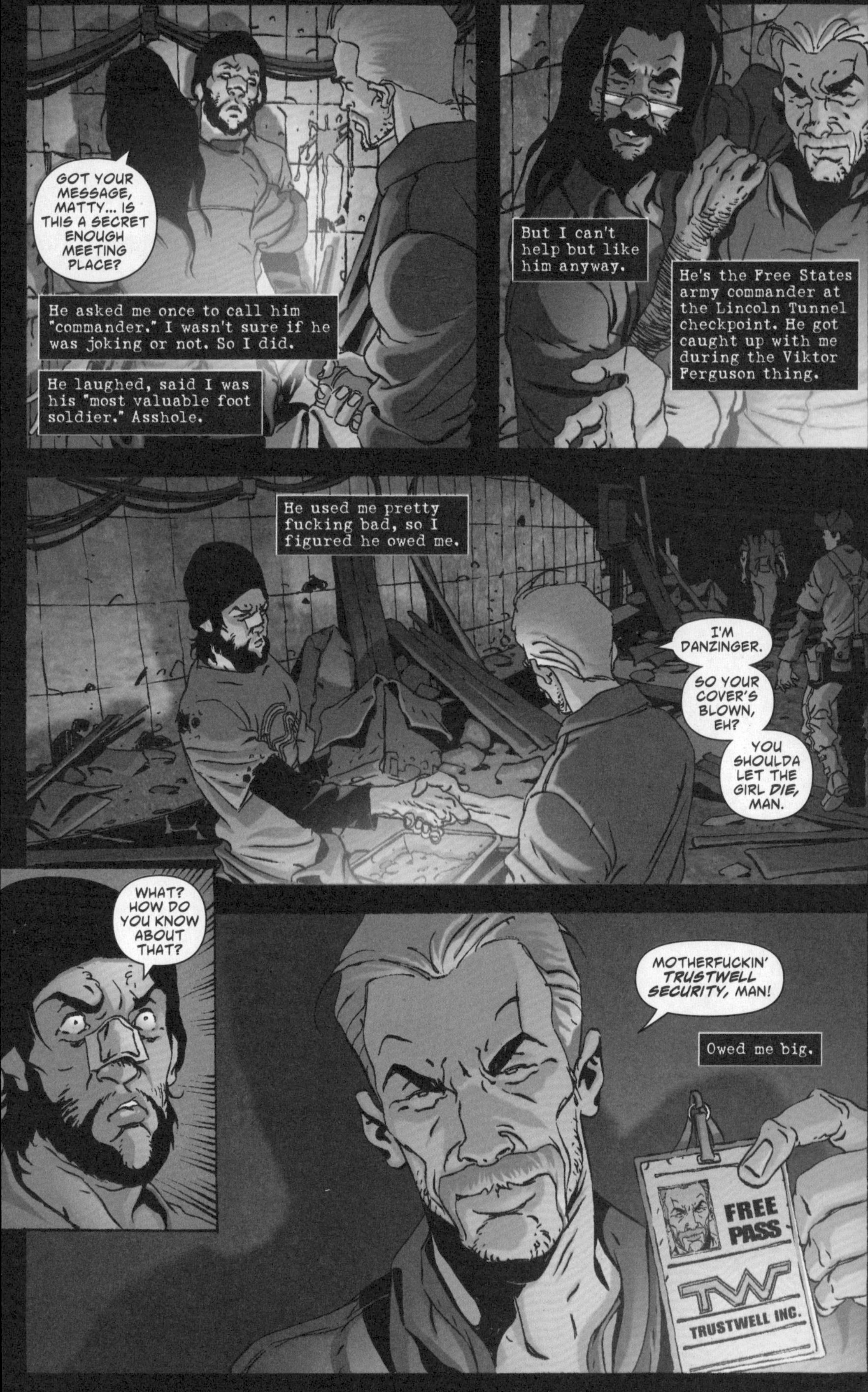
GOT YOUR MESSAGE, MATTY... IS THIS A SECRET ENOUGH MEETING PLACE?
He asked me once to call him "commander." I wasn't sure if he was joking or not. So I did.
He laughed, said I was his "most valuable foot soldier." Asshole.
But I can't help but like him anyway.
He's the Free States army commander at the Lincoln Tunnel checkpoint. He got caught up with me during the Viktor Ferguson thing.
He used me pretty fucking bad, so I figured he owed me.
I'M DANZINGER.
SO YOUR COVER'S BLOWN, EH?
YOU SHOULDA LET THE GIRL *DIE*, MAN.
WHAT? HOW DO YOU KNOW ABOUT THAT?
MOTHERFUCKIN' *TRUSTWELL SECURITY*, MAN!
Owed me big.
FREE PASS
TRUSTWELL INC.

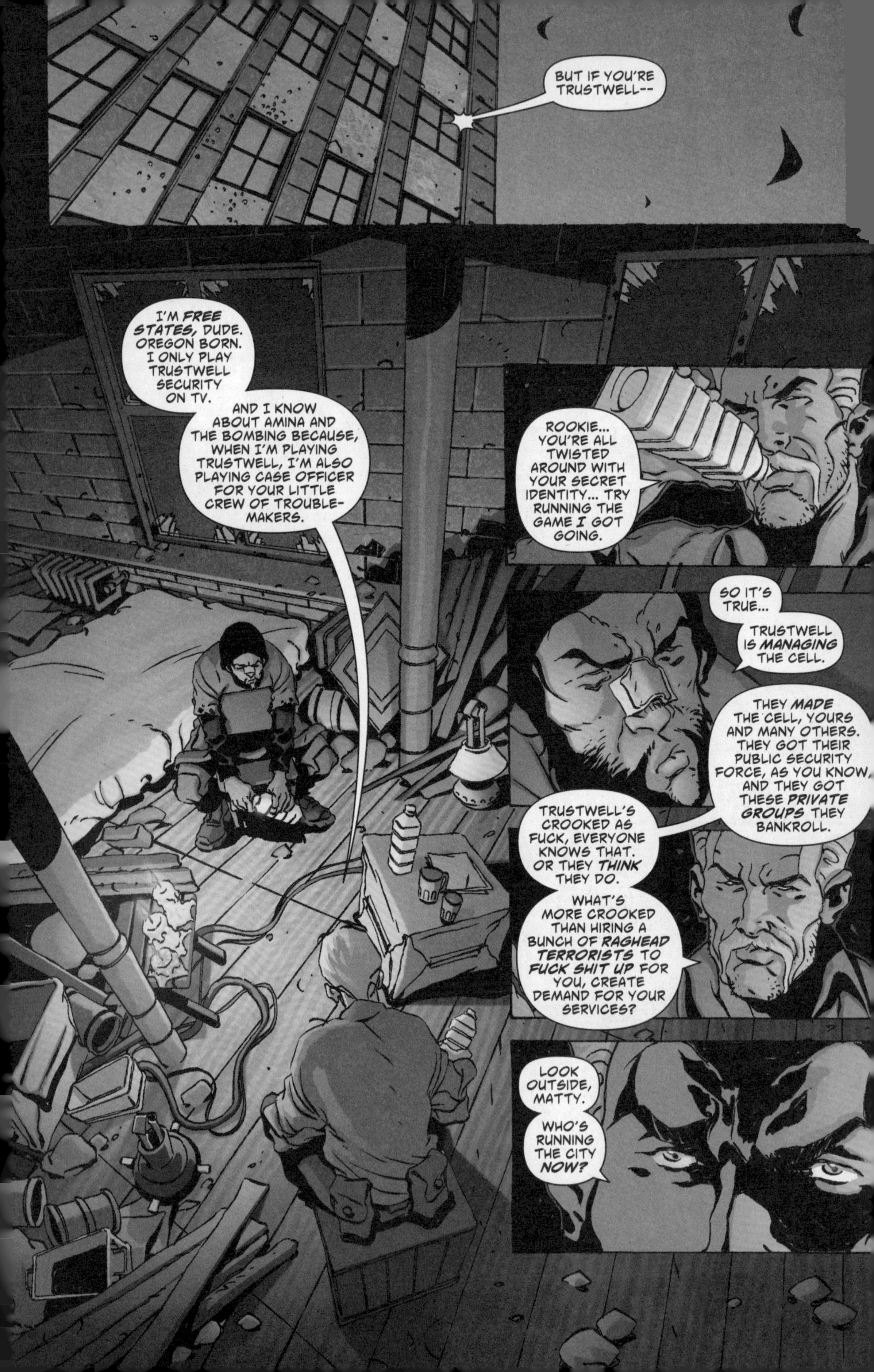
BUT IF YOU'RE TRUSTWELL--
I'M FREE STATES, DUDE. OREGON BORN. I ONLY PLAY TRUSTWELL SECURITY ON TV.
AND I KNOW ABOUT AMINA AND THE BOMBING BECAUSE, WHEN I'M PLAYING TRUSTWELL, I'M ALSO PLAYING CASE OFFICER FOR YOUR LITTLE CREW OF TROUBLE-MAKERS.
ROOKIE... YOU'RE ALL TWISTED AROUND WITH YOUR SECRET IDENTITY... TRY RUNNING THE GAME I GOT GOING.
SO IT'S TRUE...
TRUSTWELL IS MANAGING THE CELL.
THEY MADE THE CELL, YOURS AND MANY OTHERS. THEY GOT THEIR PUBLIC SECURITY FORCE, AS YOU KNOW, AND THEY GOT THESE PRIVATE GROUPS THEY BANKROLL.
TRUSTWELL'S CROOKED AS FUCK, EVERYONE KNOWS THAT. OR THEY THINK THEY DO.
WHAT'S MORE CROOKED THAN HIRING A BUNCH OF RAGHEAD TERRORISTS TO FUCK SHIT UP FOR YOU, CREATE DEMAND FOR YOUR SERVICES?
LOOK OUTSIDE, MATTY.
WHO'S RUNNING THE CITY NOW?

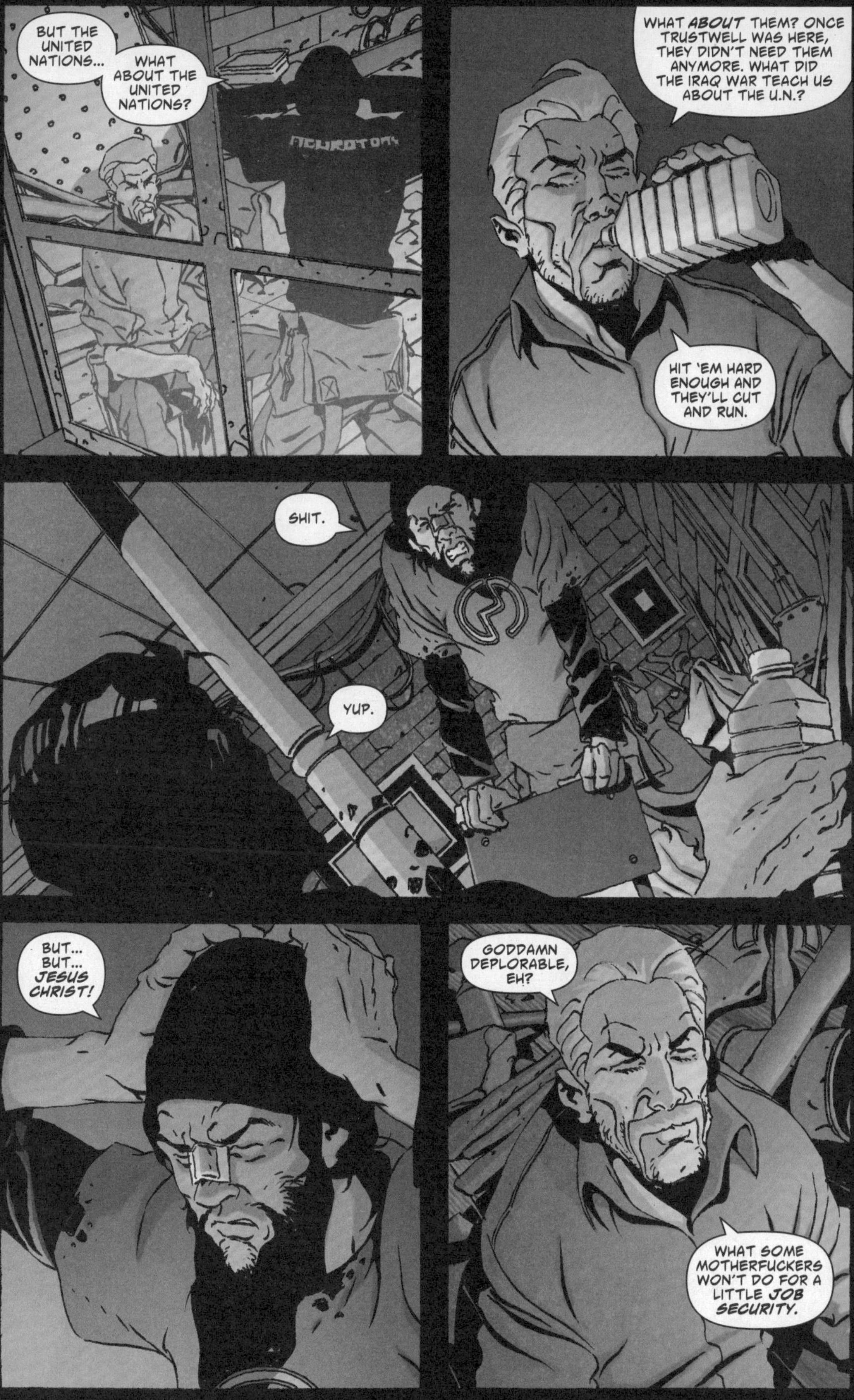
BUT THE UNITED NATIONS...
WHAT ABOUT THE UNITED NATIONS?
WHAT ABOUT THEM? ONCE TRUSTWELL WAS HERE, THEY DIDN'T NEED THEM ANYMORE. WHAT DID THE IRAQ WAR TEACH US ABOUT THE U.N.?
HIT 'EM HARD ENOUGH AND THEY'LL CUT AND RUN.
SHIT.
YUP.
BUT... BUT... JESUS CHRIST!
GODDAMN DEPLORABLE, EH?
WHAT SOME MOTHERFUCKERS WON'T DO FOR A LITTLE JOB SECURITY.

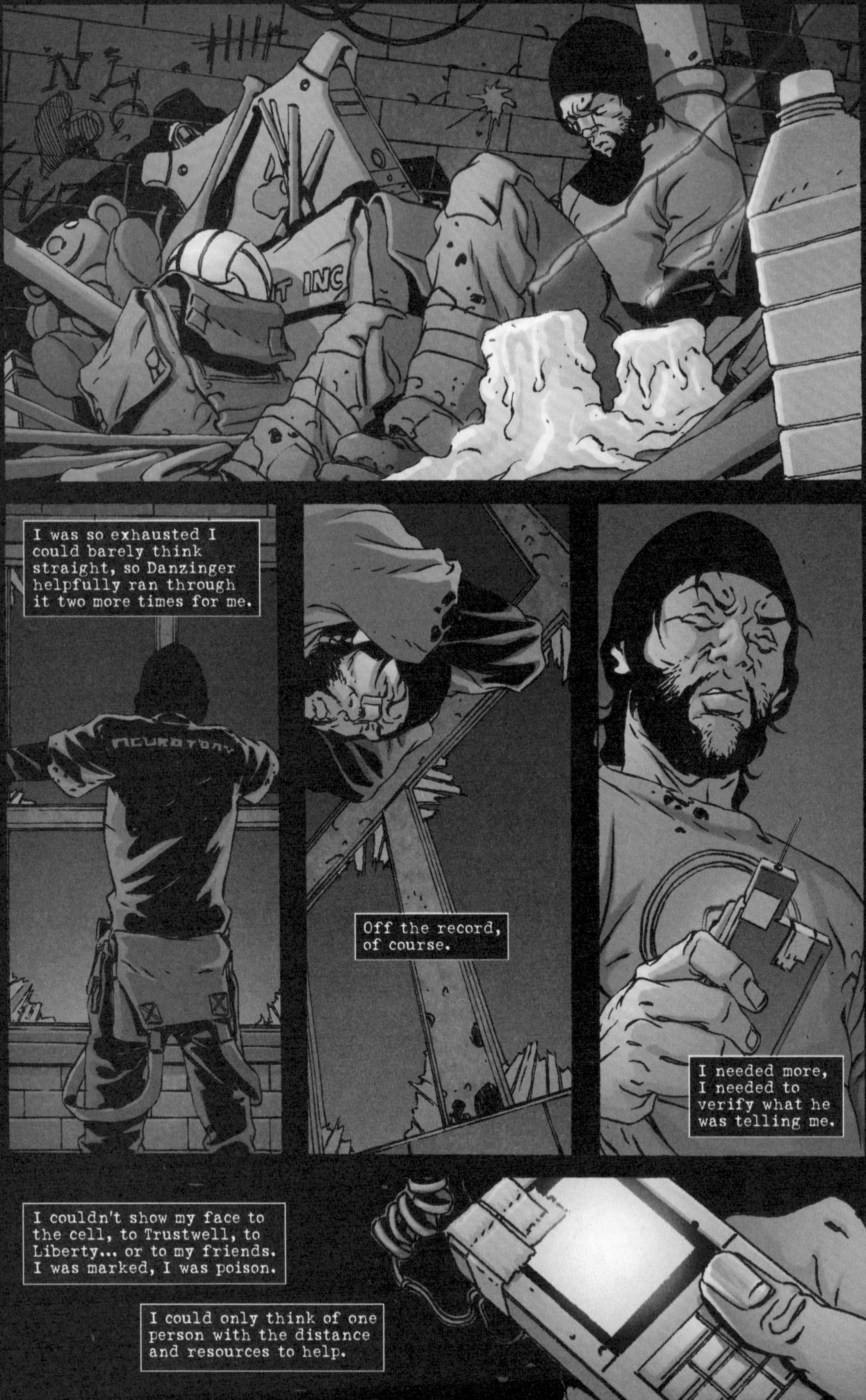
T INC
I was so exhausted I could barely think straight, so Danzinger helpfully ran through it two more times for me.
Off the record, of course.
I needed more, I needed to verify what he was telling me.
I couldn't show my face to the cell, to Trustwell, to Liberty... or to my friends. I was marked, I was poison.
I could only think of one person with the distance and resources to help.

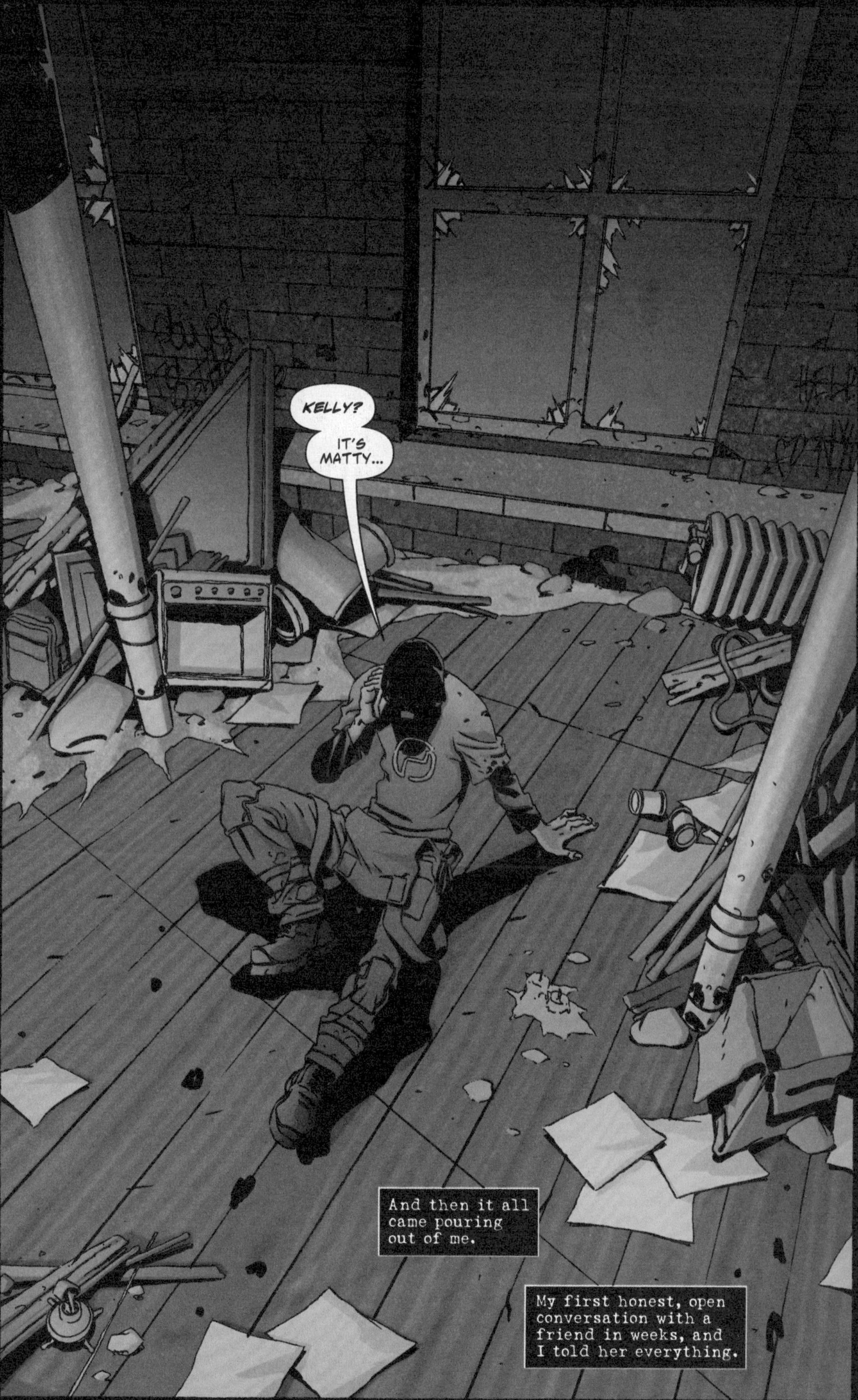
KELLY?
IT'S MATTY...
And then it all came pouring out of me.
My first honest, open conversation with a friend in weeks, and I told her everything.

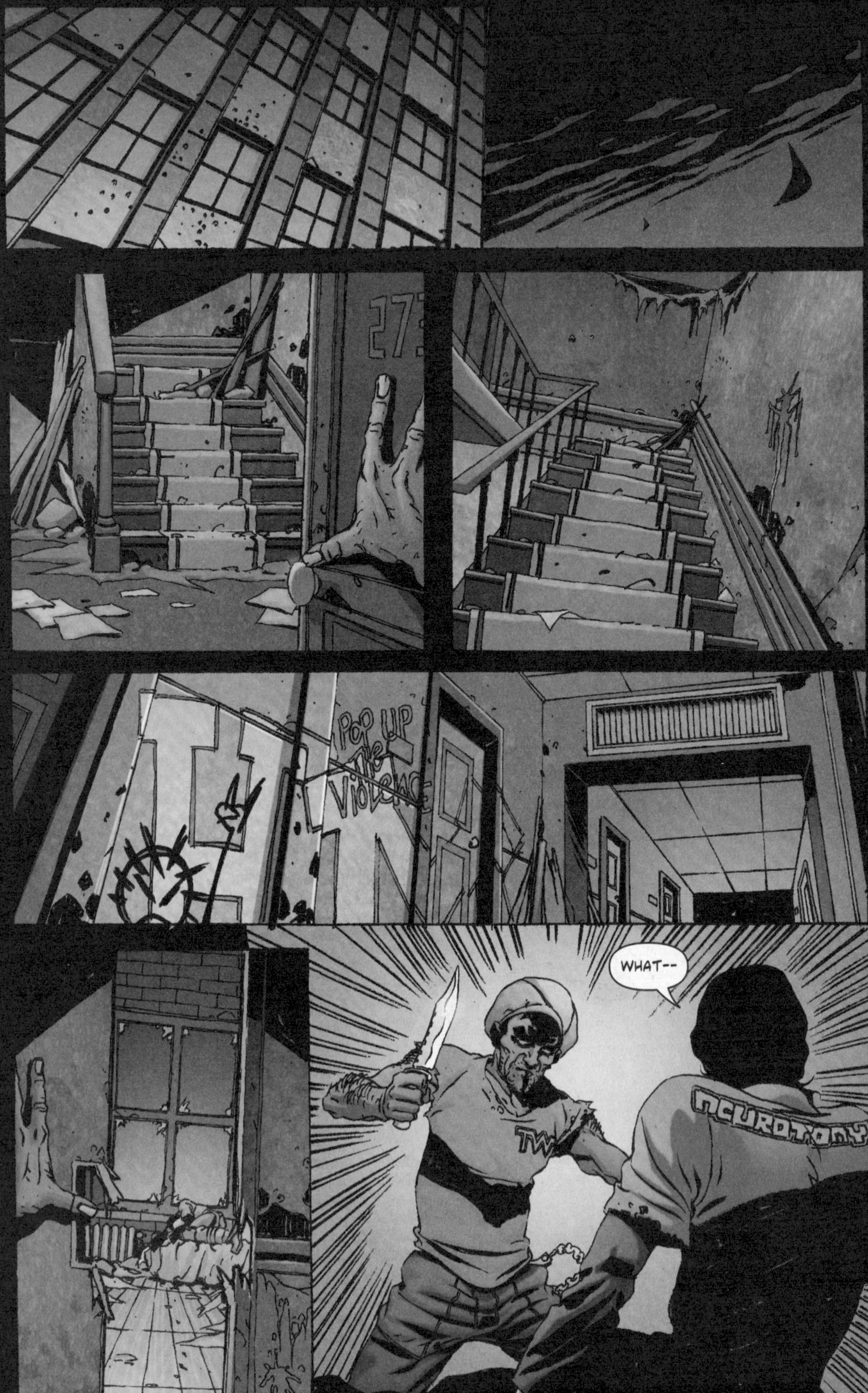
273
POP UP
VIOLENCE
WHAT--
NEUROTONY

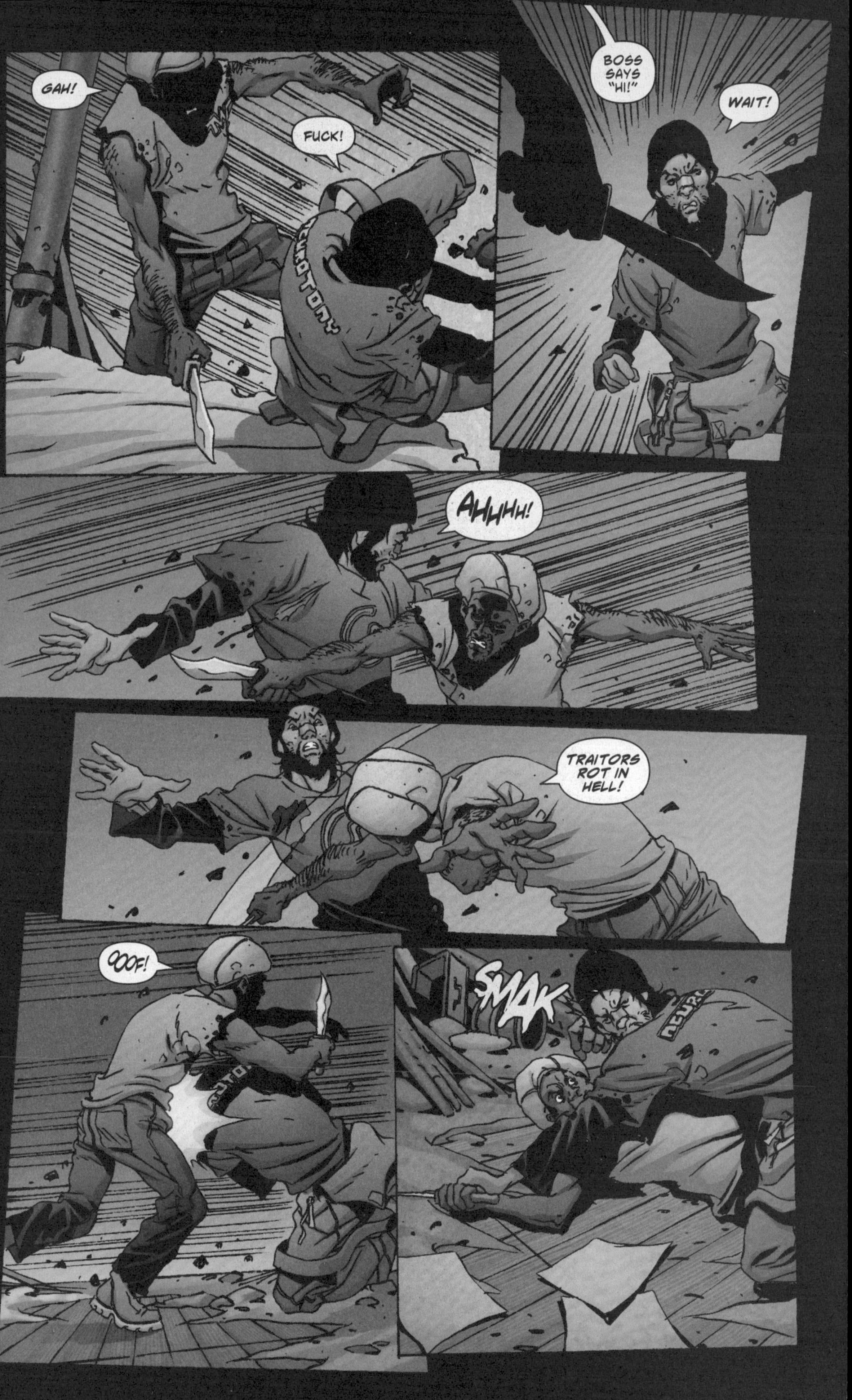
GAH!
FUCK!
BOSS SAYS "HI!"
WAIT!
AHHHH!
TRAITORS ROT IN HELL!
OOOF!
SMAK

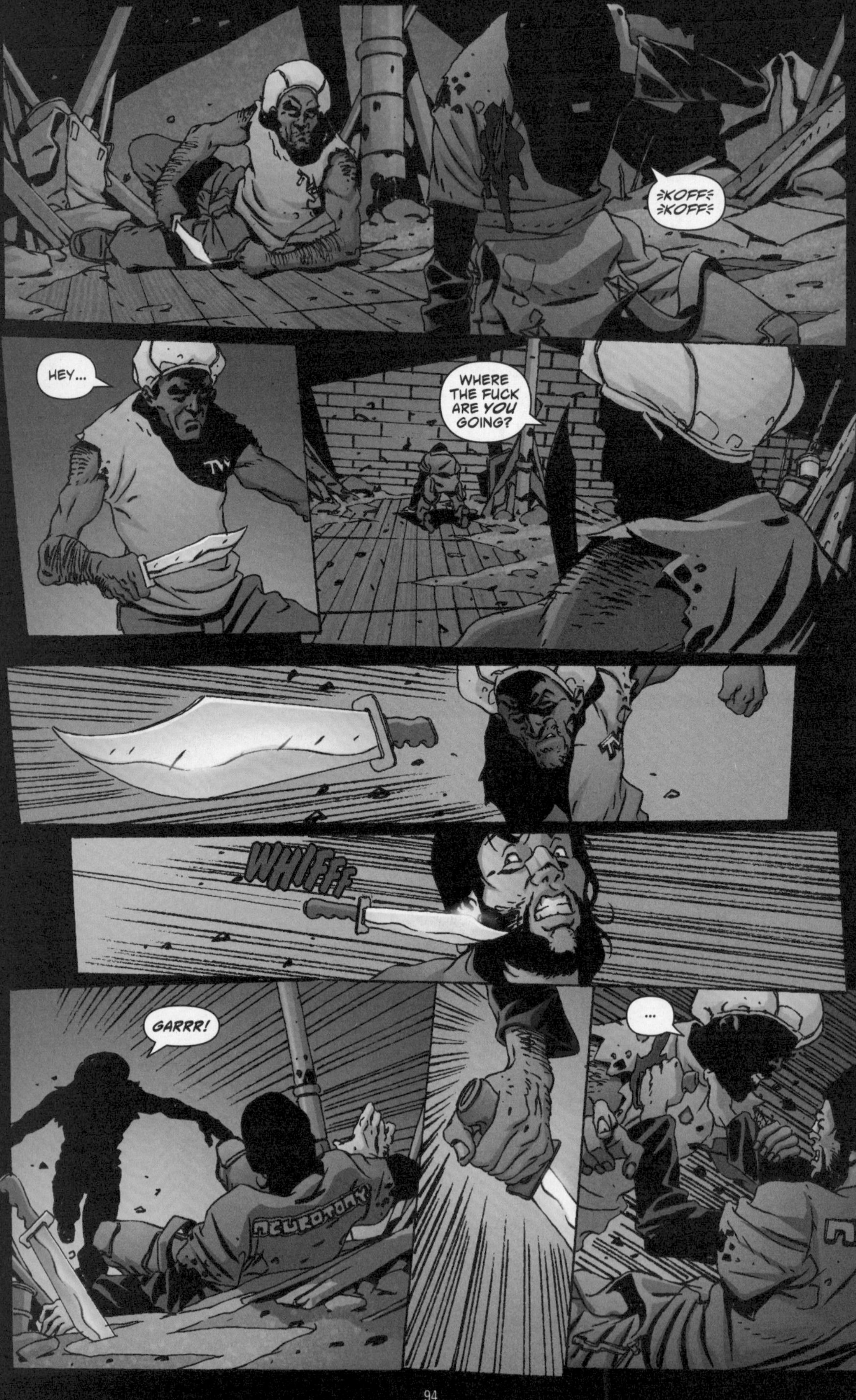
KOFF KOFF
HEY...
WHERE THE FUCK ARE YOU GOING?
WHIFFF
GARRR!
...

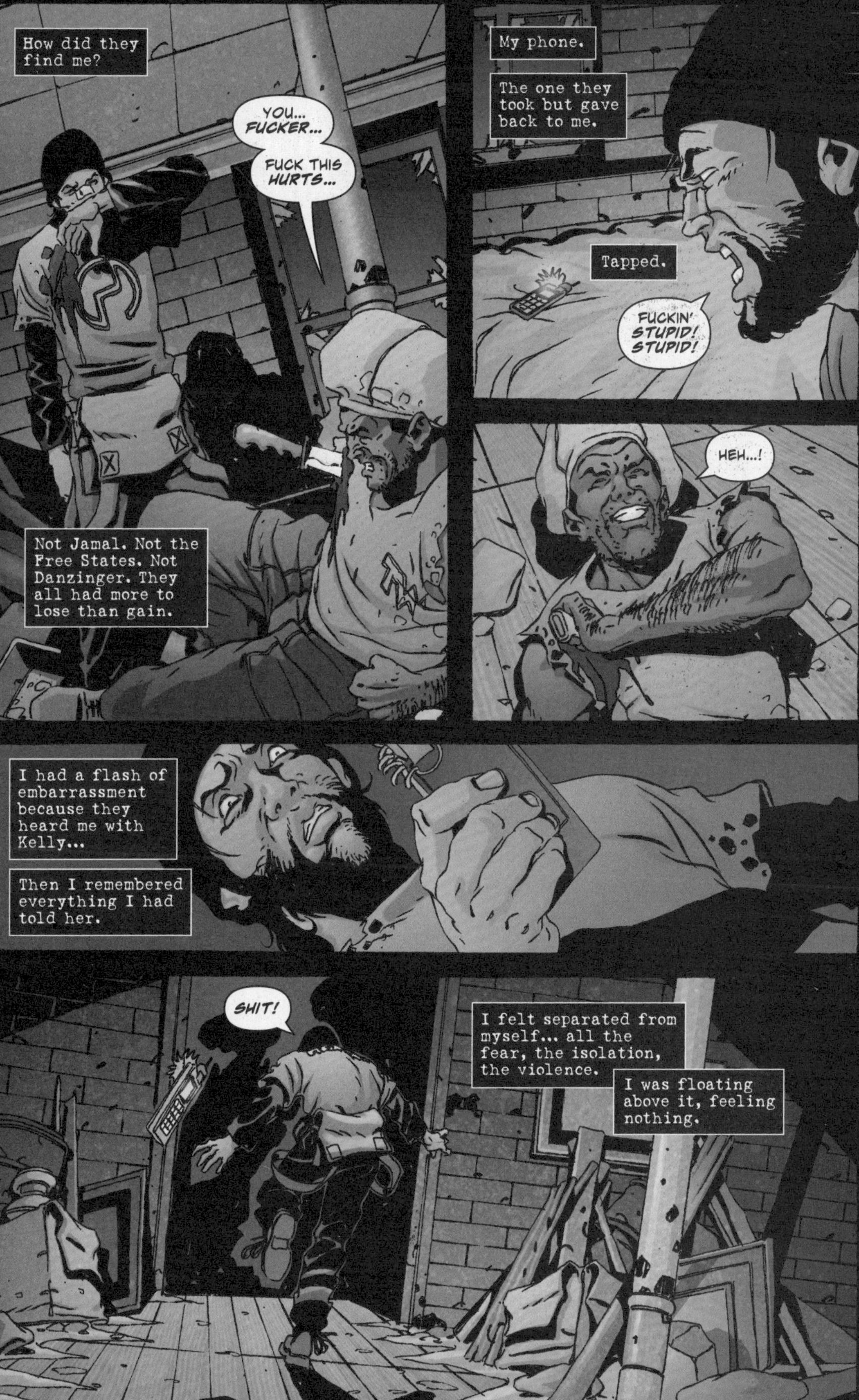
How did they find me?
YOU... FUCKER...
FUCK THIS HURTS...
Not Jamal. Not the Free States. Not Danzinger. They all had more to lose than gain.
My phone.
The one they took but gave back to me.
Tapped.
FUCKIN' STUPID! STUPID!
HEH...!
I had a flash of embarrassment because they heard me with Kelly...
Then I remembered everything I had told her.
SHIT!
I felt separated from myself... all the fear, the isolation, the violence.
I was floating above it, feeling nothing.

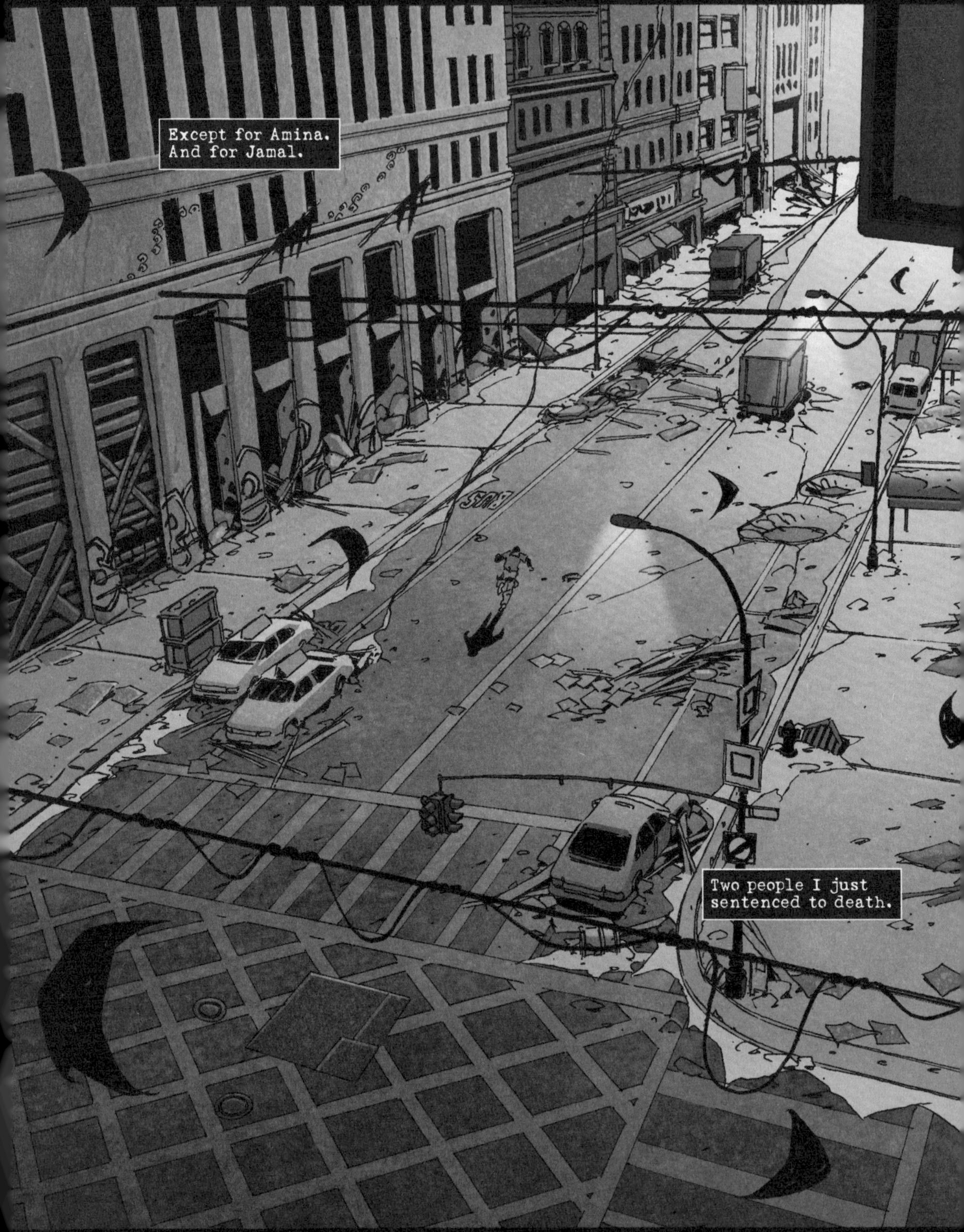
Except for Amina.
And for Jamal.
Two people I just
sentenced to death.

# CHAPTER FIVE

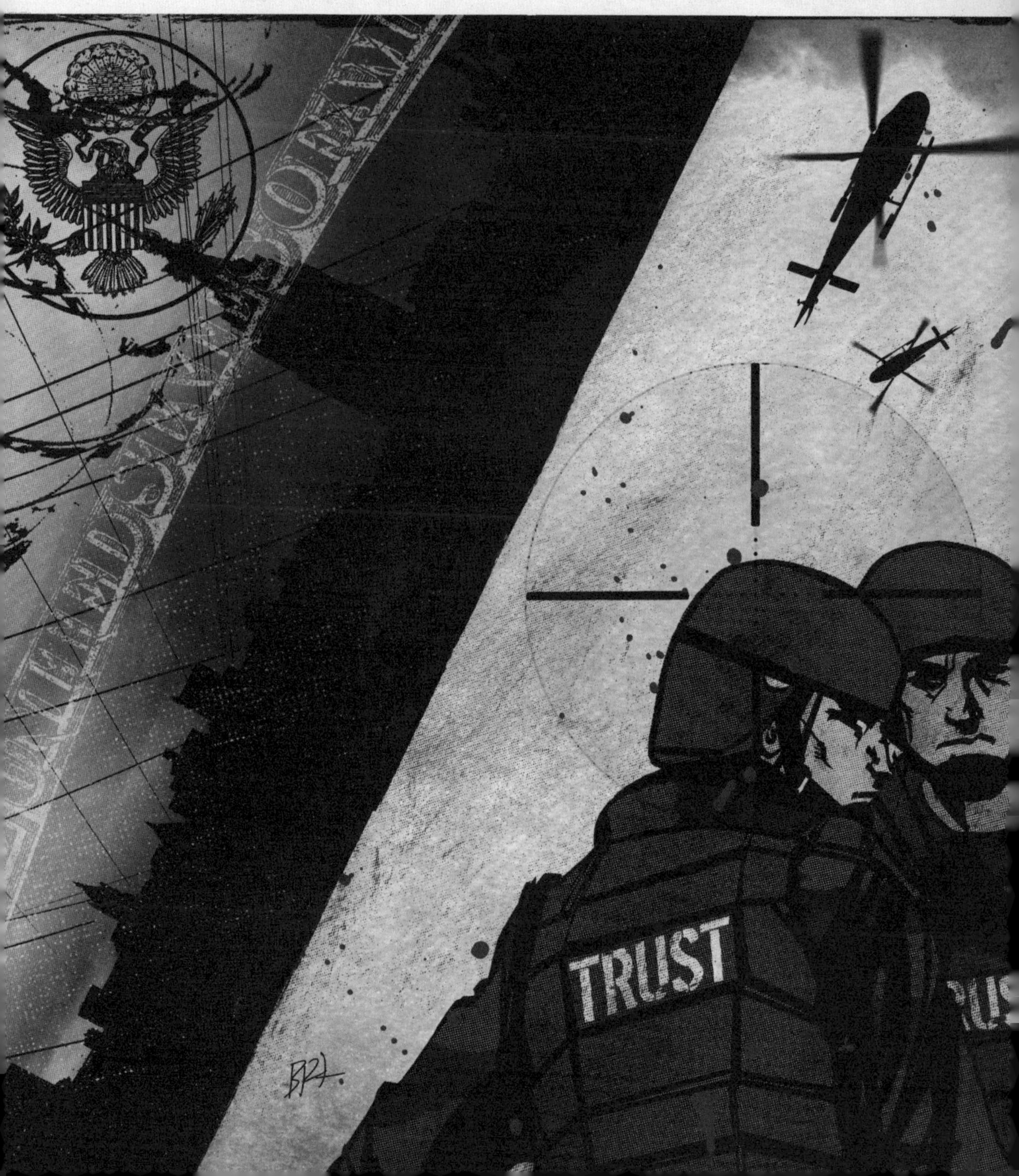
TRUST

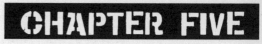

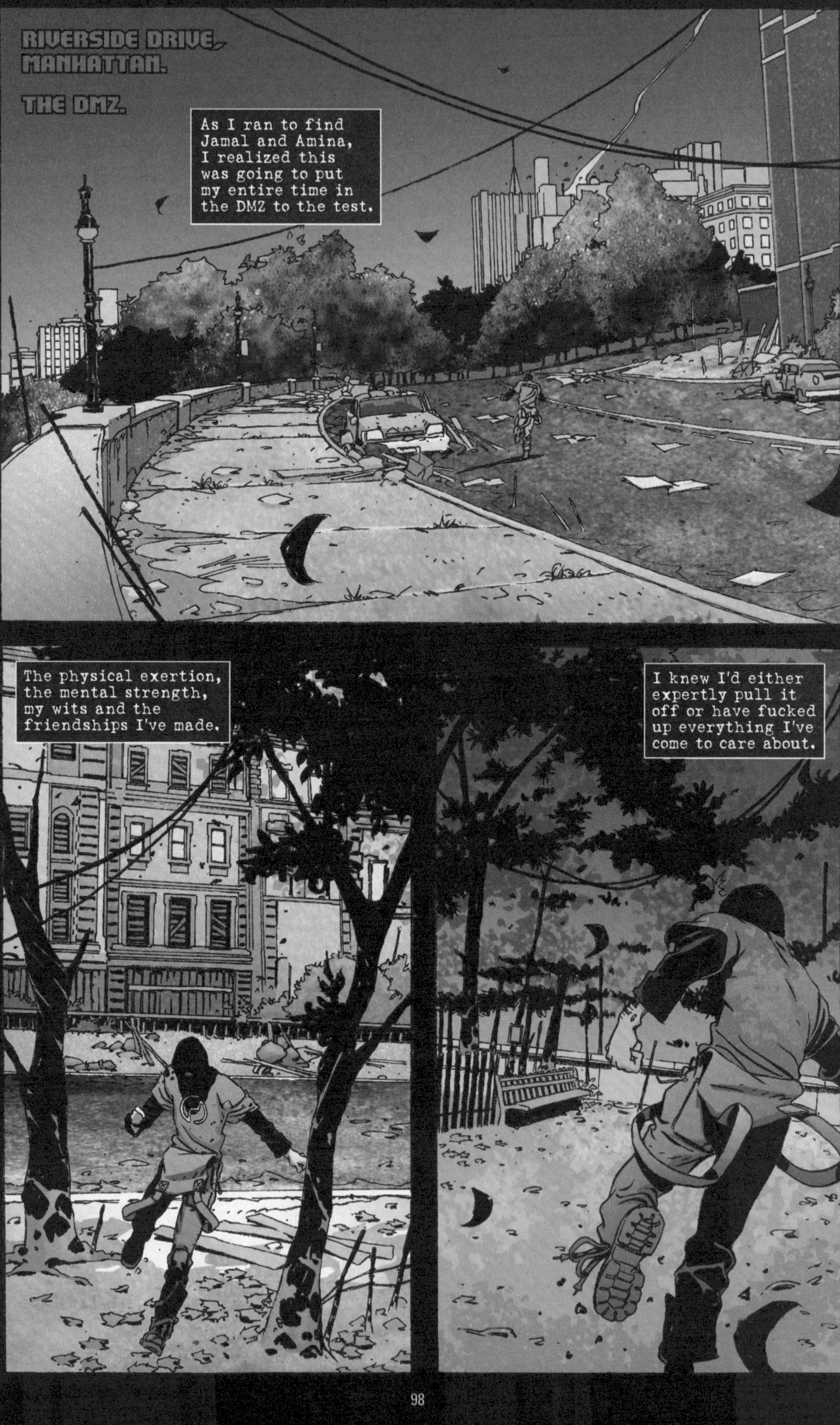
RIVERSIDE DRIVE, MANHATTAN.
THE DMZ.
As I ran to find Jamal and Amina, I realized this was going to put my entire time in the DMZ to the test.
The physical exertion, the mental strength, my wits and the friendships I've made.
I knew I'd either expertly pull it off or have fucked up everything I've come to care about.

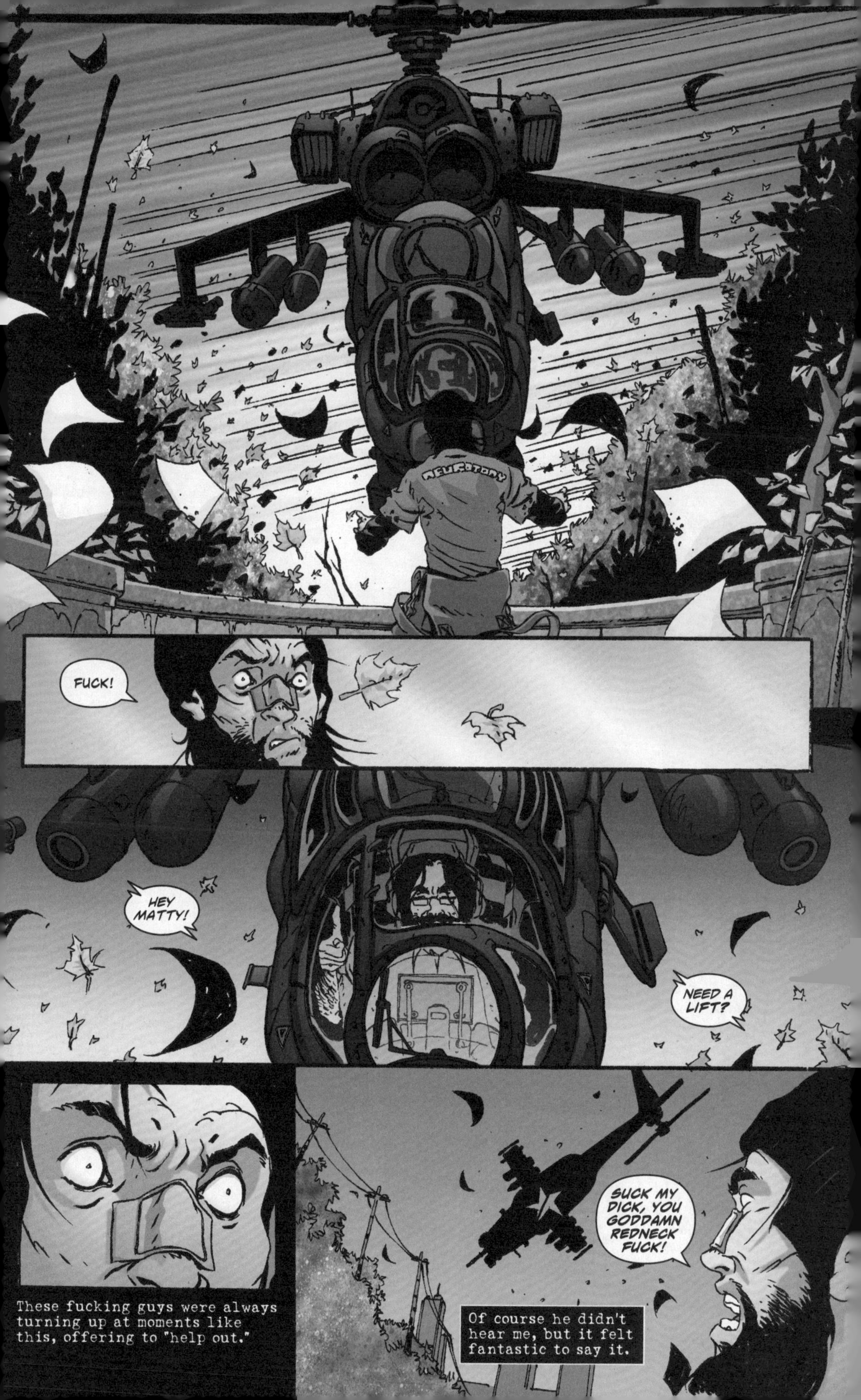
FUCK!
HEY MATTY!
NEED A LIFT?
These fucking guys were always turning up at moments like this, offering to "help out."
SUCK MY DICK, YOU GODDAMN REDNECK FUCK!
Of course he didn't hear me, but it felt fantastic to say it.

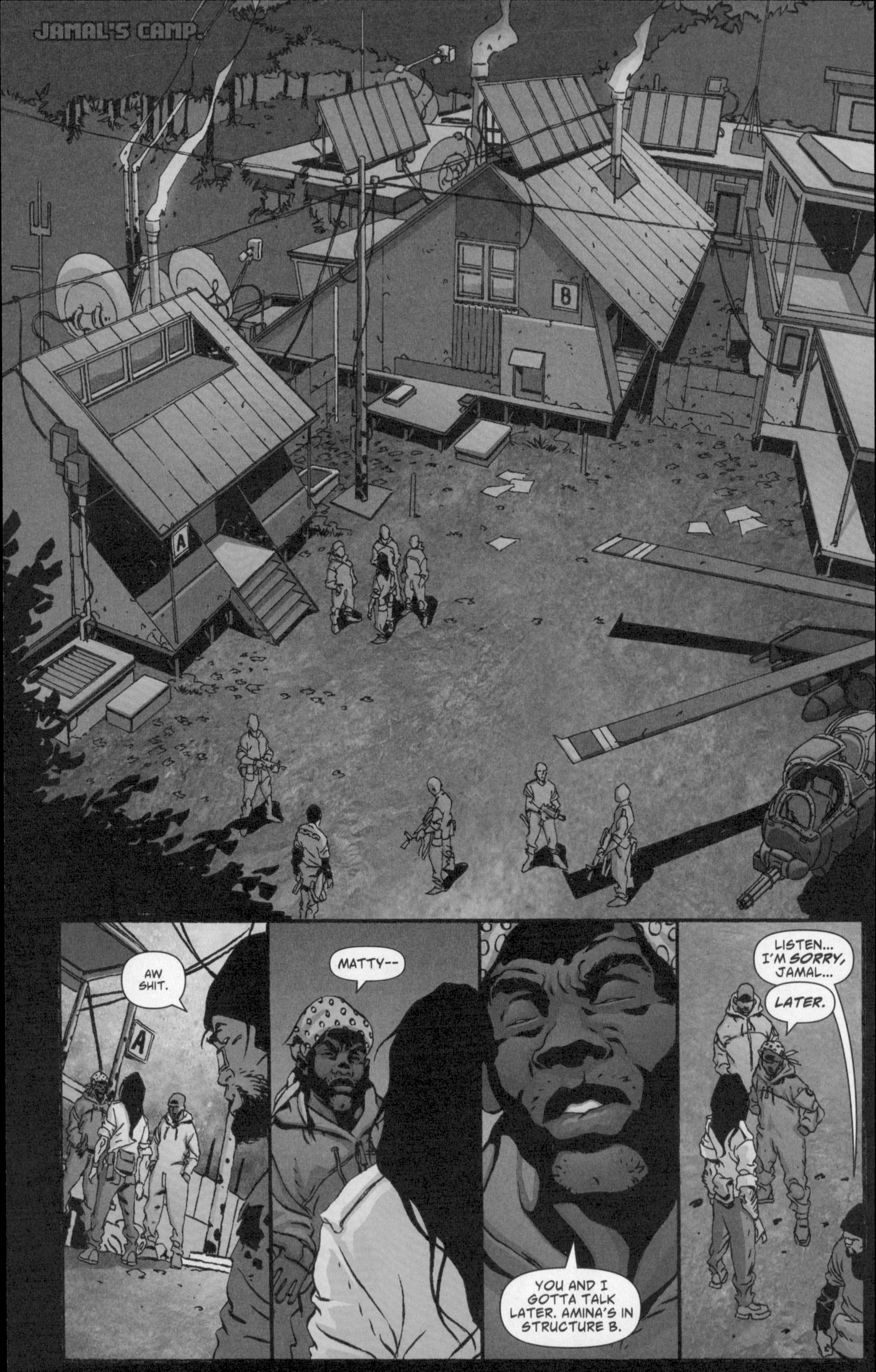
JAMAL'S CAMP.
B
A
AW SHIT.
A
MATTY--
YOU AND I GOTTA TALK LATER. AMINA'S IN STRUCTURE B.
LISTEN... I'M SORRY, JAMAL...
LATER.

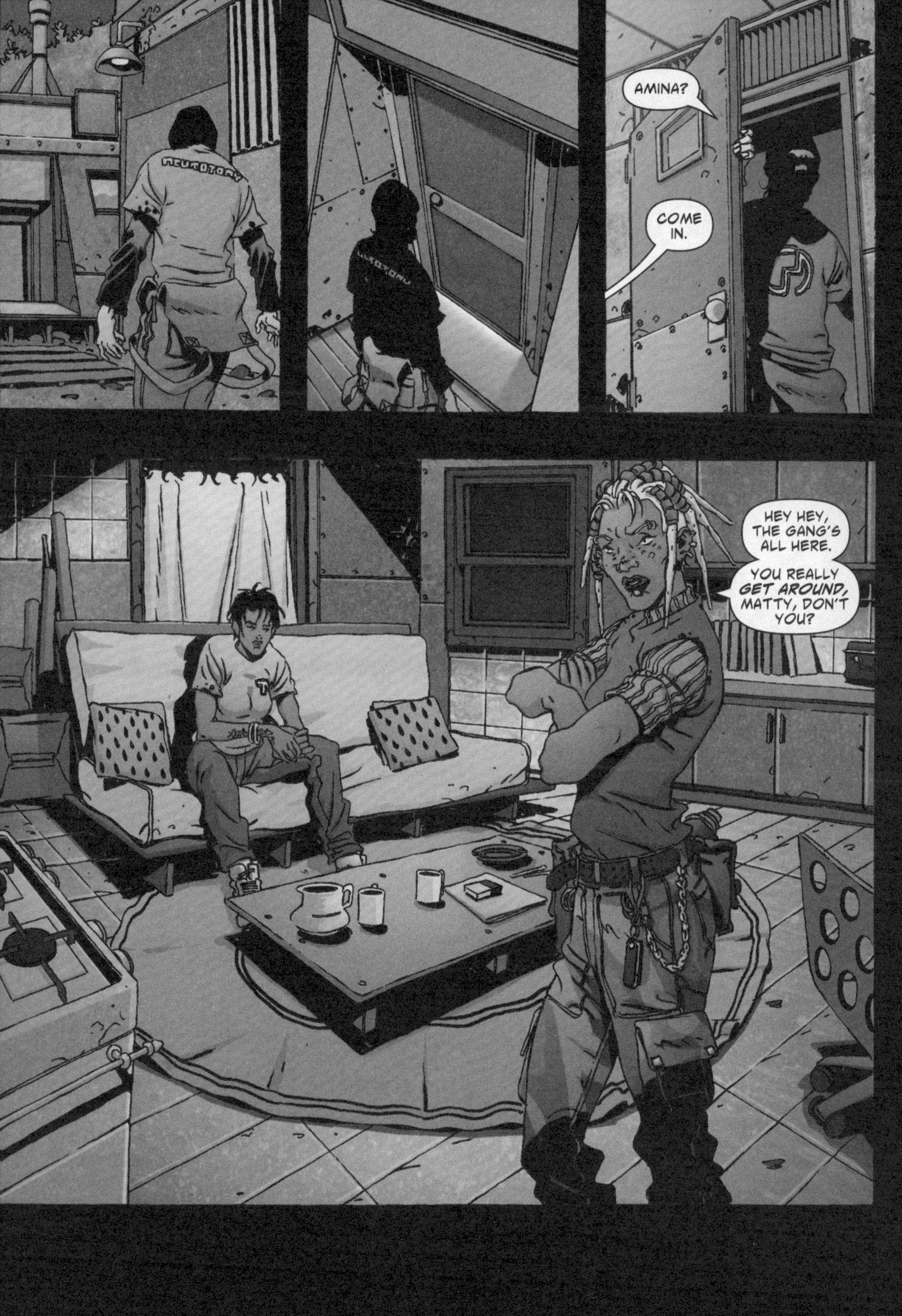
AMINA?
COME IN.
HEY HEY, THE GANG'S ALL HERE.
YOU REALLY GET AROUND, MATTY, DON'T YOU?

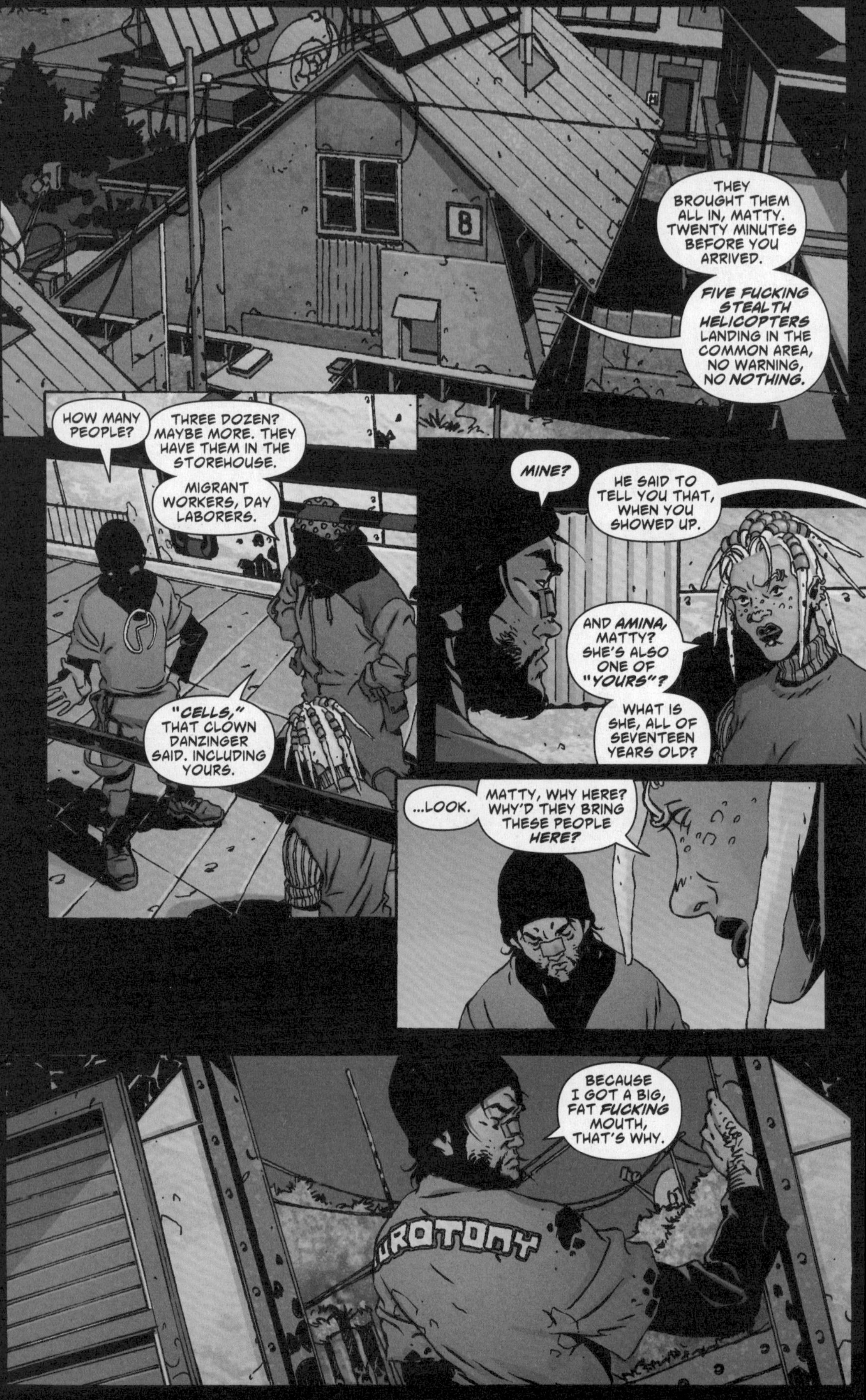

THEY BROUGHT THEM ALL IN, MATTY. TWENTY MINUTES BEFORE YOU ARRIVED.
FIVE FUCKING STEALTH HELICOPTERS LANDING IN THE COMMON AREA, NO WARNING, NO NOTHING.
HOW MANY PEOPLE?
THREE DOZEN? MAYBE MORE. THEY HAVE THEM IN THE STOREHOUSE.
MIGRANT WORKERS, DAY LABORERS.
"CELLS," THAT CLOWN DANZINGER SAID. INCLUDING YOURS.
MINE?
HE SAID TO TELL YOU THAT, WHEN YOU SHOWED UP.
AND AMINA, MATTY? SHE'S ALSO ONE OF "YOURS"?
WHAT IS SHE, ALL OF SEVENTEEN YEARS OLD?
...LOOK.
MATTY, WHY HERE? WHY'D THEY BRING THESE PEOPLE HERE?
BECAUSE I GOT A BIG, FAT FUCKING MOUTH, THAT'S WHY.

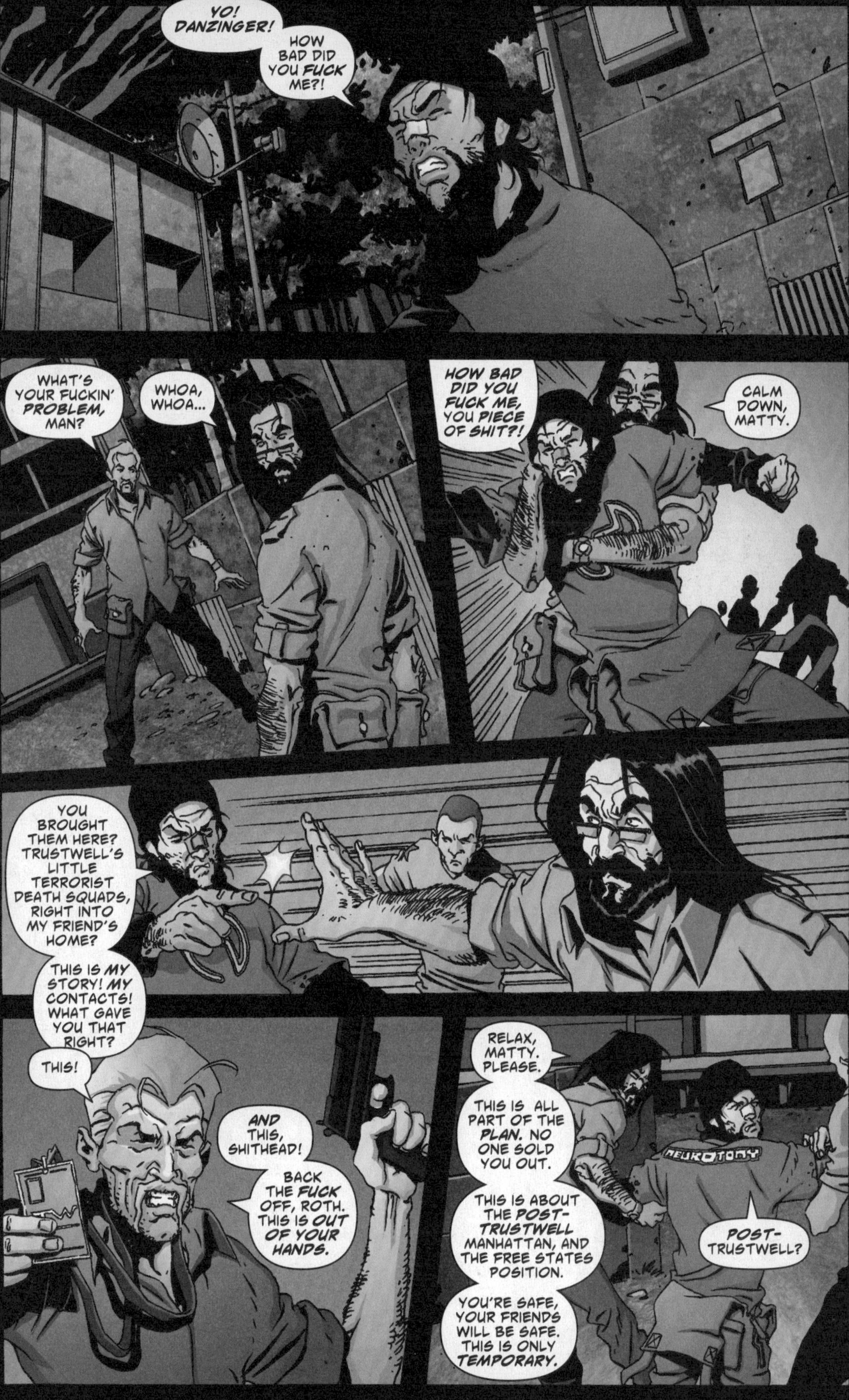
YO! DANZINGER!
HOW BAD DID YOU FUCK ME?!
WHAT'S YOUR FUCKIN' PROBLEM, MAN?
WHOA, WHOA...
HOW BAD DID YOU FUCK ME, YOU PIECE OF SHIT?!
CALM DOWN, MATTY.
YOU BROUGHT THEM HERE? TRUSTWELL'S LITTLE TERRORIST DEATH SQUADS, RIGHT INTO MY FRIEND'S HOME?
THIS IS MY STORY! MY CONTACTS! WHAT GAVE YOU THAT RIGHT?
THIS!
AND THIS, SHITHEAD!
BACK THE FUCK OFF, ROTH. THIS IS OUT OF YOUR HANDS.
RELAX, MATTY. PLEASE.
THIS IS ALL PART OF THE PLAN. NO ONE SOLD YOU OUT.
THIS IS ABOUT THE POST-TRUSTWELL MANHATTAN, AND THE FREE STATES POSITION.
YOU'RE SAFE, YOUR FRIENDS WILL BE SAFE. THIS IS ONLY TEMPORARY.
NEUROTOMY
POST-TRUSTWELL?

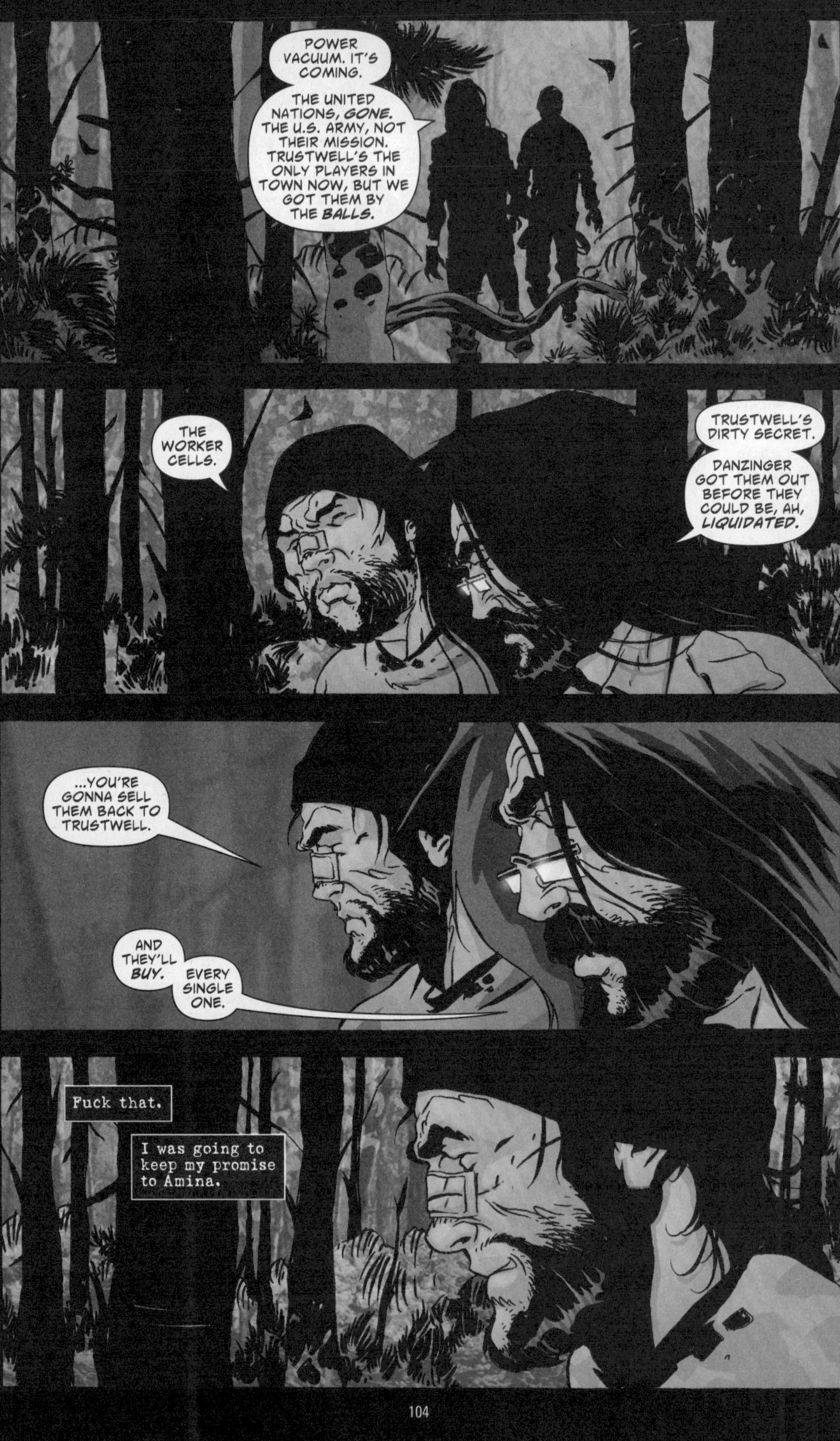
POWER VACUUM. IT'S COMING.
THE UNITED NATIONS, GONE. THE U.S. ARMY, NOT THEIR MISSION. TRUSTWELL'S THE ONLY PLAYERS IN TOWN NOW, BUT WE GOT THEM BY THE BALLS.
THE WORKER CELLS.
TRUSTWELL'S DIRTY SECRET.
DANZINGER GOT THEM OUT BEFORE THEY COULD BE, AH, LIQUIDATED.
...YOU'RE GONNA SELL THEM BACK TO TRUSTWELL.
AND THEY'LL BUY.
EVERY SINGLE ONE.
Fuck that.
I was going to keep my promise to Amina.

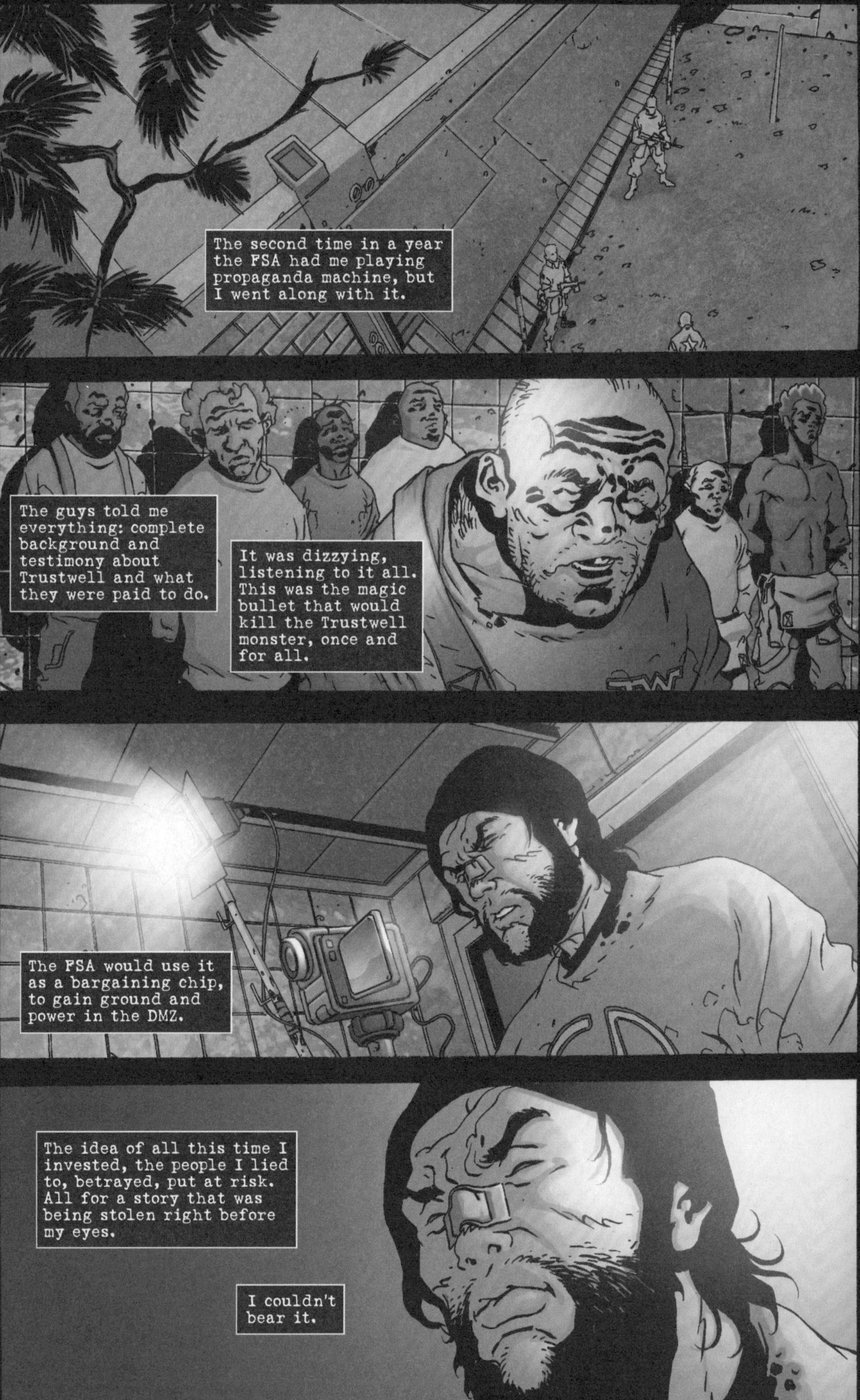
The second time in a year the FSA had me playing propaganda machine, but I went along with it.
The guys told me everything: complete background and testimony about Trustwell and what they were paid to do.
It was dizzying, listening to it all. This was the magic bullet that would kill the Trustwell monster, once and for all.
The FSA would use it as a bargaining chip, to gain ground and power in the DMZ.
The idea of all this time I invested, the people I lied to, betrayed, put at risk. All for a story that was being stolen right before my eyes.
I couldn't bear it.

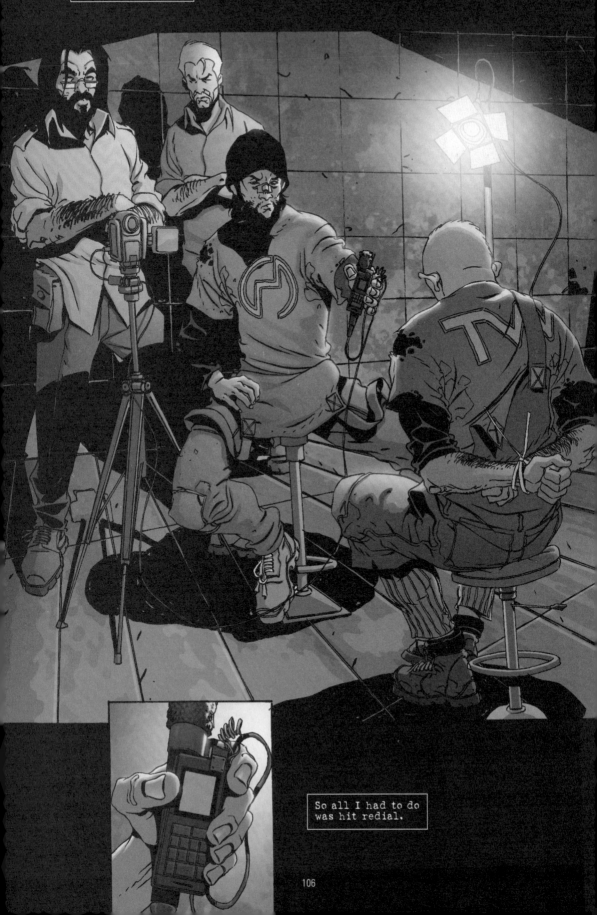

They didn't search me when I arrived.

So all I had to do was hit redial.

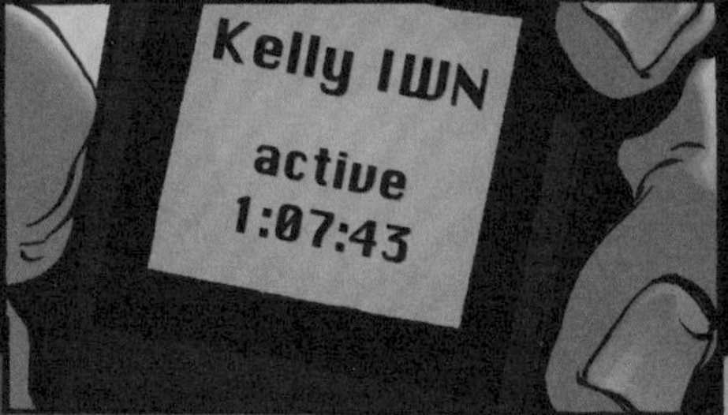
Kelly IWN
active
1:07:43

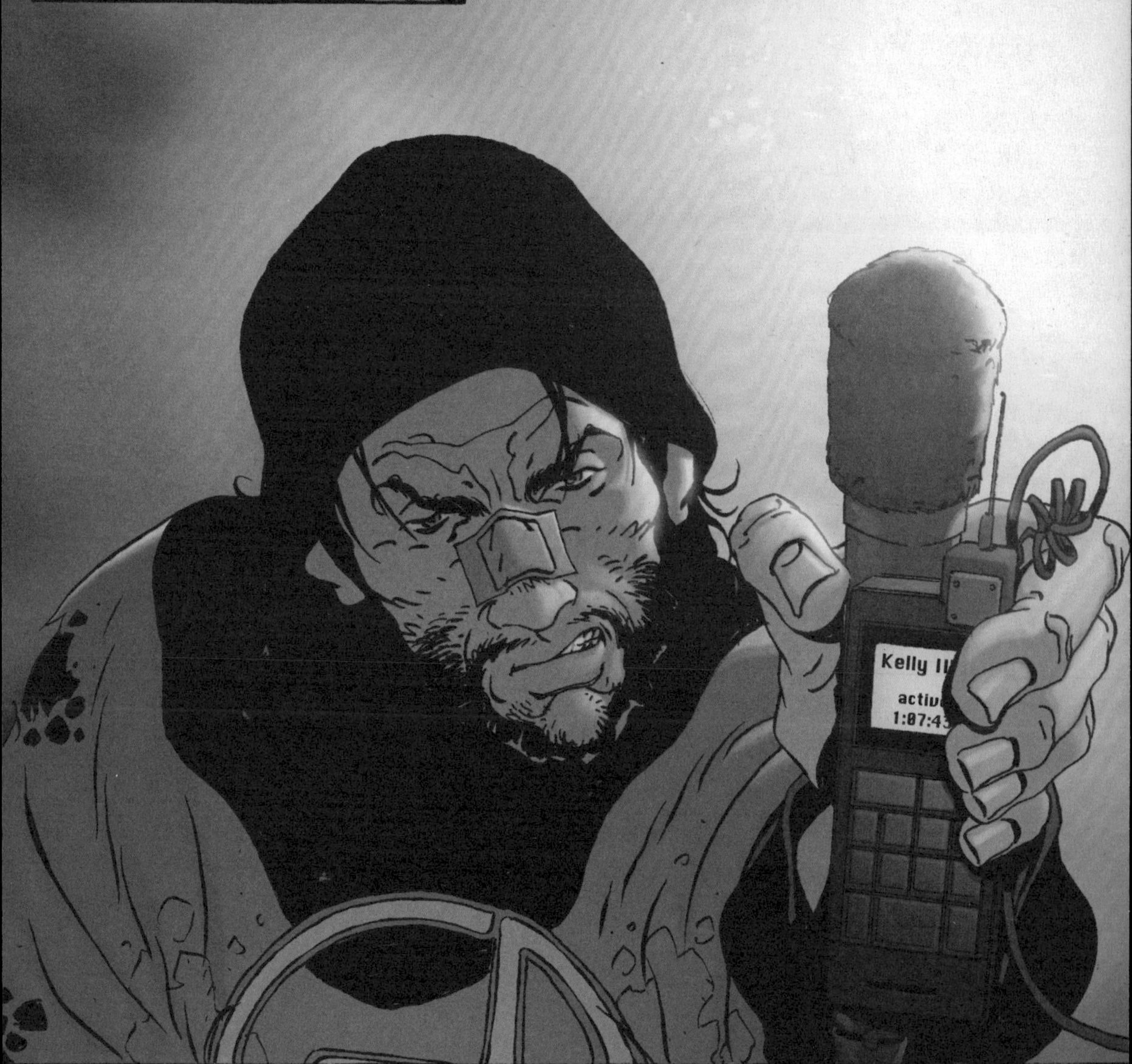
1:07:43

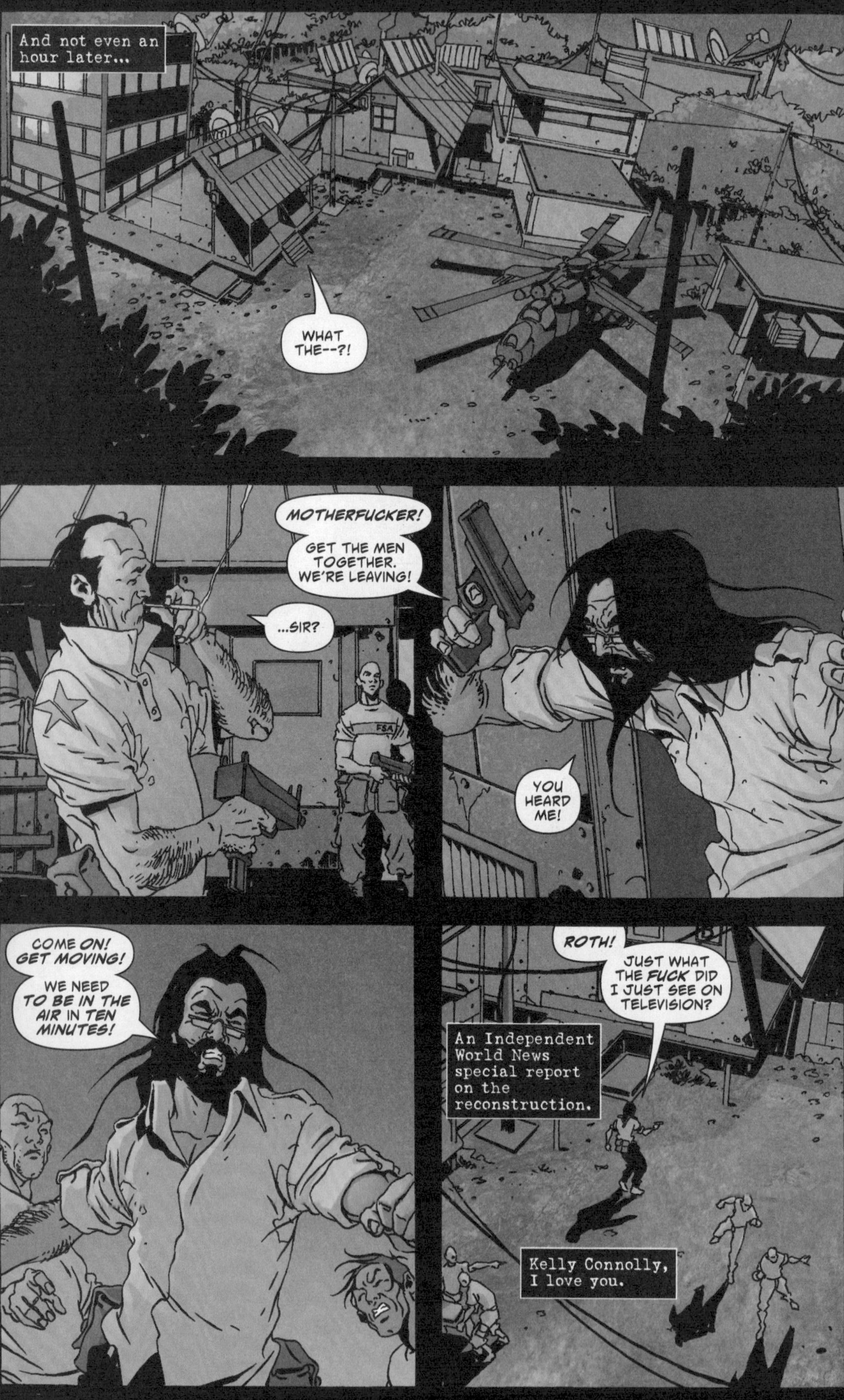

And not even an hour later...
WHAT THE--?!
MOTHERFUCKER!
GET THE MEN TOGETHER. WE'RE LEAVING!
...SIR?
YOU HEARD ME!
COME ON! GET MOVING!
WE NEED TO BE IN THE AIR IN TEN MINUTES!
ROTH!
JUST WHAT THE FUCK DID I JUST SEE ON TELEVISION?
An Independent World News special report on the reconstruction.
Kelly Connolly, I love you.

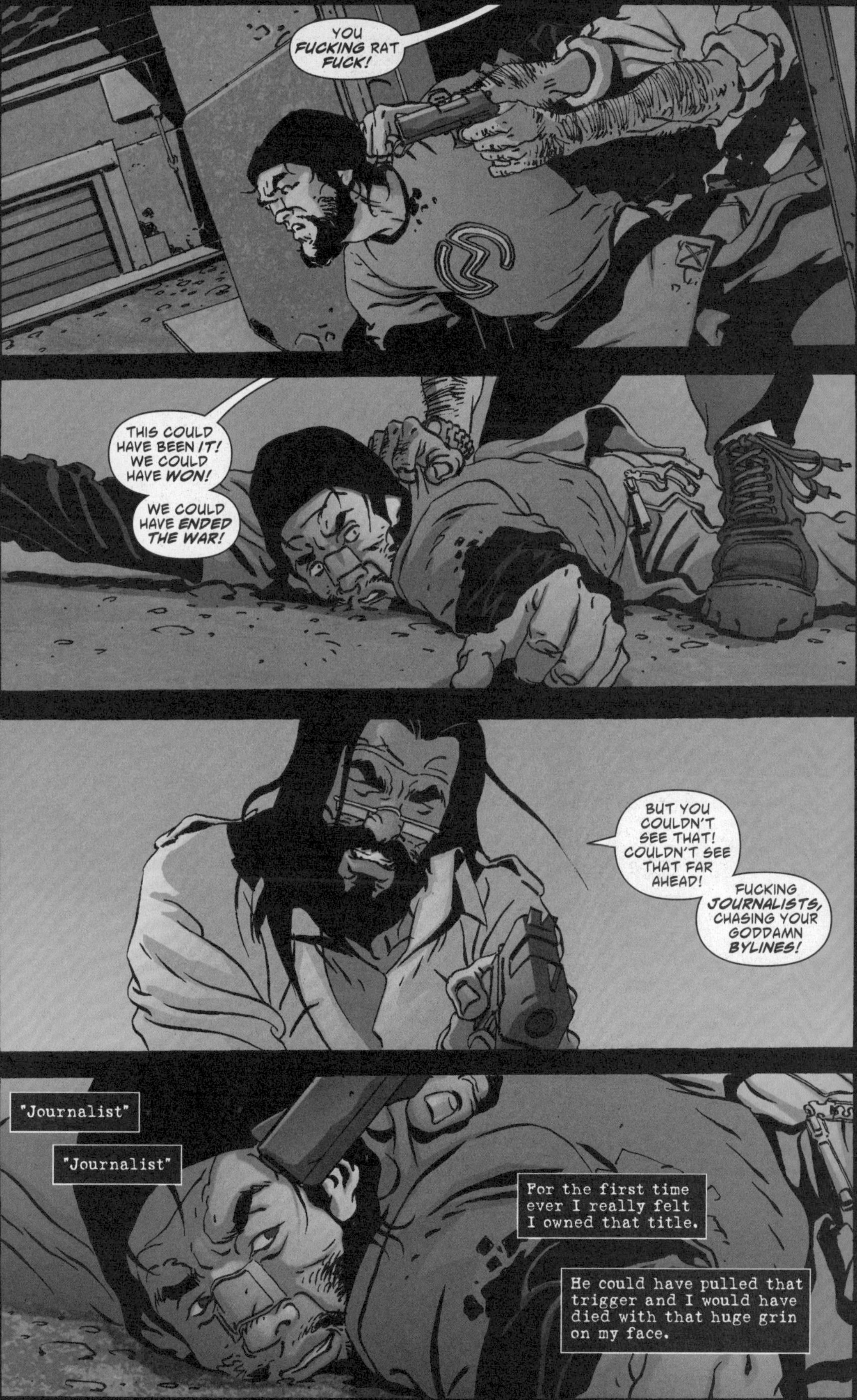

YOU FUCKING RAT FUCK!
THIS COULD HAVE BEEN IT! WE COULD HAVE WON!
WE COULD HAVE ENDED THE WAR!
BUT YOU COULDN'T SEE THAT! COULDN'T SEE THAT FAR AHEAD!
FUCKING JOURNALISTS, CHASING YOUR GODDAMN BYLINES!
"Journalist"
"Journalist"
For the first time ever I really felt I owned that title.
He could have pulled that trigger and I would have died with that huge grin on my face.

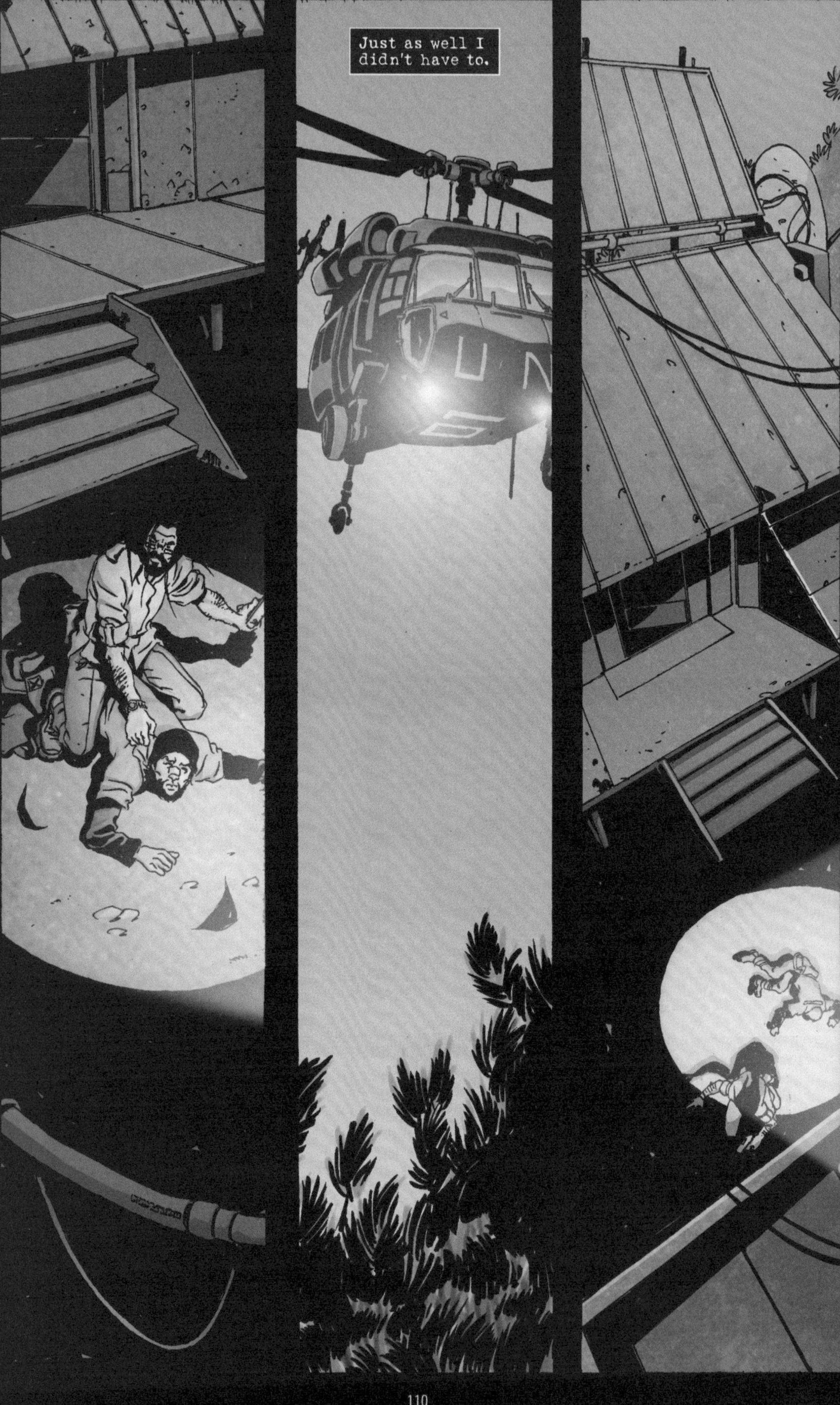
Just as well I didn't have to.

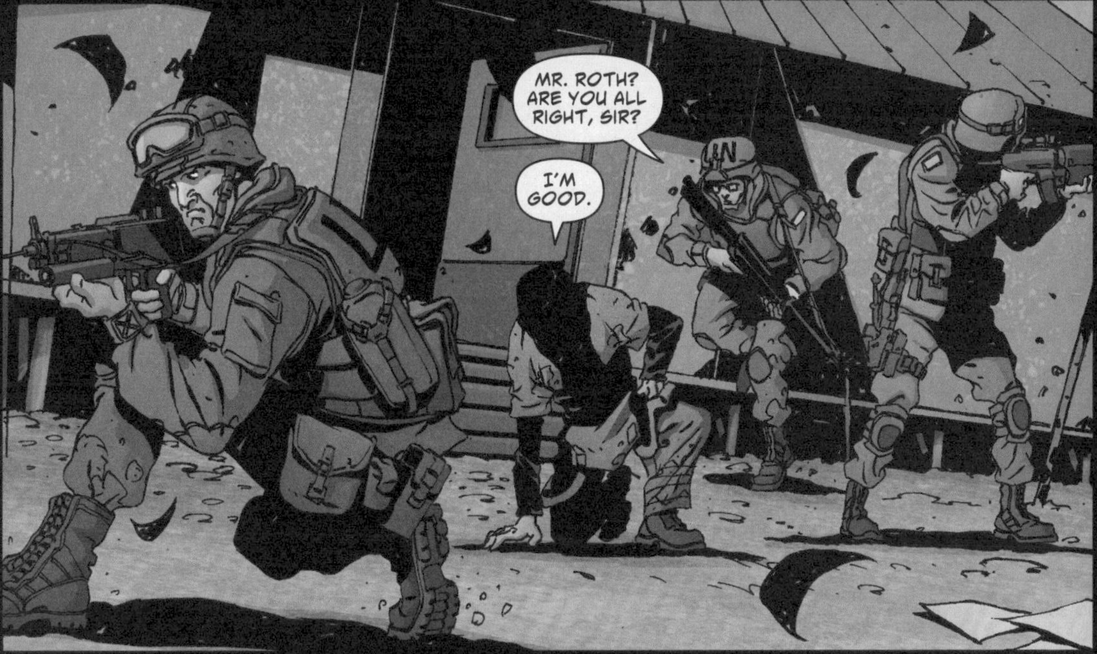
MR. ROTH? ARE YOU ALL RIGHT, SIR?
I'M GOOD.

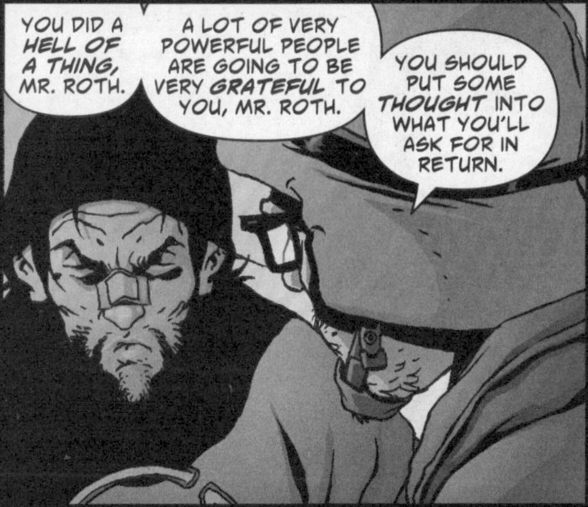
YOU DID A *HELL OF A THING,* MR. ROTH.
A LOT OF VERY POWERFUL PEOPLE ARE GOING TO BE VERY *GRATEFUL* TO YOU, MR. ROTH.
YOU SHOULD PUT SOME *THOUGHT* INTO WHAT YOU'LL ASK FOR IN RETURN.

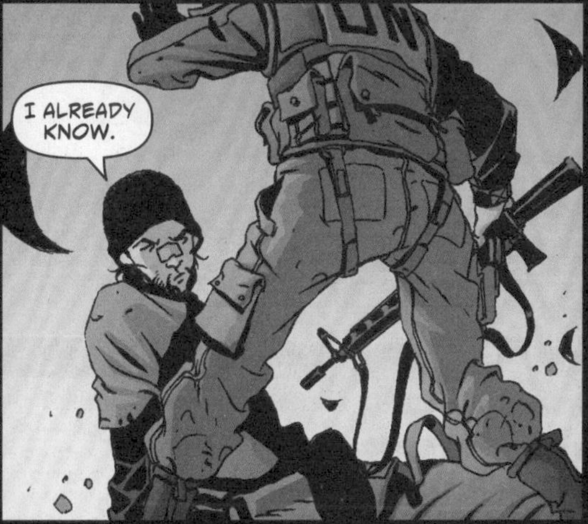
I ALREADY KNOW.

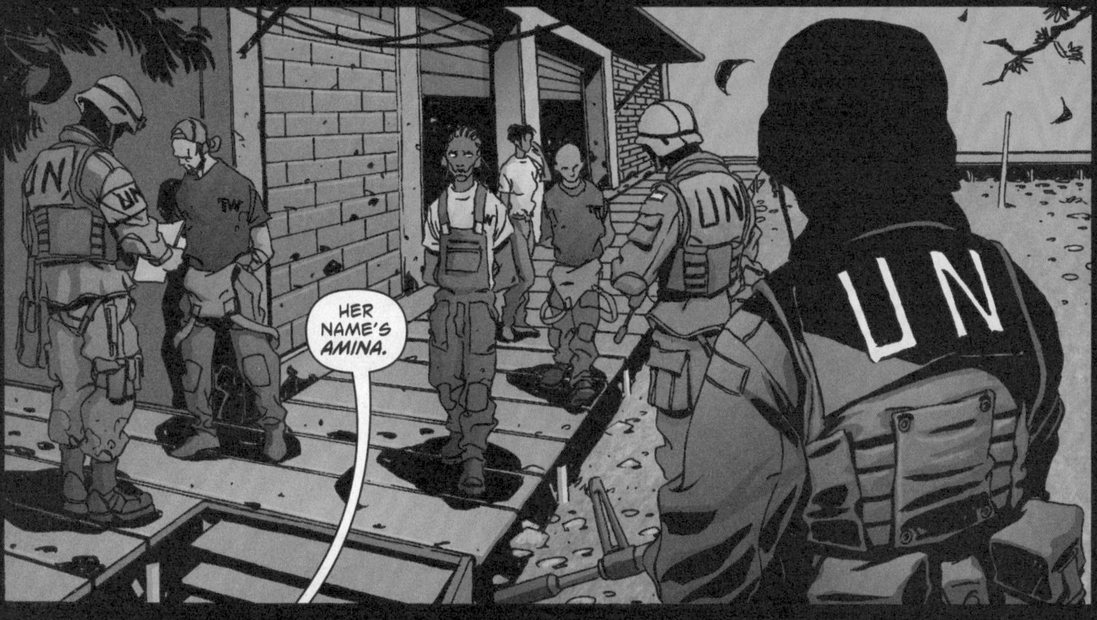
HER NAME'S *AMINA.*

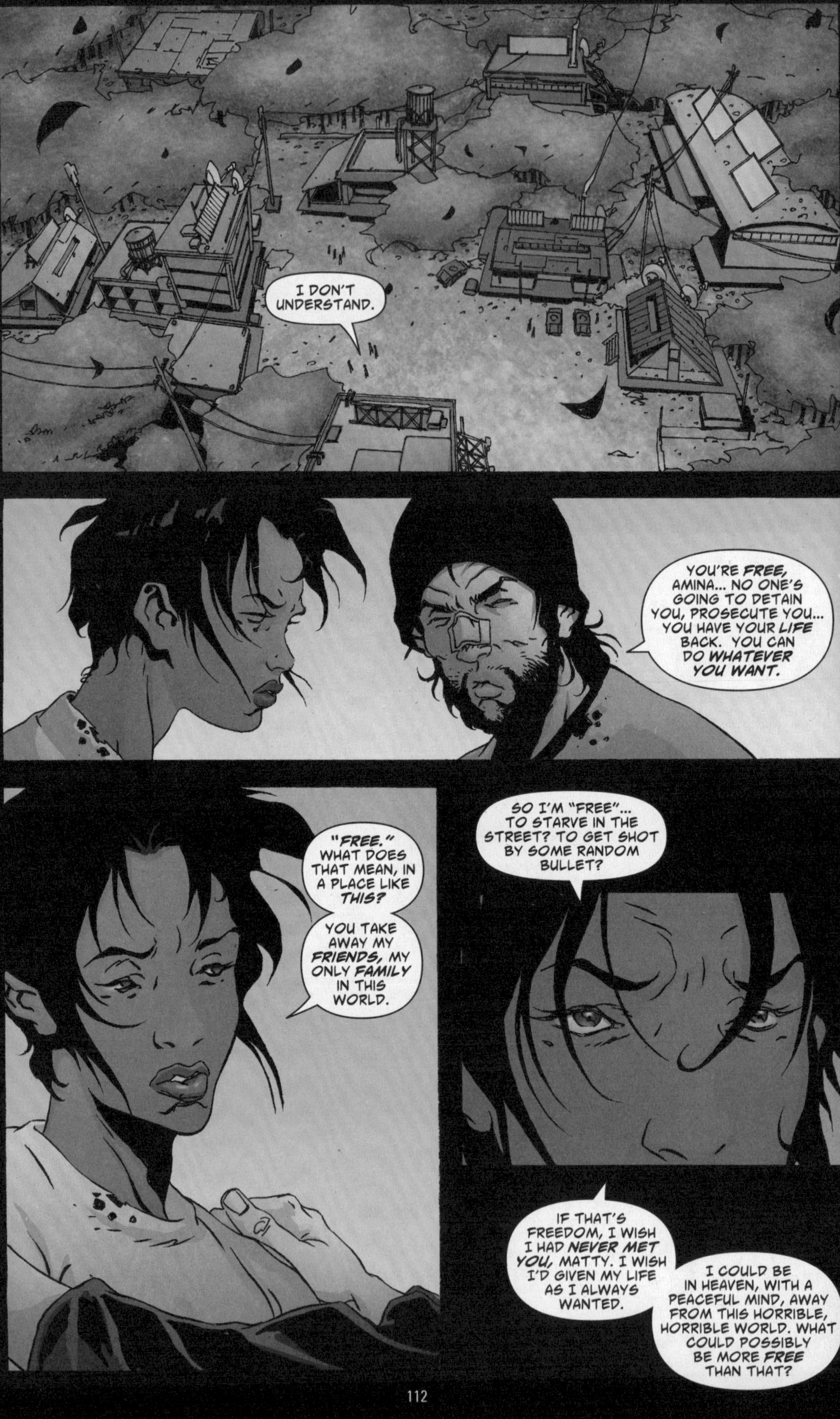
I DON'T UNDERSTAND.
YOU'RE FREE, AMINA... NO ONE'S GOING TO DETAIN YOU, PROSECUTE YOU... YOU HAVE YOUR LIFE BACK. YOU CAN DO WHATEVER YOU WANT.
"FREE." WHAT DOES THAT MEAN, IN A PLACE LIKE THIS?
YOU TAKE AWAY MY FRIENDS, MY ONLY FAMILY IN THIS WORLD.
SO I'M "FREE"... TO STARVE IN THE STREET? TO GET SHOT BY SOME RANDOM BULLET?
IF THAT'S FREEDOM, I WISH I HAD NEVER MET YOU, MATTY. I WISH I'D GIVEN MY LIFE AS I ALWAYS WANTED.
I COULD BE IN HEAVEN, WITH A PEACEFUL MIND, AWAY FROM THIS HORRIBLE, HORRIBLE WORLD. WHAT COULD POSSIBLY BE MORE FREE THAN THAT?

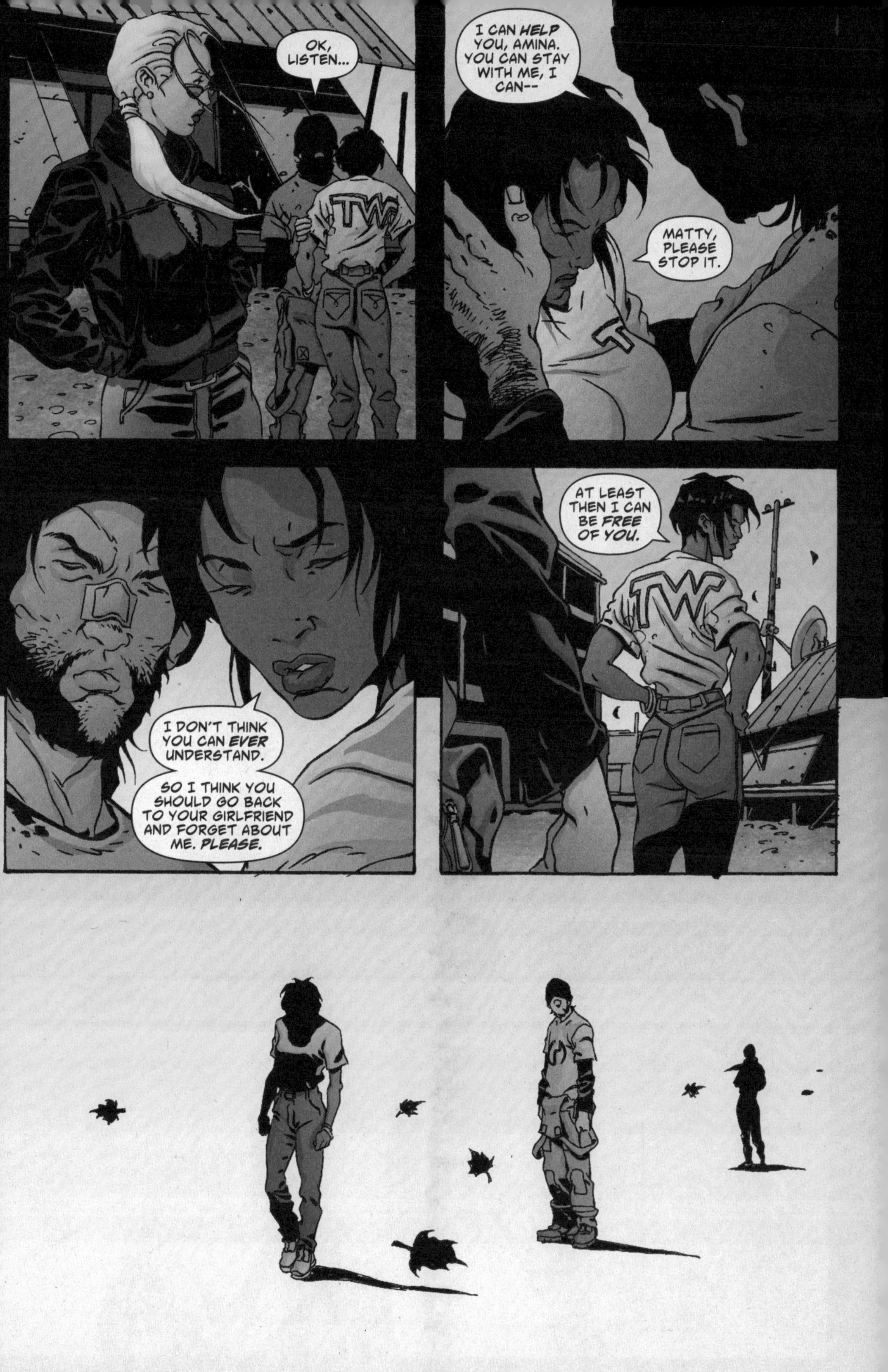
OK, LISTEN...
I CAN HELP YOU, AMINA. YOU CAN STAY WITH ME, I CAN--
MATTY, PLEASE STOP IT.
I DON'T THINK YOU CAN EVER UNDERSTAND.
SO I THINK YOU SHOULD GO BACK TO YOUR GIRLFRIEND AND FORGET ABOUT ME. PLEASE.
AT LEAST THEN I CAN BE FREE OF YOU.

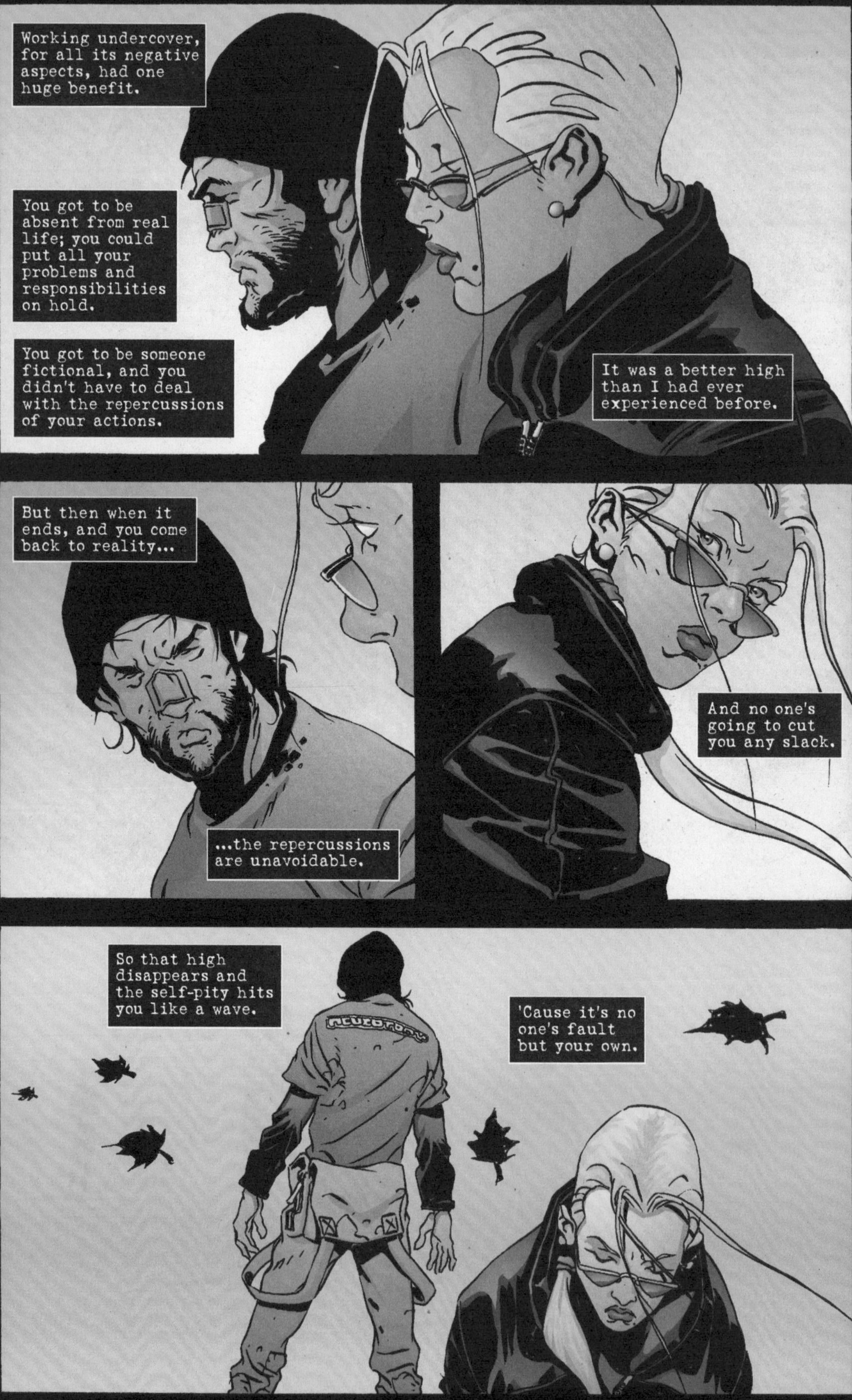

Working undercover, for all its negative aspects, had one huge benefit.
You got to be absent from real life; you could put all your problems and responsibilities on hold.
You got to be someone fictional, and you didn't have to deal with the repercussions of your actions.
It was a better high than I had ever experienced before.
But then when it ends, and you come back to reality...
...the repercussions are unavoidable.
And no one's going to cut you any slack.
So that high disappears and the self-pity hits you like a wave.
'Cause it's no one's fault but your own.

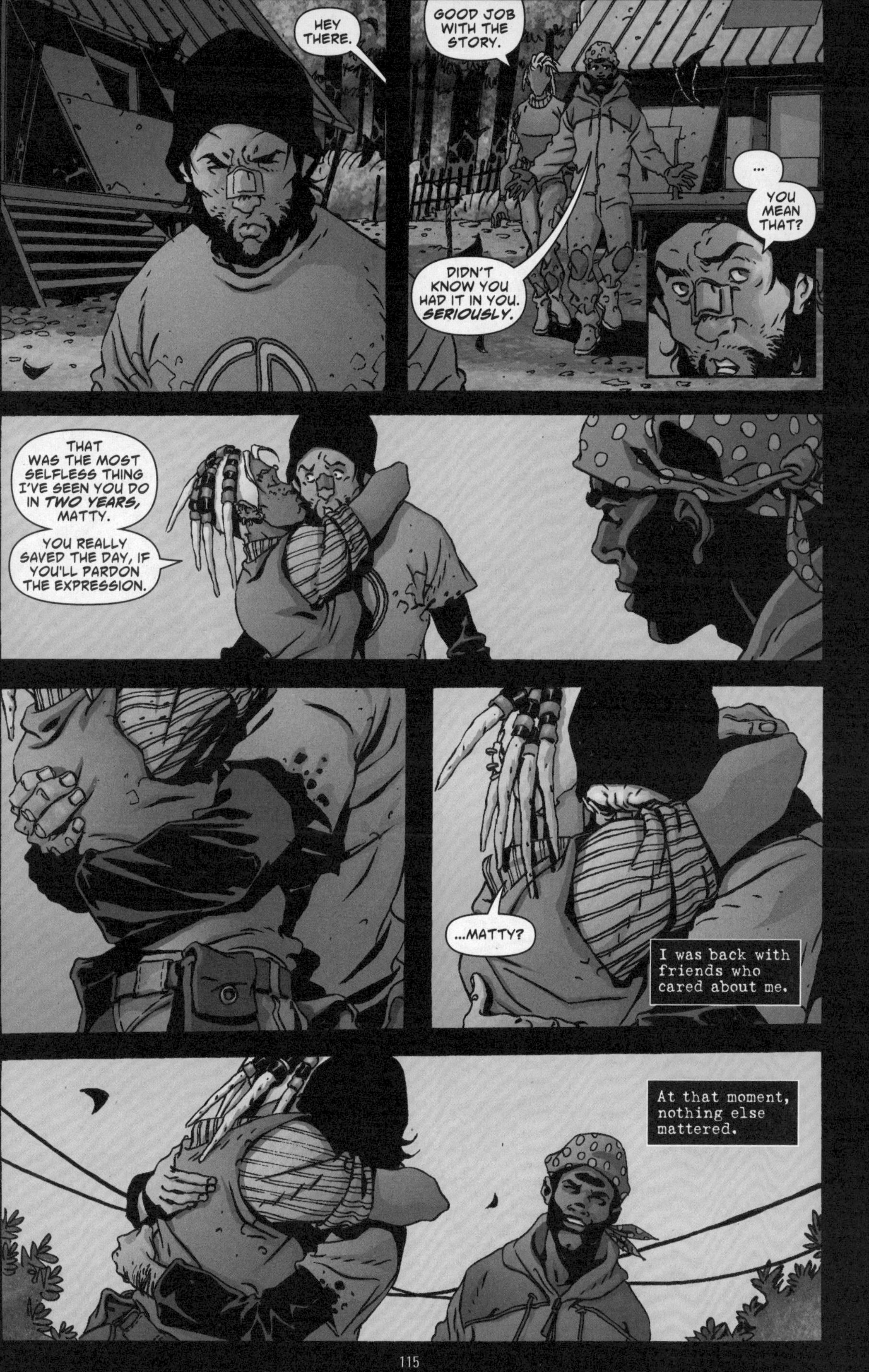
HEY THERE.
GOOD JOB WITH THE STORY.
DIDN'T KNOW YOU HAD IT IN YOU. SERIOUSLY.
...
YOU MEAN THAT?
THAT WAS THE MOST SELFLESS THING I'VE SEEN YOU DO IN TWO YEARS, MATTY.
YOU REALLY SAVED THE DAY, IF YOU'LL PARDON THE EXPRESSION.
...MATTY?
I was back with friends who cared about me.
At that moment, nothing else mattered.

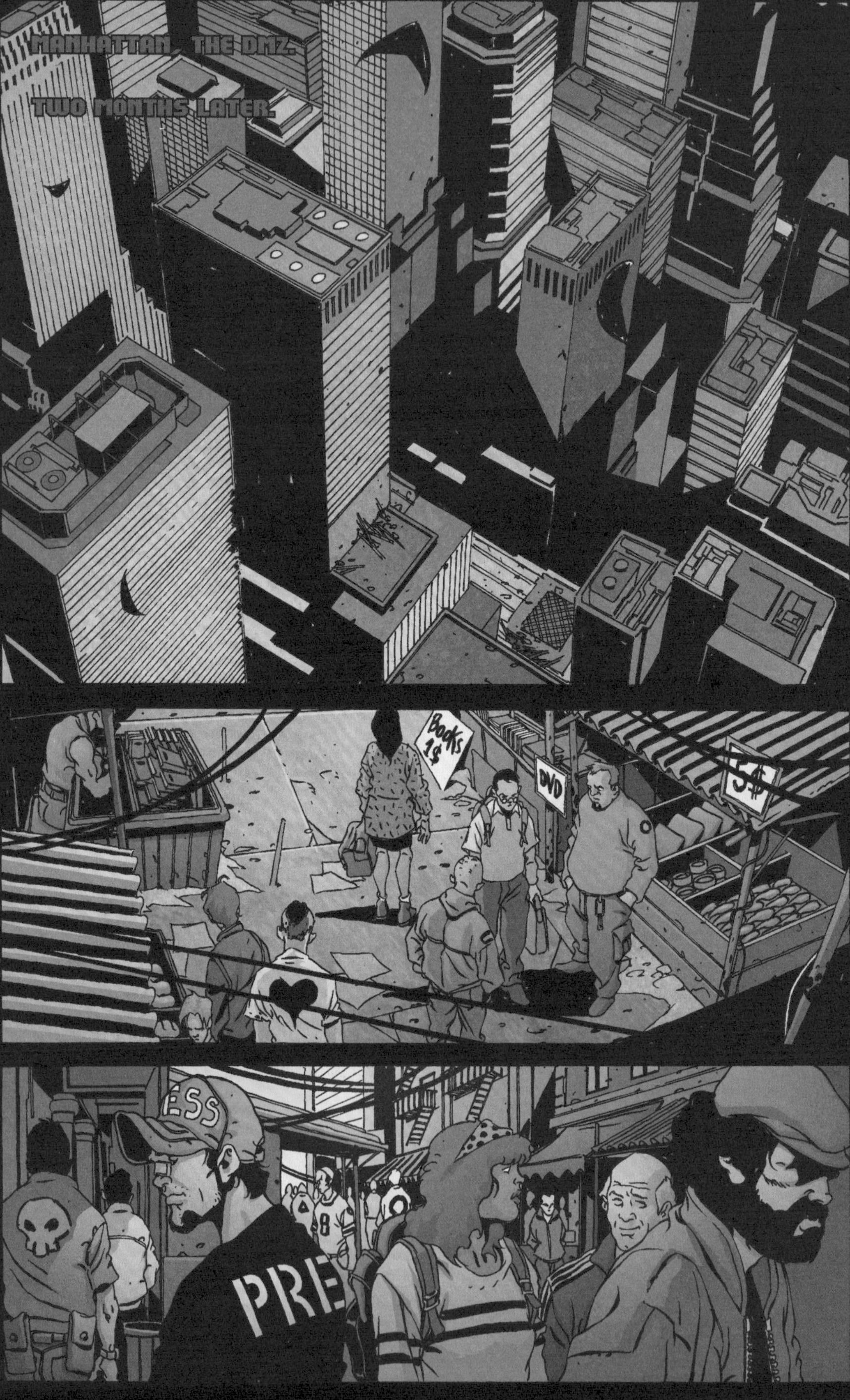
MANHATTAN, THE DMZ.
TWO MONTHS LATER.
Books 1$
DVD
5$
ESS
PRE

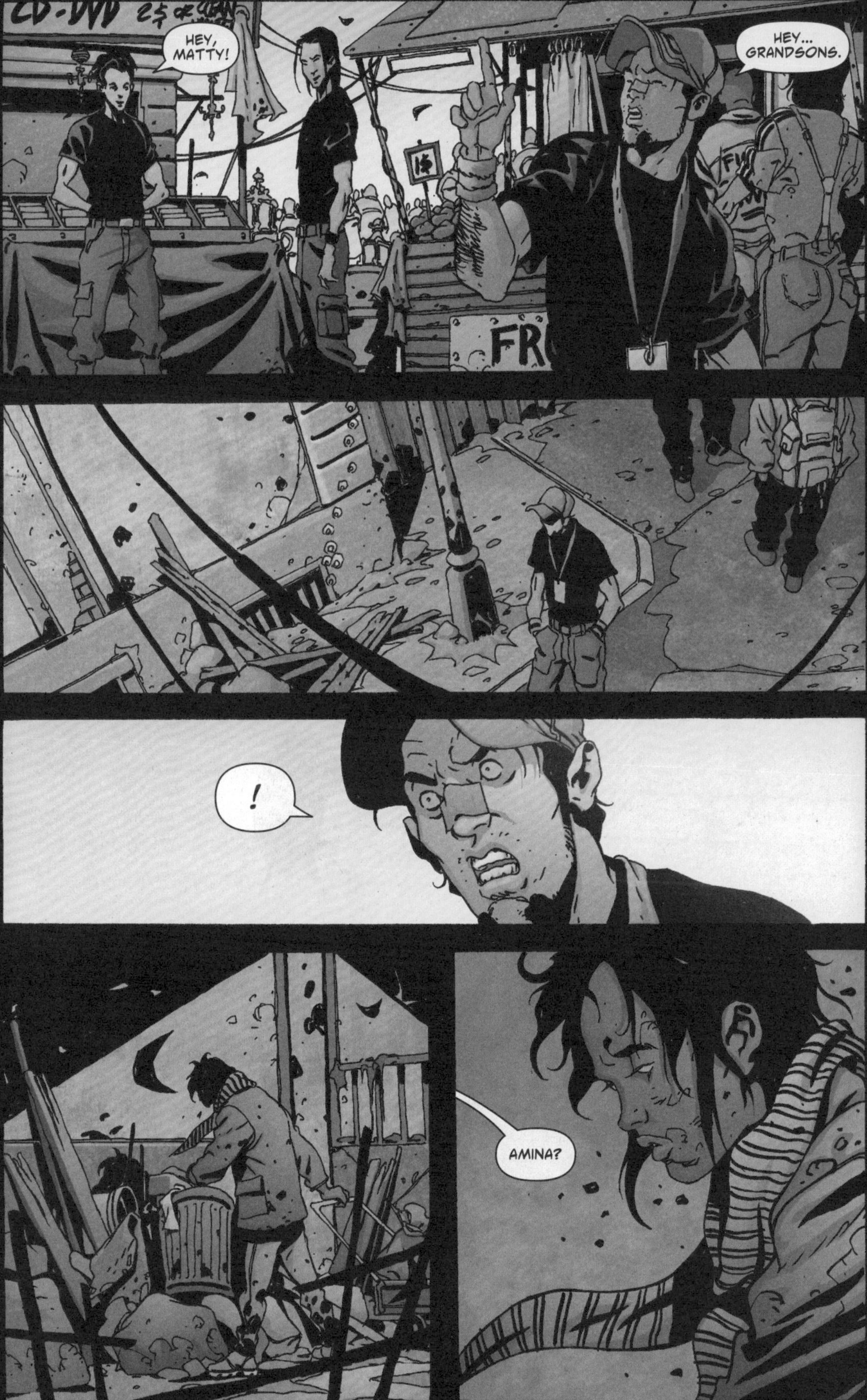
CD-DVD
HEY, MATTY!
HEY... GRANDSONS.
FR
!
AMINA?

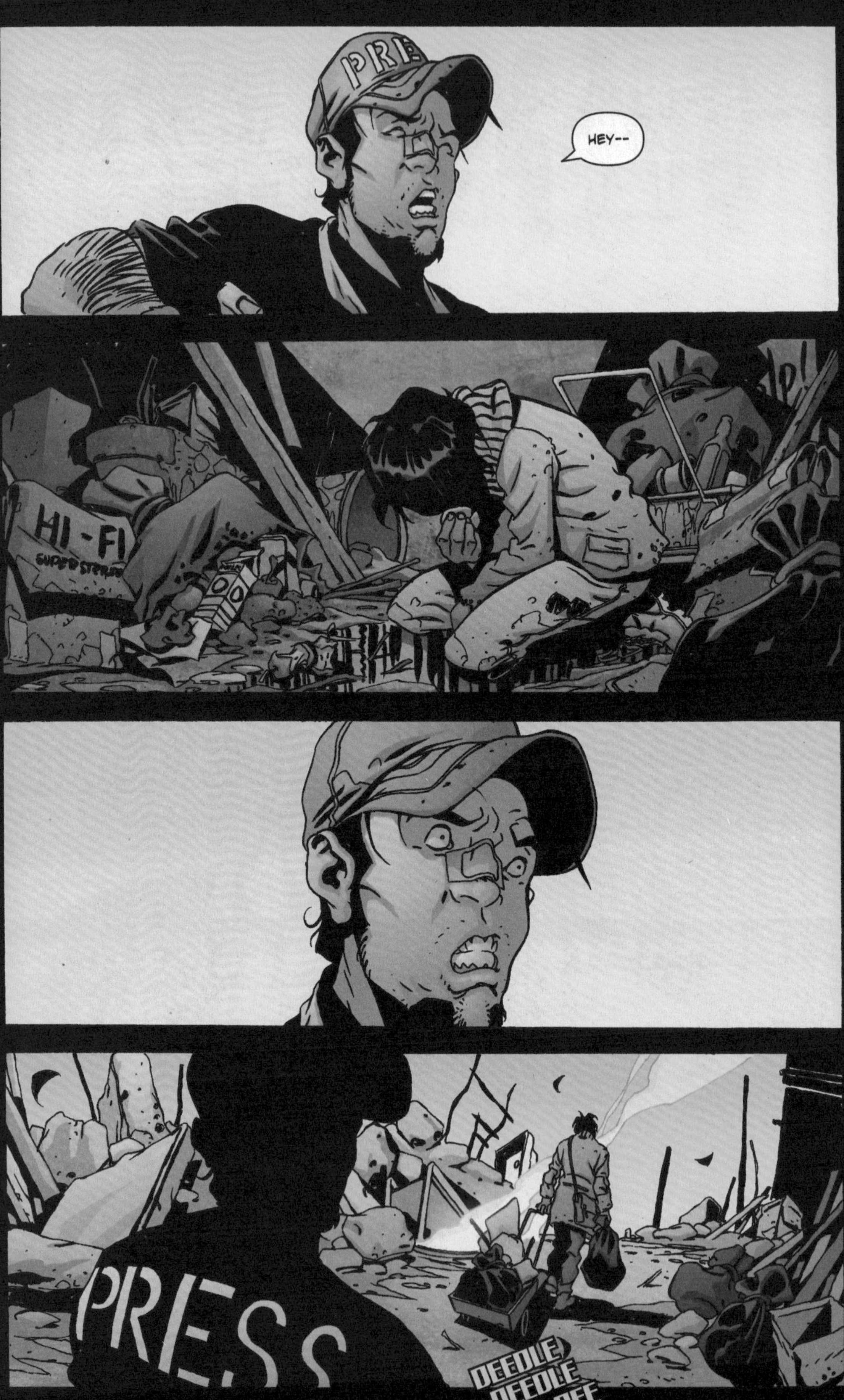
HEY--
HI-FI
PRESS
DEEDLE DEEDLE DEE

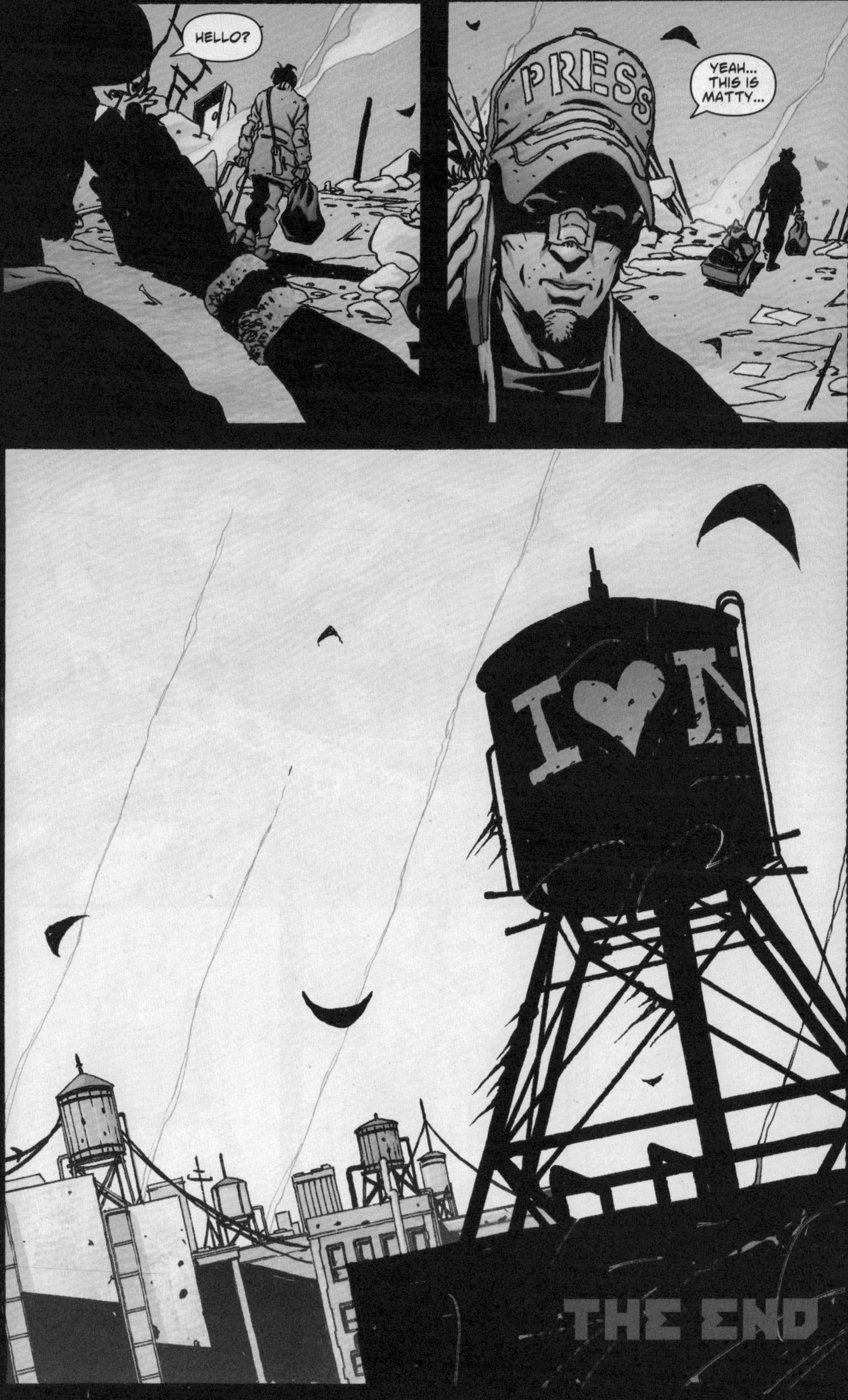
HELLO?
PRESS
YEAH... THIS IS MATTY...
I
THE END

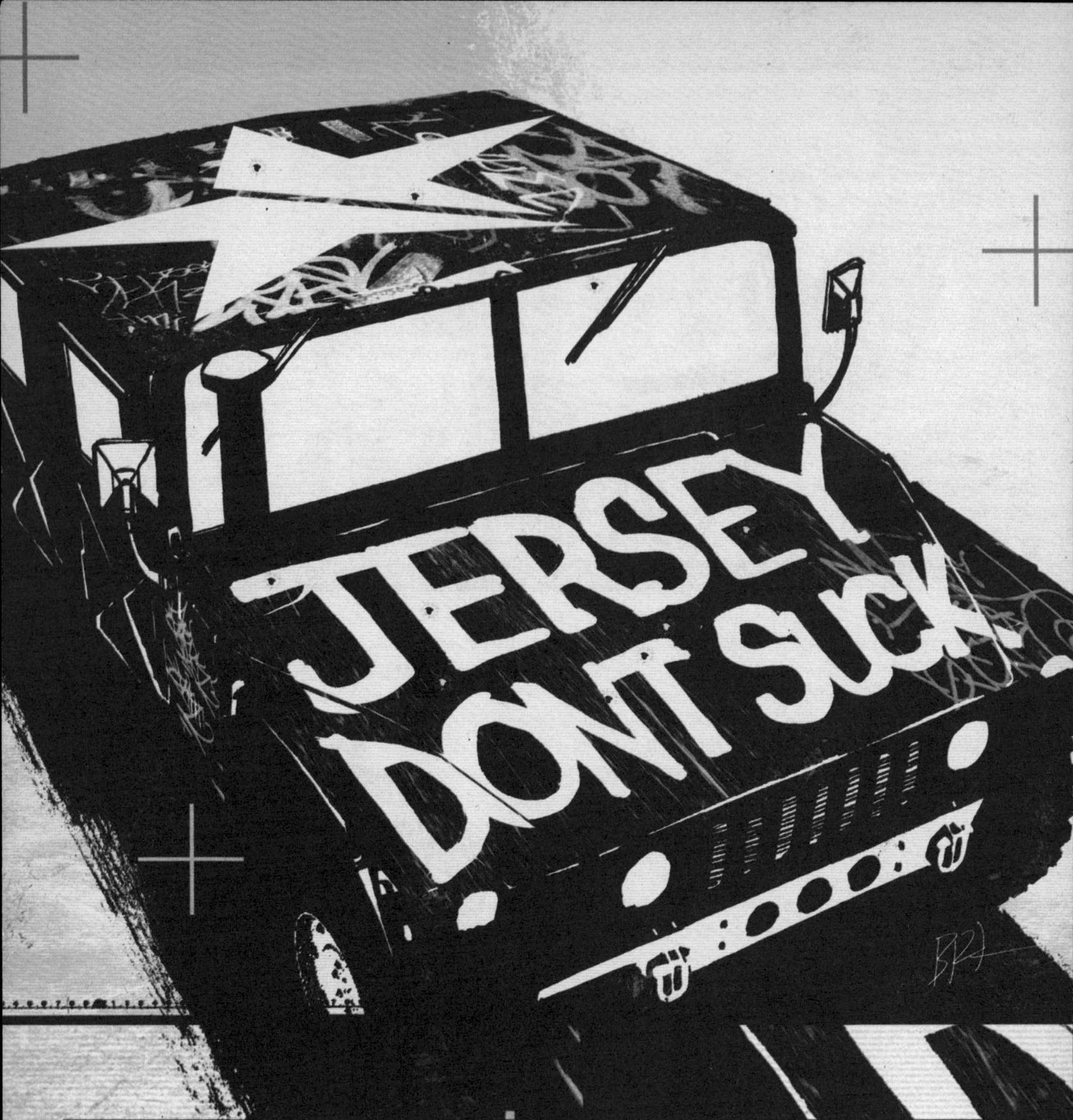
JERSEY
DONT SUCK

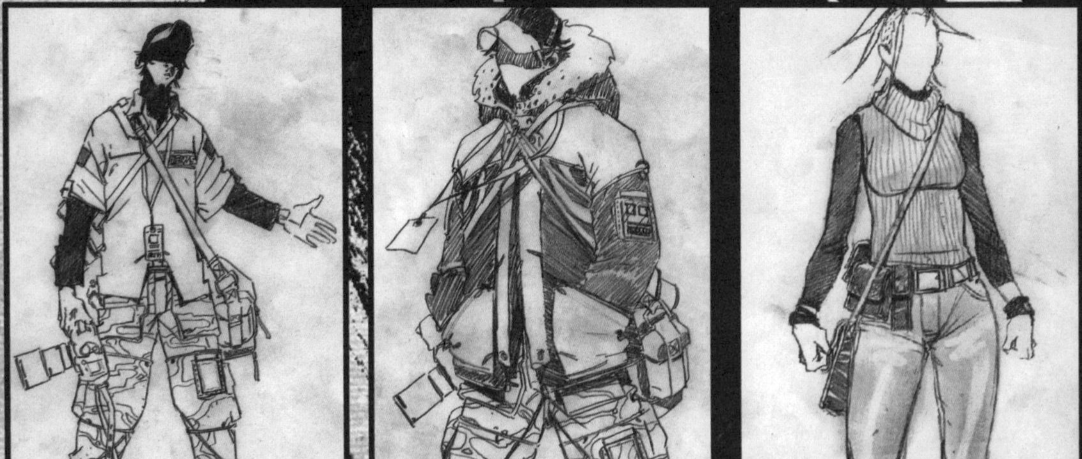

*Above:* Alternate cover DMZ #7. Art by Brian Wood *Below:* Character designs by Riccardo Burchielli

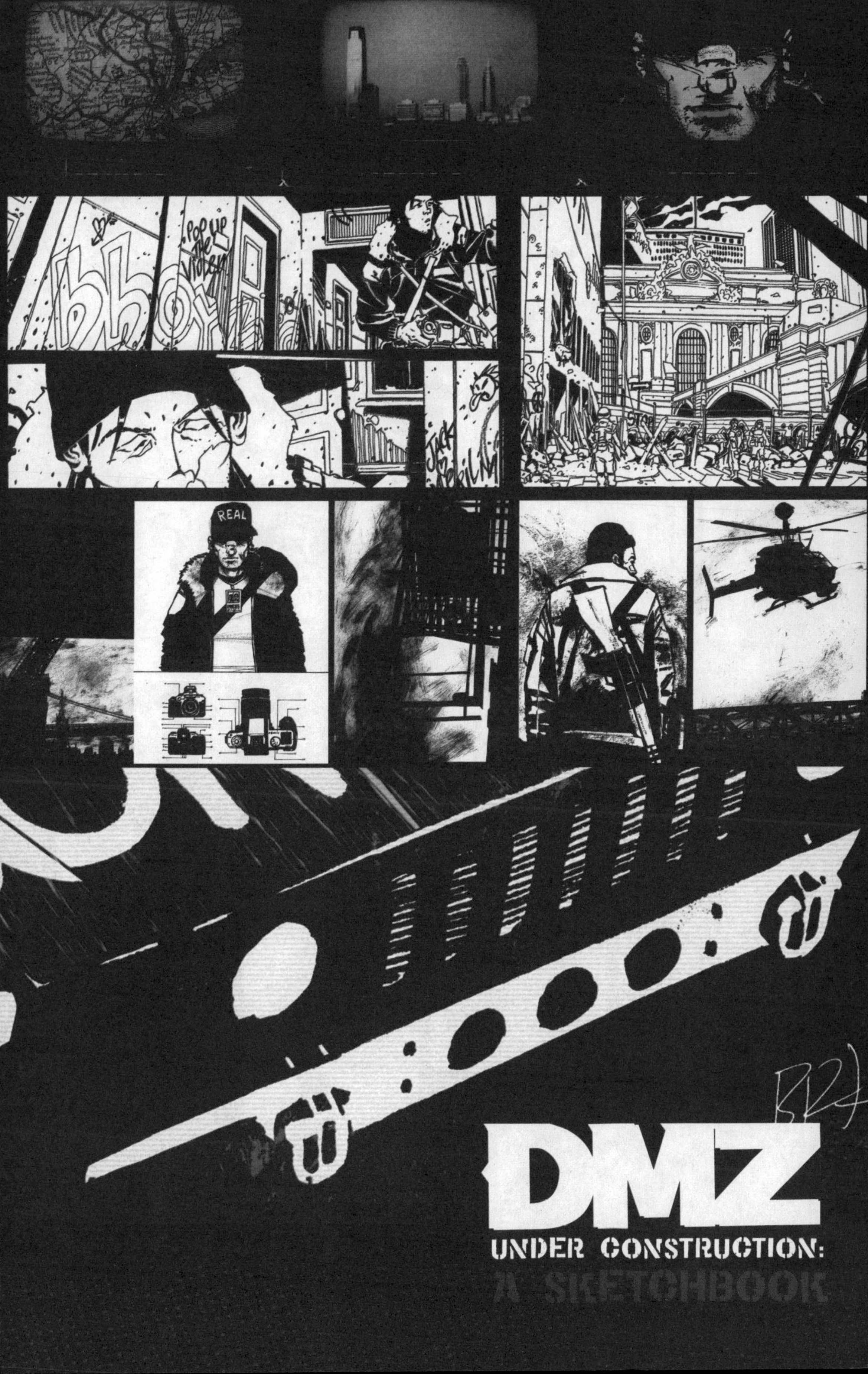
REAL
DMZ
UNDER CONSTRUCTION:
A SKETCHBOOK

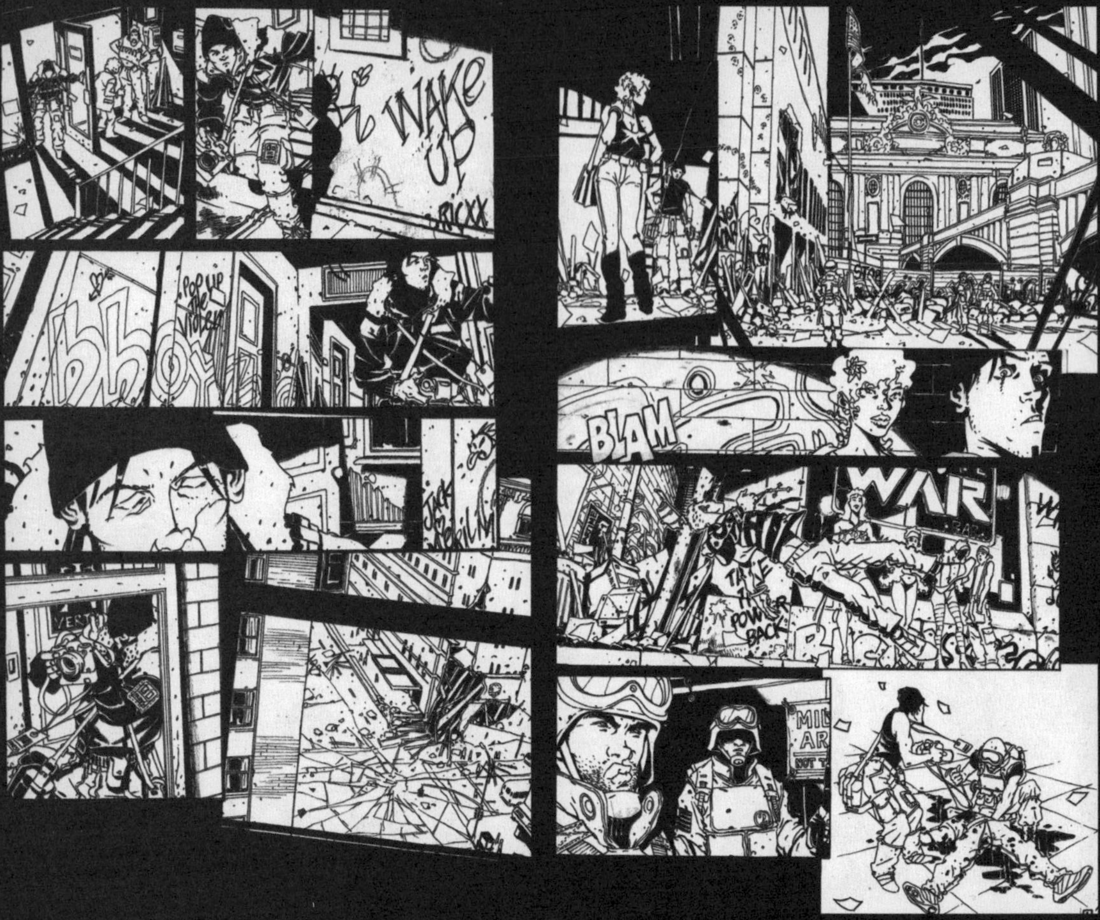

WAKE UP
BLAM
WAR
TAKE THE POWER BACK

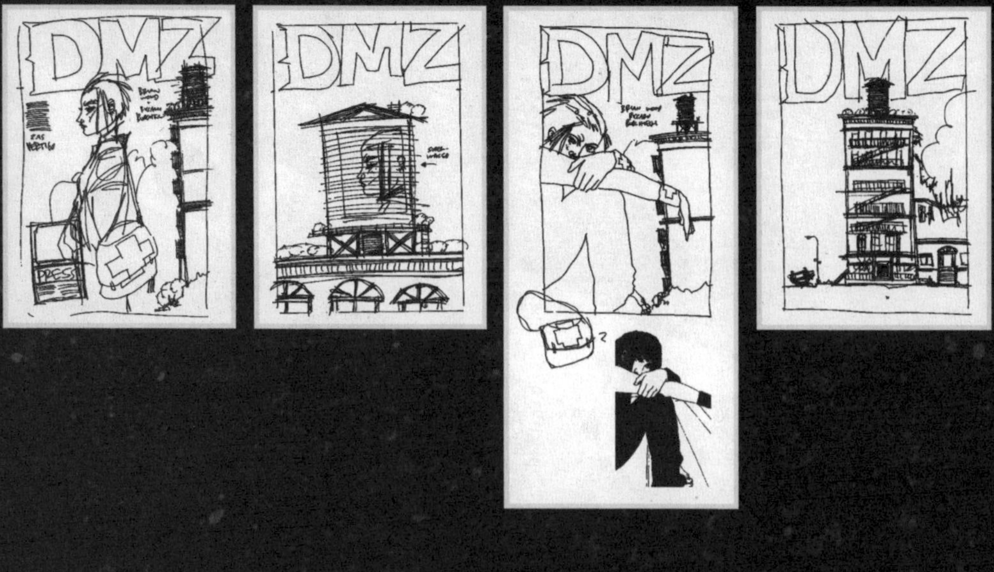

DMZ
PRESS
DMZ
DMZ
DMZ

*This page, above:* Original sample pages by Burchielli *Below:* Alternate cover sketches DMZ #2 by Wood
*Opposite page:* Character designs (Matty)

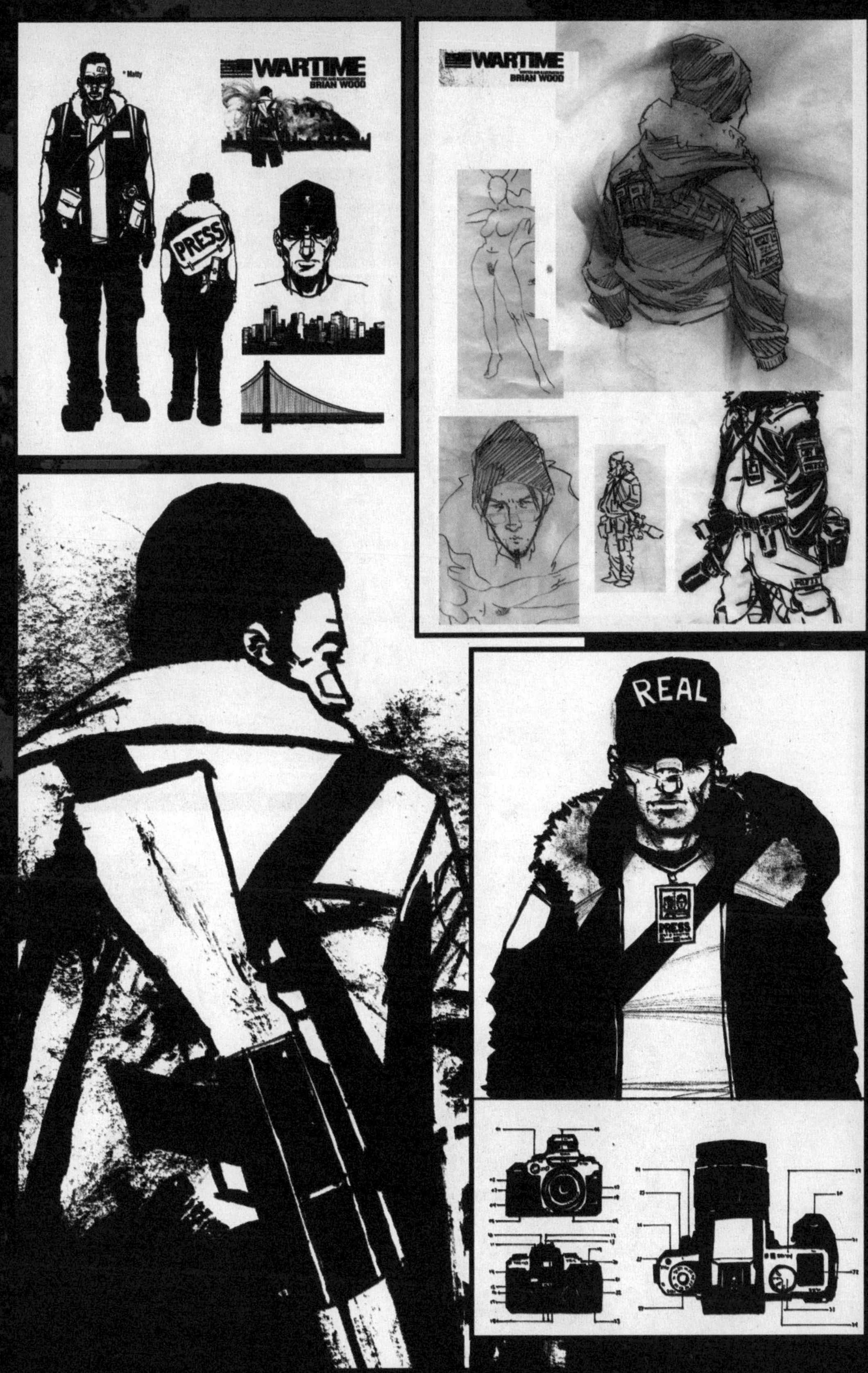
WARTIME
BRIAN WOOD
PRESS
WARTIME
BRIAN WOOD
REAL
PRESS

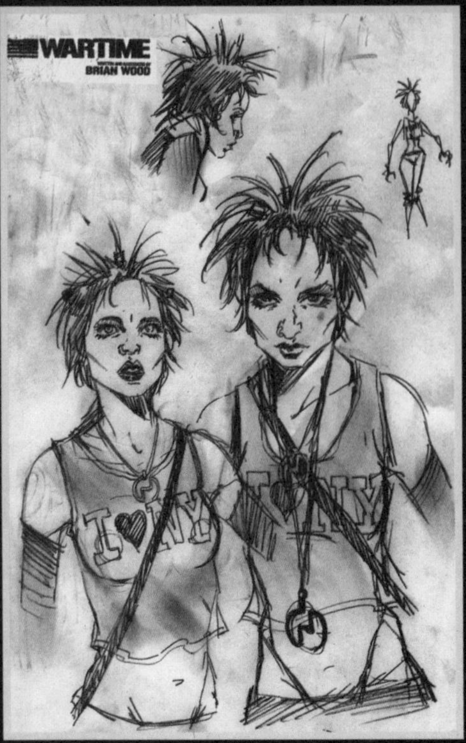
WARTIME
BRIAN WOOD

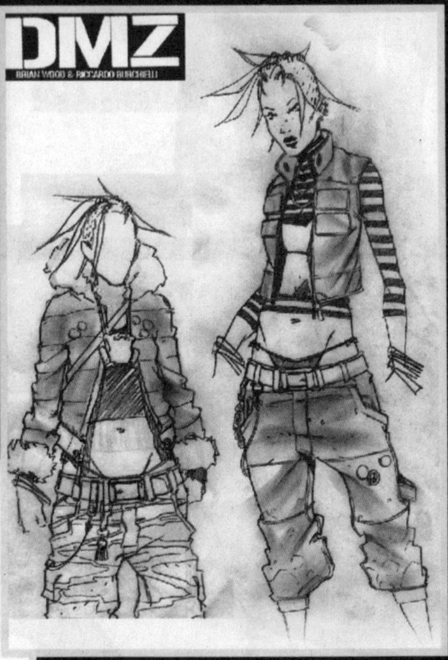
DMZ
BRIAN WOOD & RICCARDO BURCHIELLI

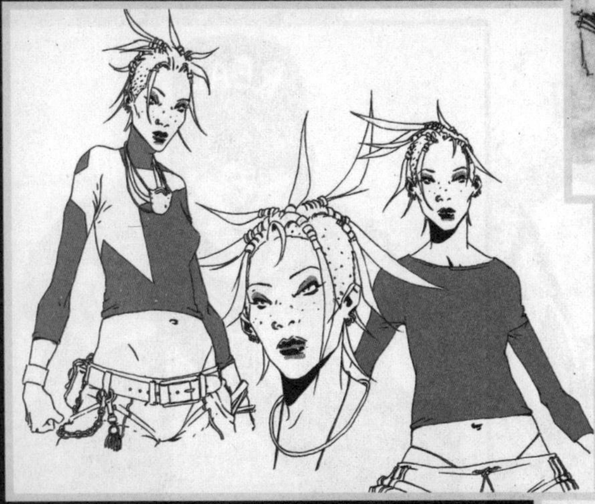

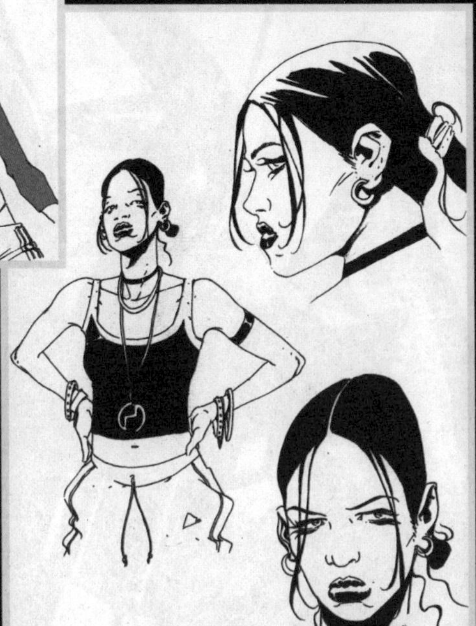

*This page:* Various Zee incarnations by Burchielli

# DMZ#11
**Zee - med student design + artist take on current design**

**prepared for Will Dennis    6-20-06**
**by Kristian Donaldson**

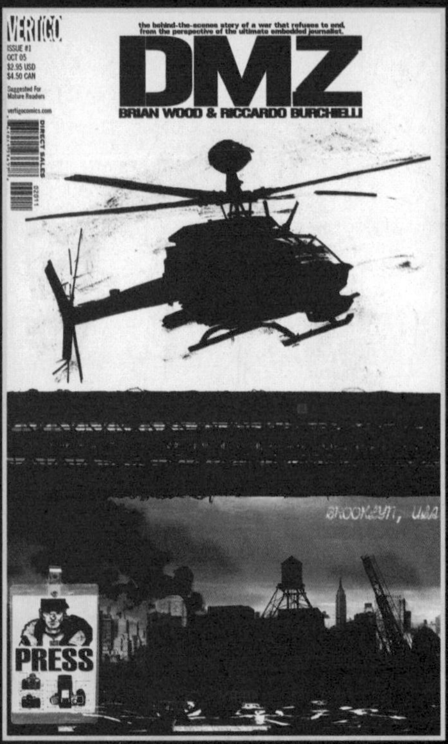
VERTIGO
ISSUE #1
OCT 05
$2.95 USD
$4.50 CAN
Suggested For Mature Readers
vertigocomics.com
the behind-the-scenes story of a war that refuses to end, from the perspective of the ultimate embedded journalist.
DMZ
BRIAN WOOD & RICCARDO BURCHIELLI
BROOKLYN, USA
PRESS

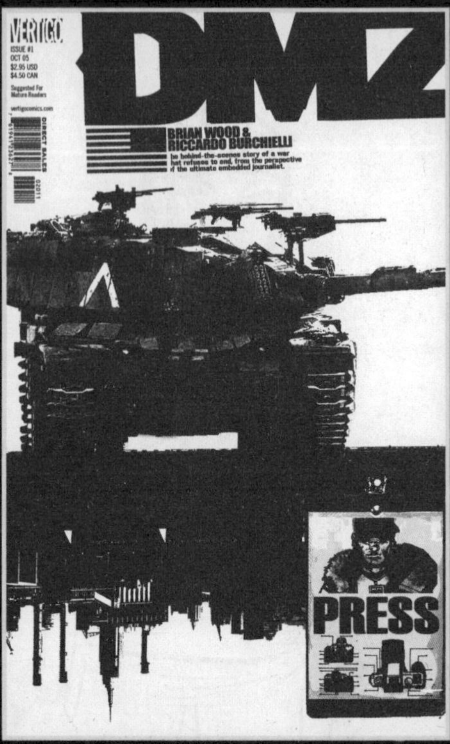
VERTIGO
ISSUE #1
OCT 05
$2.95 USD
$4.50 CAN
Suggested For Mature Readers
vertigocomics.com
DMZ
BRIAN WOOD & RICCARDO BURCHIELLI
PRESS

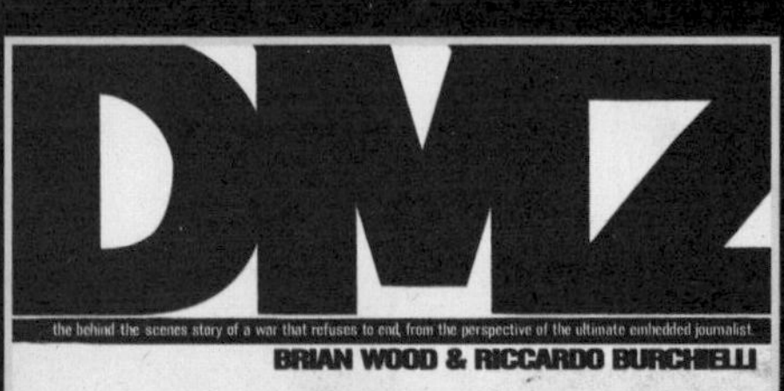
DMZ
the behind-the-scenes story of a war that refuses to end, from the perspective of the ultimate embedded journalist.
BRIAN WOOD & RICCARDO BURCHIELLI
PRESS

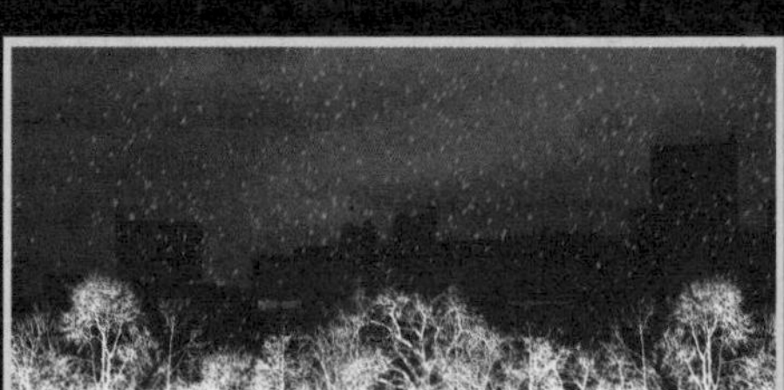
VERTIGO
DMZ
BRIAN WOOD & RICCARDO BURCHIELLI
the behind-the-scenes story of a war that refuses to end, from the perspective of the ultimate embedded journalist.

*This page:* Alternate cover designs, DMZ #1-4 *Opposite page:* Cover sketches and comps, DMZ #14-16

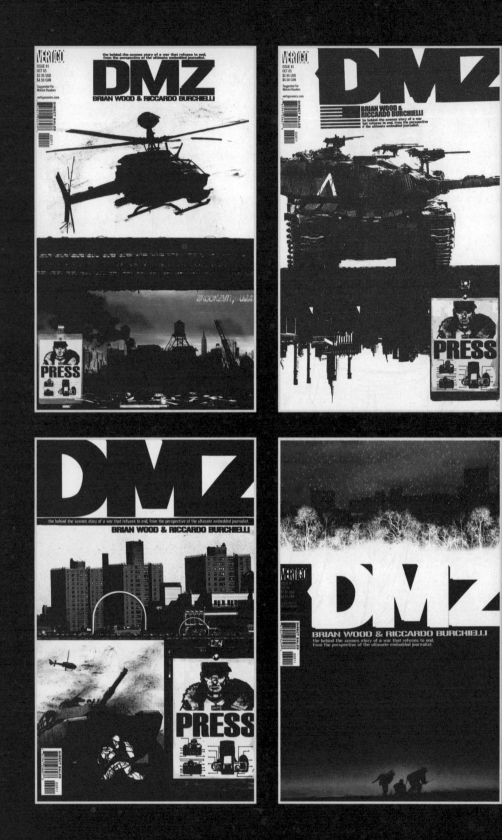

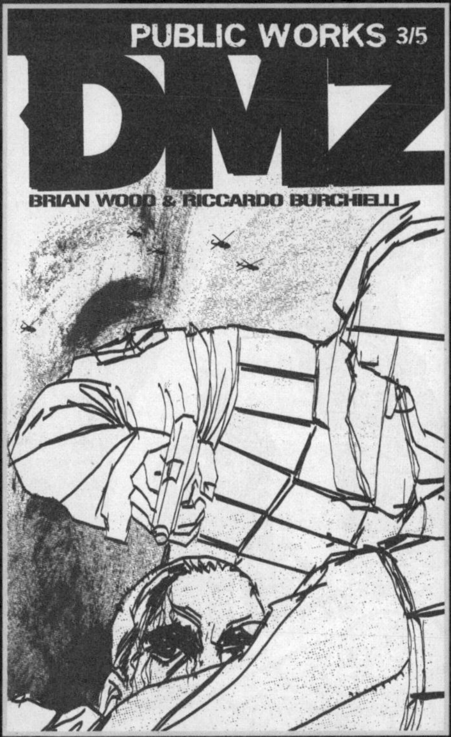
PUBLIC WORKS 3/5
DMZ
BRIAN WOOD & RICCARDO BURCHIELLI

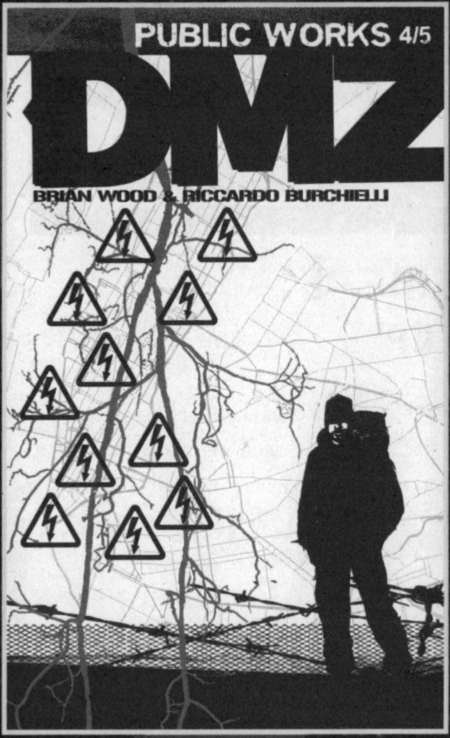
PUBLIC WORKS 4/5
DMZ
BRIAN WOOD & RICCARDO BURCHIELLI

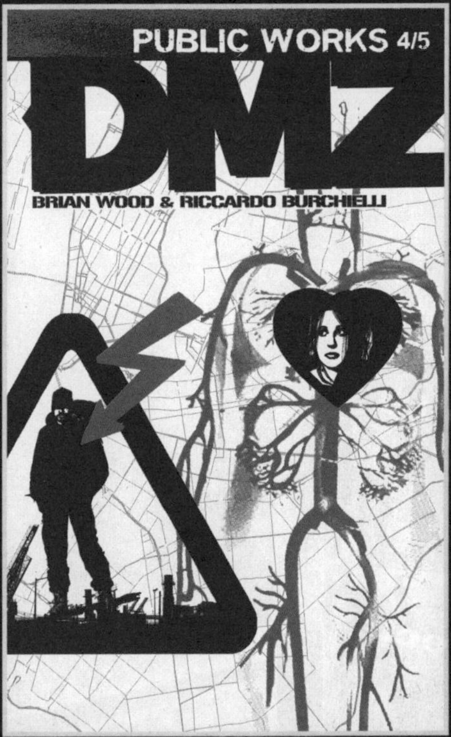
PUBLIC WORKS 4/5
DMZ
BRIAN WOOD & RICCARDO BURCHIELLI

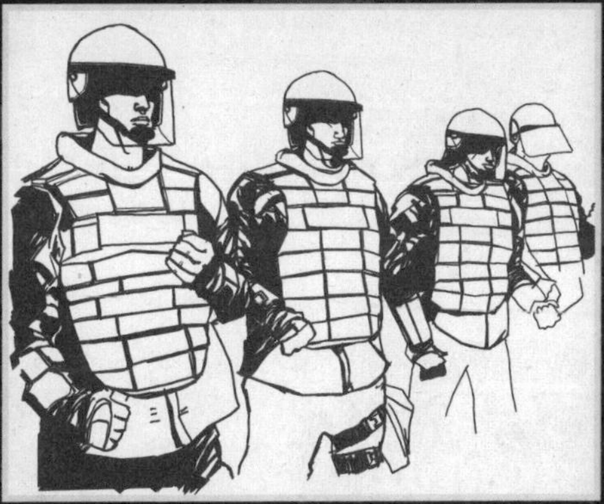

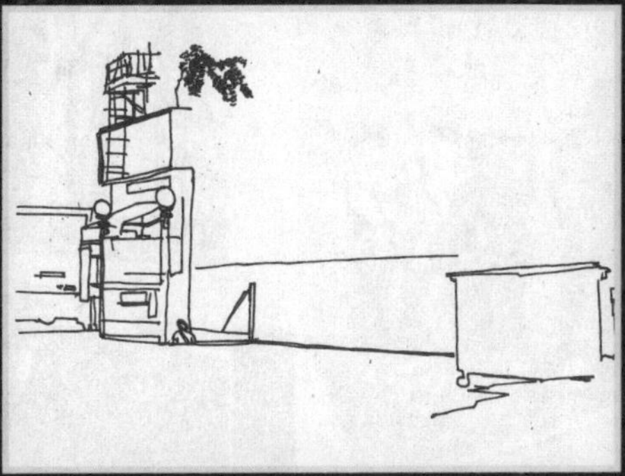